My Parrot, My Friend

An Owner's Guide to Parrot Behavior

Bonnie Munro Doane
and Thomas Qualkinbush

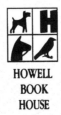

HOWELL
BOOK
HOUSE

Dedicated to the Memory
of
Richard Schubot
A man who had many parrot friends
whose emotional and physical welfare
were the ultimate concerns of his life

Library of Congress Cataloging-in-Publication Data

Doane, Bonnie Munro.
   My parrot, my friend : an owner's guide to parrot behavior / Bonnie Munro Doane and Thomas Qualkinbush.
        p.   cm.
   Includes bibliographical references and index.
   ISBN 0–87605–970–1
   1. Parrots—Behavior. 2. Parrots—Training. I. Qualkinbush, Thomas. II. Title.
   SF473.P3B58 1995
   636.6'865--dc20   94-24718   CIP

Manufactured in the United States of America

ISBN 978-1-68442-184-8 (pbk.)

Acknowledgments

This book is not the sole product of its authors. Many who have not had direct input are an integral, though perhaps unrecognized, part of such a project. Families certainly qualify for this category, and for their support and help we are most grateful.

Numerous friends have provided support and encouragement when the going got rough. Those among them who are also aviculturists were willing and welcome soundboards for ideas and concepts. We deeply appreciate the clients who brought their parrots to Parrot Responsive to repair and strengthen relationships with their birds. They are to be congratulated for their willingness to seek a better way, and without them this book would not have been possible.

Dr. Scott McDonald, DVM, provided many of the photographs used in this book. His time and generosity are deeply appreciated. Mr. Scott Schubot, director of The Avicultural Breeding and Research Center, and his late father, Mr. Richard Schubot, also contributed photographs, for which we are most grateful.

Martha Vogel Lucenti supplied line drawings. In spite of her busy schedule as an assistant art director of *Country Living,* and being a new wife, she once again came through with flying colors. Our thanks to her.

Many thanks to Diane Schmidt, noted photographer and photojournalist. A number of her pictures appear in the text, illuminating not only the behavioral modification process, but also the stunning beauty of parrots.

To Dr. Irene Pepperberg of the University of Arizona, our deep gratitude for the time she spent reviewing the manuscript, despite her enormous teaching, research and lecturing responsibilities. Her comments were invaluable; we are most appreciative of these, and of her kindness in helping us.

To friend and editor Seymour Weiss, many, many heartfelt thanks. No authors have ever been blessed with a better editor. His belief in this book and its usefulness means more than words can ever convey.

Acknowledgments

We also wish to thank Dana Zaremba, facility manager for Parrot Responsive. She functioned as friend, assistant and general factotum. Her willingness to help regardless of the task, and her perceptiveness and respect for the parrots in training were invaluable. It is Dana's arm that appears in the parrot bite photograph in Chapter 2. And although she did not deliberately offer up her arm as a sacrifice to provide an illustration for the book, her good humor regarding the episode does her great credit!

To all of these wonderful people we owe a debt of gratitude, and emphasize that any errors are ours alone. Their support, criticism and friendship have made this book possible in large part, and their contributions have been a real and material blessing to us.

And last, our thanks and gratitude to all the parrots who share our lives and the lives of our readers. They have given us more than they know. They have taught us wonderful things about how two species can share and grow together.

Contents

Foreword

Would you like to join me on a journey of discovery? We will explore a place where the ideas of yesterday's parrot keeping become obsolete, and a brand-new adventure of growth and happiness for you and your parrot(s) replaces the routine of everyday existence. You may ask if there is such a place, what has kept us from going there? Simple: the human assumption about what we call the way we've always done things. Habits that have led us to believe our early conditioning with parrots were right. We convince ourselves our way is best, based on the human ego that stubbornly resists the inner voice that tells all of us there must be something better.

There is nothing in Nature that proves it cares more for the human species than other species. We may one day vanish as quickly and as radically as thousands of other life forms before us. But whatever we have in common with other living things, there is one peculiarity that is ours exclusively: We are the only species in Nature working toward its own destruction. Until man addresses the problem of his determination to cover the earth with his own kind, those who love and provide for parrots may prove to be the only safe havens for such living works of nature's art. Culturally speaking, there are far more Rembrandts in the world today than there are certain species of parrots (e.g., the Spix's macaw). An artist may reconceive the beauty and genius of a work of art though its first material expression be destroyed, but when the last individual of a race of living things breathes no more, another Heaven and another Earth will have to be created before such a one can be again.

Interaction with living things is a basic human instinct, which, when rediscovered and encouraged, allows the genuine self to let the magic of the universe flow freely. By doing so we consciously touch other life forms with feelings of good intentions, sincere respect and a willingness to help. It is only then that we are able to contact all forms of life pleasantly, with consideration, with the heart of a helper and the mind of a student.

It is difficult for today's parrot enthusiasts to grasp the realization that only three decades ago we did not even have books dealing with the very rudimentary requirements of keeping a pet parrot alive and healthy. In the last twenty-five years many informative writings have been published, each giving the author's singular method of husbandry; but in each I have noticed the most important ingredient was wanting. It was often skirted, ignored or passed over. At best it was hinted at and then only from the *human* standpoint.

But at last it has come!

The authors have parted the veil of mystery with this new, innovative and thought-provoking text. Finally, we are allowed, no—compelled, to look into the very heart of that obscure nature of the unseen relationship that exists between a parrot and *its* human.

They have dared to throw down the barriers of taboo—the same disallowance that has made advancement in any field a laborious task for the few possessed of Creative Impulse. To those who will not listen, such inspiration does not speak. This presupposes man's superiority. It results in stunted personalities void of the joy experienced from free, uninhibited communication with all Life. Thoreau defined this when he wrote "All things do exist in mutual relationship to one another."

For the reader to proceed let us consider two points: First, that human beings all over the earth have this curious idea that they ought to behave in a certain way, and cannot really get rid of it. Second, that they do not in fact behave that way; if they know the rules of nature, they break them. Acceptance of these two facts provides the foundation of all clear thinking about ourselves and determines our reaction to fellow living creatures whose right to exist should be as obvious as our own. This is the truth all highly evolved cultures have come to recognize. It separates us from the troglodyte consciousness still evident in today's modern world. They are often the insentient beings we encounter, those who cannot give or receive loving feelings, yet long to do so.

In this monumental work, the authors have presented us step-by-step workable principles to arrive at what the ancient Chinese called the Tao: The Way, in which the universe goes on, The Way in which things everlastingly emerge into space and time. It is The Way every caring person evolves in imitation of cosmic progression, harmonizing feelings to that great exemplar of selflessness. Those who know the Tao can hold that to call a parrot delightful is not simply to recognize a psychological fact about one's own emotions at the moment, but to discern a quality that demands a certain response whether or not we make it. Einstein called this cosmic religious feeling and emphasized its importance, "In my view, it is the most important function of art and science to awaken this feeling and to keep it alive in those who are receptive to it." Some parrot keepers appear only partially awake to this very necessary feeling.

After fifty rewarding years of an ongoing romance with parrots of every type, it is my opinion the authors have reached the highest peak of awareness in their presentation, and, if read and experienced, promises to lead the serious psittacine student into a richer and far more rewarding relationship with parrots, and, for that fact, with all life everywhere.

Ramon P. Noegel
Founder and Director of Life
Fellowship Bird Sanctuary

1

Introduction

The purpose of this book is to help people and parrots mend and strengthen existing relationships and to facilitate optimum development of new relationships.

Parrots are wild animals. Whether wild-caught and imported or domestically bred and hand reared, parrots today are at best only three or four generations away from 35 to 38 million years of wild inheritance. The earliest known parrot fossil was found in England and consists of fragments of the end of the tarsometatarsus (analogous to the arch of the foot in humans). Parrot fossils from France are approximately 26 million years old, and Australian psittacine fossils have been dated at between 17 and 26 million years. Fossil records from Africa belonging to the Pliocene period (1.5 to 7 million years ago) have been identified. And South American parrot fossils found thus far appear to have made their debut about 1.5 million years ago.

Parrots have been around a very long time, and if current hypotheses formulated by paleontologists such as Bakker, Paul and Horner are correct, all birds, including parrots, are the direct lineal descendants of dinosaurs (Bakker 1986; Horner 1988; Paul 1988).

Although the parrot is a creature that seems comfortable with people, adapting well to a family setting, its long evolutionary history has equipped it superbly to survive in its range countries. Instinctive and learned behaviors acquired in the wild allow the parrot to forage, attract a mate, defend the nest and its young and escape predation. However, these skills are not necessarily an asset in domestic surroundings, but may become a liability to the relationship of the bird and its human companions in situations the parrot perceives as threatening. In such cases, instinctive and learned behavior may be used in maladaptive ways, leading to serious behavioral problems such as fear biting,

A mated pair of Major Mitchell's Cockatoos (*Cacatua leadbeateri*) display to each other. *Aviculture Breeding and Research Center*

perseverative screaming, feather mutilation and sexual aggression. (Perseverative behavior is behavior that is meaningless and repetitive.) In the breeding situation, such birds may destroy eggs and young.

This book will explore the psychology of psittacine behavior, the development of maladaptive problems and how they can be changed through behavioral modification. Parrots are highly intelligent birds with evolutionarily developed flock behavior, which makes them ideal as companion animals for many people. If one recognizes the concept of "another" intelligence: an intelligence different from but parallel to human intelligence, finely honed to allow survival and social interaction, then one becomes aware of the possibility of a mutually beneficial interface of two separate systems—human and psittacine.

In addition, parrots seem to be at the beginning of the road to domestication. This is especially true now that very few imported exotic birds will be available in the pet trade. Soon, anyone wishing to own one of these delightful birds will be obtaining a parrot bred and hand reared in civilization. It is inevitable that some selective breeding will occur, either intentionally or not, for personality traits desirable in a companion animal. (Although this is not a consideration, or even desirable, for the captive propagation of endangered

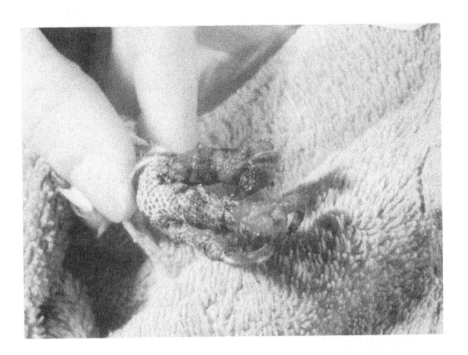

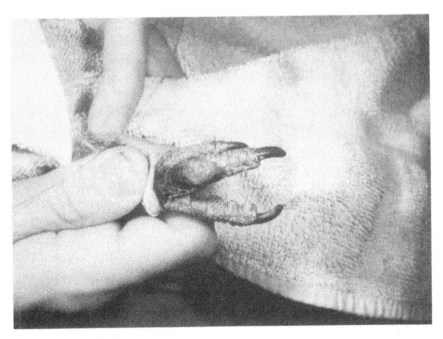

Two Amazon parrots demonstrating self-inflicted foot injuries. *Scott McDonald, DVM*

species whose progeny will eventually be the subjects of reintroduction into their range countries, a sweet-natured bird is much in demand as a family companion.)

However, it will be many years before parrots (excluding budgerigars and cockatiels) can be considered domestic in the sense that a cat or dog is domestic. They may always retain their aura of the exotic, the mysterious, the pagan. This is probably part of their appeal. Perhaps we wish to live with these birds because by living with the unknowable, we attempt to make it knowable, thereby possessing, being a part of it, controlling it. Or perhaps we recognize, on some atavistic level, that these birds were our companions when we had not yet descended from the trees in some African forests.

But for the present, our parrots are wild. They relate to us because they wish to, not because it has been bred into them. A good relationship with a parrot will always be one of mutual agreement, never of the owner and the owned. The term *owner*, as used in this book, implies "guardian": one who protects, defends, preserves, champions. A parrot's "owner" is that bird's patron and mentor, never its enslaver or conqueror.

Providing the insight and skills to deal successfully with birds requires not a cookbook approach, but a thorough grounding in the concepts that govern behavior and its modification. Each parrot is highly individual, despite the general characteristics for its species. Further, parrots do not develop problems in a vacuum, but in settings containing many variables. These variables include the relationships of their humans with each other, as well as the individual and collective relationships of those humans with the parrot.

The authors feel that basic knowledge of family dynamics theory is germane to the study of psittacine behavioral problems. It contains striking parallels that may be used with good effect in understanding and modifying problems. We wish the reader to understand that we are *not* saying that parrots are little people. We *are* saying that humans and parrots share social traits that, when understood, provide a framework the owner can use effectively to create a mutually satisfying relationship with an avian companion. And that further, this approach will provide a satisfying, happy life for the parrot. The mutually beneficial interface of the human/canine and human/feline systems is so accepted that no one questions it. The mutually satisfying, advantageous meshing of human/parrot systems is still viewed as somewhat serendipitous, a "gift of the gods," as it were, or dependent on the "animal magic" possessed by the fortunate and gifted few. Nothing could be further from the truth. There is no sorcery or witchcraft involved in a good relationship with one's parrot. Rather, it is the natural flowering based on principles that govern all relationships, whether they be with other people or with animals.

The application of good parenting skills to the socialization of the newly weaned parrot is a very sound way to effect the beneficial functioning of the people/parrot system interface to which we refer. Because of this, consideration of such principles will be reviewed to explore their specific applicability to "bringing up baby."

Many avoidable problems arise between birds and people because often individuals acquire one of these intelligent animals as a companion, not realizing the degree of emotional and physical care they require. They do not understand that disciplinary techniques used with dogs, for example, are not only inappropriate with birds, but absolutely counterproductive. For instance, hitting a biting parrot with a newspaper is abusive. It is not understood by the bird in terms of cause and effect. And it will inevitably lead to severe emotional trauma, escalated aggression or complete withdrawal.

Prospective parrot owners need to know which parrot will fit their needs and lifestyles. They should have basic knowledge of what to expect from a hand-reared parrot, as opposed to a wild-caught bird. An understanding, for example, of a parrot's need to chew—and appropriate ways to satisfy this need—will prevent much distress and thousands of dollars' worth of damage to household furnishings and equipment.

Collectively, the authors have many years of experience with parrots: as pet owners, breeders and professionals working with parrot behavior problems. Experience in family counseling techniques and human growth and development have also been a part of our background and have contributed to the approach and philosophy that guides our work with these birds. The authors hope to provide the reader with sound basic concepts applicable to parrot psychology and behavioral problems. In this way, each person will be able to decide what will work best with his parrot in his own unique situation, rather than being confronted with a list of "how-to's" that may or may not be applicable to the specific situation. A good comparison would be the old saying, "Give a man a fish and he will eat today. Teach him how to fish and he will eat for a lifetime."

To this end readers will find a broad range of material presented for their information and use. We will discuss the general personality traits of parrot species commonly kept as pets, as well as an overview of genus characteristics. The concept of pair-bonding and its importance to the parrot/human relationship will be explored. What a domestically bred, hand-reared parrot is—and more important, what it is *not*—will also be included.

The principles of behavioral modification and their application to parrots with maladaptive problems will be covered, as well as an overview of various accepted approaches and specific techniques that may be helpful. Specific techniques will often be presented within the context of case studies that will cover the parrot's presenting problems, a history of bird and owner, an analysis of problem development, creation of a modification protocol and follow-up. In this way, the reader will be able to understand how specific techniques appropriate to particular situations are developed for the individual.

We will also include material to help the reader understand how parrots grow and develop intellectually, socially and emotionally, and parrots' use of speech (both cognitive and imitative) will be discussed. These topics will be presented against a background of cognitive ethology, as well as experiential observation and anecdotal evidence.

Throughout the book, various topics will be examined as they relate to parrots in the domestic setting. Discussion of the use of psychotropic drugs to modify problems of sexual aggression and perseverative behavior will be included, and ethical considerations of such approaches (still not common) will be examined. The issues involved with an owner's decision to place his parrot in a breeding program as a last resort to refractory problems will be addressed. This is important because of the moral imperative to manage the existing captive gene pools of various species as well as possible, given the need to propagate these birds in captivity. Unless good genetic flock health is maintained, captive breeding will only postpone extinction, not prevent it. The breeder/seller of parrots also needs to examine his responsibility in placing birds in suitable homes. Issues such as educating prospective owners about what these birds require, the responsibility involved and species-specific personality traits will be included. All these issues will probably raise more questions than answers, but on such questions are new directions and solutions formulated. This is good and necessary and can only benefit the parrots who rely on us, as do children, for the best quality of life that we are able (and morally obliged) to provide them.

A Greater Sulphur-Crested Cockatoo (*Cacatua galerita galerita*) fluffs its feathers before preening. *Avicultural Breeding and Research Center*

2

Which Parrot Is for You?

"But no one ever told me these things." Often those who have acquired parrots as companions make this statement, sometimes in amused chagrin, sometimes in disappointment. Parrots are among the finest companions, but only for those who have "done their homework." Having a good relationship with a parrot requires that the would-be owner investigate which of the 350-some

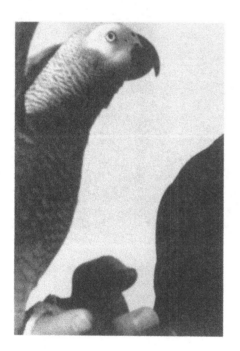

It is not my goal to hurt you...This writing is attributed to an African Grey Parrot named GoTizo. Her name, in the native lanugage of the African region from which she comes, means "Voice of Human." The entire piece is titled "Do Parrots Talk?" *Diane Schmidt*

species of this tribe will best fit his lifestyle. It also requires that the owner make the necessary commitment to the bird's emotional as well as physical health. Owners must recognize that even though the parrot is tame, even perhaps hand reared, it is not domestic in the sense that a cat or dog is. Parrots are intelligent creatures with a wild genetic heritage that have learned to adapt, with varying degrees of success, to the domestic setting.

This chapter is intended to help the reader make the necessary choices and decisions about acquiring a parrot as a companion. Knowing beforehand what a mutually enjoyable relationship with a parrot entails is the best way to ensure the desired results. These results can rarely be achieved when a bird is bought on impulse, or with the mistaken notion that it is a "low-maintenance" pet.

WHAT MAKES A PARROT A DESIRABLE PET?

Parrots carry with them an element of mystery. Living in close proximity with an essentially wild animal provides a sense of closeness with nature that is increasingly rare in urban society. Parrots, indeed all birds, have incredibly ancient lineages. They are probably direct lineal descendants of dinosaurs, making them modern dinosaurs. The eyes of birds seem to reflect an ancient wisdom, a "collective consciousness" at which we geologically young humans can only guess. There is so much we do not know about parrots.

The beauty of most parrots is undeniably an important factor in their desirability as pets. Many also have a characteristically regal bearing that enhances plumage and displays it to perfection. The marvelous color combinations possessed by parrots are a direct and dramatic contrast to the often drab colors of our native songbirds. It is interesting that even among dedicated birdwatchers, there is often much more excitement at having spotted a scarlet tanager than a dun-colored cowbird. People are visually drawn to dramatic colors.

The fact that all birds possess feathers also draws people to them. Feathers imply flight, which always fascinates us. The power of flight confers a lifestyle so different from our earthbound one that we can only guess at what it must be like. Birds live in the midst of this mystery. By sharing our lives with them, we vicariously experience something of a lifestyle that will always be impossible for us to achieve.

Parrots are extremely intelligent. As with dogs or cats, this makes them very attractive as companions and friends. It has been stated by those who work with parrots on the behavioral/learning level that they may possess the intelligence of a five-year-old child. Other researchers opine that parrots may be at least equal in intelligence to whales and dolphins. Parrots, jays and crows are generally acknowledged to be the most intelligent of all birds, and even have some concept of numbers—a concept that is difficult even for chimpanzees and gorillas to grasp.

Most people associate the ability to mimic with parrots and believe that this is their most important characteristic. Although many parrots do have the ability to mimic, not all do so. Even within the species known for outstanding talking ability (African Grey Parrots, Yellow-Naped Amazons, Blue-Fronted Amazons, Yellow-Fronted Amazons and Double Yellow-Headed Amazons), this ability varies tremendously among individuals. While this is accounted for in part by the bird's genetic predisposition to talk, it is also dependent to a large degree on the bird's experience in its domestic setting. Additionally, it may no longer be accurate to speak of the parrot's ability to "mimic." Many who have long and close relationships with their birds commonly report that their parrots use cognitive speech. In other words, the bird knows what it is saying and uses speech appropriately on many occasions.

The work of Dr. Irene Pepperberg with Alex, an African Grey Parrot, has demonstrated beyond any doubt that some birds, at least, have the ability to learn concepts and employ them appropriately in the majority of cases. Naturally, to know that one's bird may be able to communicate on a deeper level than mere mimicry is a compelling reason to share one's life with such a parrot. However, as fascinating as this potential is, it is far better to have a parrot with a steady, affectionate nature. If the bird also talks, so much the better. "Pretty is as pretty does!"

In some ways, parrots can become our mirrors, although we are usually not aware of this on a conscious level. Nevertheless, this phenomenon exists. For example, we have noticed many times that when people have the good fortune to live with a happy, healthy parrot in a state of mutual enjoyment, these same people also have good relationships with their children. They seem to have related in the same way to their birds as to their children, with the same happy results!

The companionship of parrots is a gift from them to us. Not genetically programmed to give us their friendship or loyalty, nevertheless, many, many of them do. This offering should not be undervalued or trivialized. To have a friendship with such a bird means a conscious commitment on the owner's part to return the same degree of loyalty, trust, concern—all of the components that nurture a satisfactory relationship. Individuals who ignore this truth forfeit their parrots' friendships. Comradeship with a parrot is never a question of the owner and the owned. It is always an alliance based on mutual agreement and trust.

The issue of status should be mentioned in connection with parrot ownership. Buying a parrot because it is "macho," expensive, rare, amusing or different is irresponsible. The same can be said of acquiring one as an ornament. These birds are intelligent, sentient creatures whose lives have intrinsic value to themselves, aside from any other attribute they may possess that makes people want them. True, people do purchase parrots for the wrong reasons—their rarity and expense is sometimes used to proclaim the economic status of their owners—but the parrot acquired for such reasons inevitably experiences emotional and physical tragedy. Parrots are not throwaways, to be possessed because they are "trendy." The only true justification for sharing one's life with any animal is the honest desire to provide enhanced quality of life through commitment to its emotional and physical well-being.

EXPECTATIONS: THE WILD-CAUGHT PARROT VS. THE DOMESTICALLY BRED, HAND-REARED PARROT

The person wishing to acquire a parrot to share his life has two sources from which to choose: the wild-caught import market and the domestic market. As conservation of parrots in their range countries assumes increasing urgency, the availability of imported birds has waned. And as advances in husbandry and health care make it possible to breed exotic birds with increasing success, breeders are producing more domestically bred, hand-reared parrots. To be sure, a hand-reared parrot youngster has the *potential* to become a better pet than a wild-caught bird that may already have been fully adult at the time of capture and is thus much less amenable to learning the skills necessary for happy adaptation to life in a family setting. However, when discussing the companion potential of the hand-reared bird, certain limitations must be recognized, since most people have unrealistic expectations of such a parrot. The following is a discussion of what can and cannot be expected of both wild-caught and domestic parrots.

Let us first talk about the wild-caught parrot. This bird, as the term obviously implies, has been trapped in its range country by a variety of methods and sold to a broker, who in turn sells the bird to an importer in the United States or other country to which the bird is not indigenous. There are serious ethical and moral issues surrounding such practices, and these have been addressed and corrected by federal legislation as well as by international treaties such as CITES (Convention on International Trade in Endangered Species of Flora and Fauna).

Although it can be very difficult to gentle a wild-caught parrot, it is not impossible to do so; indeed, some of these birds have become dear companions, flourishing in the family setting. It is far more common, though, for the owner to find that he does not possess the time, skill, patience and physical courage to effect such a result. To teach a wild animal to live in the unfamiliar surroundings of captivity requires change, on the part of bird *and* owner, and since the experiences involved in change are frequently painful and inconvenient, it may seem, at least in the short term, more pleasant and less trouble to avoid them. As a result, the parrot often lives a solitary life in its cage, ignored and poorly cared for, as its humans lose interest in a creature whose sole aim in life appears to be aggression and hate.

This is not to say that all individuals who purchase a wild-caught parrot will experience this. Those who have had great success in helping such a bird become a happy, outgoing avian friend state that they would not have missed such an experience for the world. The bonding that occurs between parrot and human in such a circumstance is unique and cannot be duplicated with any other companion animal. Nevertheless, it is not recommended that those other than the extremely experienced ever attempt to gentle a wild parrot. The potential for serious damage to both bird and person is too great, and the chance of success far too small, to justify such an undertaking.

All of the foregoing logically leads us to the question of the hand-reared parrot. Such birds are imprinted at birth, or shortly thereafter, on humans. If the bird has been reared by a human surrogate from the moment of hatching, it will have never known others of its kind, unless it had clutchmates that were also being hand reared. If the baby was removed from the nest for hand rearing between three to four weeks of age, the same imprinting occurs. Because the bird has not learned defensive responses toward humans as a baby, it readily accepts companionship with people. So the parrot will never bite, right? It will never pick its feathers, or pull them out, or mutilate itself, right? It will never scream like a wild bird, right? It will never become aggressive when it matures sexually, right? *Wrong!!!!*

And hereby hangs the tale concerning the domestically bred bird: It is tame, but *not* domestic. The mere fact that it was bred in captivity *does not mean it is a domestic animal.* It merely means that the bird is tame when it is weaned and sold as a companion. *It does not mean that the bird will stay this way.* Three or four generations of captive breeding will not erase 35 or 40 million years of wild genetic heritage. What domestic breeding *does* mean is that the parrot has the potential, given *informed* human companions, of remaining a delightful pet all

Which of these two African Grey Parrots is imported/wild-caught, and which domestically bred and hand-reared? The bird on the left is wild and is about three days into his "petting" work. When working with such birds, we must be cautious, yet not allow ourselves to be manipulated into backing off by the threatening posture. The other Grey is co-author Thom Qualkinbush's personal pet. Here, she illustrates that she's aware of her own wild heritage and is the emotional support her wild counterpart needs. *Diane Schmidt*

its considerably long days. However, if the bird's owner does not apply knowledge, caring and sound behavioral psittacine psychology, the bird will not only fail to fulfill its companion potential, but will usually revert to wild behavior (especially at sexual maturity), and subsequently develop serious behavior problems. A wild animal capable of inflicting injury can become a safety risk if it has no fear of humans. Hand-reared parrots have *no* fear of people.

There are, of course, many species of parrots that, because of their genetically determined temperament, are more docile and less inclined to extreme independence and aggression. Nevertheless, it is appropriate and necessary to outline here the Golden Rules for "bringing up baby." Acquiring a cuddly, newly weaned parrot and bringing it home is just the beginning. Observance of the following guidelines will help immensely in developing a good, long-term relationship with your hand-reared parrot.

The reader may, at first glance, feel that such guidelines are too stringent for use with a very young parrot. However, remind yourself that you will be dealing with a highly intelligent animal with a tremendous capacity to learn, and an innate desire to fit in comfortably with its flock—in this situation you, your family and your other pets. Additionally, consider that you would never bring home a new kitten and neglect to teach it to use a litter pan because it was "too young." You would never purchase a puppy and wait until it was "old enough" to withstand the rigors of being taken outside to accomplish elimination. Firm, loving guidelines must be set for all young animals in order to allow them to learn what is expected of them in the domestic setting. It is much easier to prevent potential problems than to correct them once they have become established, maladaptive behavior. The following guidelines will sometimes vary for different species and individuals, but are generally applicable to most parrots.

GUIDELINES FOR HANDLING A NEWLY WEANED PARROT

1. Purchase a waist-high training stand immediately. This will be money well spent, and an invaluable training tool.

2. Make sure the parrot's primary flight feathers are clipped by someone competent to do so.

Note the submissive posture of the Umbrella Cockatoo (*Cacatua alba*) on the right. The submissive mode is the behavior to look for when taming a parrot. It's quite natural for parrots to assume either a dominant or submisssive role when socializing. Many people feel guilt if their parrots seem to appear submissive. A more productive and positive attitude is to respect the parrot's submission to your dominance. This is when the parrot is most receptive to physical contact. *Diane Schmidt*

3. Bring the bird home, place it in its cage and let it adjust to cage, surroundings, family members and other pets. The time this takes varies with the individual bird. One to four days is usually enough. Do not spend too much time with the parrot too soon (see #5 below).

4. The first time the bird is allowed out of the cage, limit the time. This reduces the stress the parrot may feel at first. It also establishes from the beginning that you are in control, as expressed by the fact that *you* determine when the bird is returned to the cage.

5. Do not initiate routines with the bird that you will be unable to continue. For example, if you will not always be able to take the parrot out of its cage immediately after you arrive home from work, do not do it just because the parrot is new to your household.

6. Do not open the cage door and let the bird come out, climb to the top of the cage or go back into the cage by itself. The bird must learn that you are the one to determine when and if these activities are to be allowed. Therefore *you* must be the one to place the parrot where you want it to be. This establishes you as the person in control of the relationship just as a parent does with a child.

7. Once the parrot has been removed from its cage, hold it on your hand for a brief period before proceeding to other activities with it.

8. Do not allow the parrot to bite, even playfully. This includes nibbling. Birds do not discriminate, at least at first, between inanimate objects and tender flesh. Further, the parrot must never be allowed to view the use of its beak on a person as acceptable behavior, no matter what the circumstances.

9. Do not allow the parrot on your shoulder for at least a week after it is home. Some parrots should never be allowed on the shoulder.

10. Do not allow the bird on your shoulder unless you place it it there. Remove it when *you* choose the time for this.

11. Teach the parrot to come on *and off* your hand or arm on command.

12. Do not allow the parrot to roam the floor. This presents a safety risk for the bird and encourages it to set its own rules for what it will or will not do, giving the parrot, not you, control of situations.

13. Introduce the parrot to as many new foods as possible. Fruits, vegetables and most human foods are fine, but avoid junk food, foods high in fat, and alcohol.

14. Do not introduce the parrot to seed if this has not already been done. Later on, it can be used as an *occasional* treat.

15. Set aside time each day as playtime, in addition to training time.

An Amazon parrot with properly cliped wings. This parrot will not be able to gain altitude but will be able to flutter safely to the floor if it should attempt to fly from cage or training stand. *Scott McDonald, DVM*

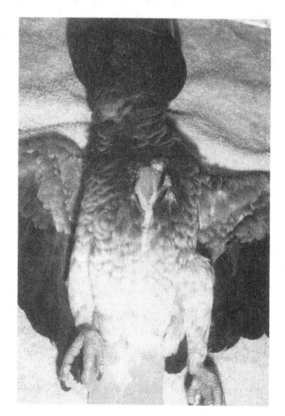

Failure to properly clip this African Grey Parrot's wings caused it to fall and fracture its breastbone. *Scott McDonald, DVM*

16. Start setting behavior guidelines for your new parrot as soon as possible. This establishes what is expected of it at the outset and prevents undesirable behavior from becoming hard-to-break habits.

ACQUIRING ADULT, PREVIOUSLY OWNED PARROTS

Often one will be tempted to rescue a parrot that has been found in less than ideal circumstances, or purchase a bird from someone who no longer wants it. This last can be especially tempting because the price asked is frequently below what one would pay a pet store or breeder. In either case the reader should understand both the potential hazards and drawbacks and the fact that it usually makes no difference whether the parrot was originally hand reared or wild caught relative to problems you may encounter.

The difficulty in taking on such parrots is that more often than not, they have serious problems. Occasionally, there may be legitimate truth to the seller's explanation that genuine health problems preclude continued ownership of the parrot. It is more than likely, though, that the bird screams incessantly, picks its feathers or has become aggressive.

Often the parrot's problems have been created unwittingly by a well-intentioned but misinformed owner, and changing these behaviors can be frustrating and expensive. Indeed, the would-be new owner's chances of successfully altering such behaviors without professional help is very slim in the majority of cases, especially since the sheer size of some of the large parrots greatly magnifies their problems.

Compounding the problem is the fact that these intelligent birds are often skillful con artists. What you see is not always what you get. Behaving with utmost charm and sociability during a first encounter, they may, upon arriving in their new homes, change into convincing copies of the devil incarnate.

If you feel compelled to acquire such a bird, seek professional help as soon as you get the bird home, for unless you are extremely skilled in working with parrots such as these, you are almost certainly doomed to failure. This is sad for the new owner but a tragedy for the bird, for its future will consist of being shuffled from place to place, never having a chance to learn better ways of relating and experiencing the pleasure and security of a good rapport with people.

CHILDREN, ADOLESCENTS, YOUNG ADULTS AND PARROTS

Parrots are not throwaway playthings. Probably the most important factor in keeping a parrot emotionally healthy is routine provided by a consistent caretaker. This ensures stability of diet, hygiene, schedule and handling. Children, adolescents and young adults cannot provide this. *Parrots need stability.* This cannot be stressed too strongly.

For the obvious reason given above, children and parrots do not mix. Understandably, parents want to give their children experience with the animal world. Often, a large component of this desire is to "teach the child responsibility." If you feel a pet is a necessary part of your child's learning and growing process, a cat or dog is a much better choice. In fact, it is the *only* responsible choice. Children are unable to reason in adult ways (for example, cause and effect) until they are approximately four years old. Parrots cannot reason that a child is physically more fragile than an adult. The sudden gestures and loud exclamations and vocalizations of children are often interpreted by parrots as serious threats, and they will frequently react by biting (no matter how tame). Potential harm to the child from even the most friendly parrot is not worth the risk. The potential harm to the parrot, both physically and emotionally, are not worth the risks, either.

Misinformation creates the erroneous belief that because a parrot is tame, it is domestic, in the sense that cats or dogs are domestic. Parrot owners who believe this also believe that their birds would never inflict damage on them or their children. When a child then places the parrot in a threatening situation and the bird retaliates, the parrot is then labeled as untrustworthy and dangerous. We contend that such unrealistic attitudes lead to tragedies for both child and bird.

We are reminded of an incident that could have had terrible consequences. The parents of a two year old had several large parrots, among them a macaw. On one occasion, the child inserted her hand into the macaw's cage, and it bit her so badly that for quite some time physicians were uncertain whether she would ever regain the use of her fingers. Fortunately, the incident had a happy ending and the child suffered no permanent impairment, but the outcome could have been just as easily the opposite.

Another situation comes to mind that indicates the inability of some adults to understand the maturity needed to care for a parrot. One of the authors received a telephone call from a very distressed woman who had bought a medium-sized, hand-reared parrot for her son. The child, according to her, was longing for a pet, and had been persistent about it for long enough to convince her of his sincerity. She confided that her son was extraordinarily bright and advanced for his age, so she had no misgivings about purchasing the bird for his birthday. However, after having the parrot for nearly four months, both mother and child were very disappointed. The woman stated that her child could not handle the bird without being bitten. The boy was now afraid of the parrot, as was she. After hearing this sad story, the author finally had an opportunity to ask how old the child was. The mother replied that he had just turned four years old!

When children and parrots are developing a relationship, they need *close* supervision. A large parrot may cause serious injury to a child. Young children must learn how to behave around parrots. It is the adult's responsibility to prevent injury and emotional trauma to both child and parrot. *Thom Qualkinbush*

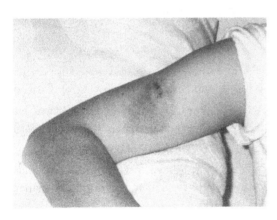

Parrots' beaks are to be respected. Although this injury was very unpleasant and painful, it could have been much worse. What if that had been a five-year-old child's finger? Please supervise vulnerable children and parrots, and help educate adults of the dangers as well as the pleasures of parrot ownership. *Steve Isenberg*

Generally, where adolescents and young adults are concerned, the inability of either to provide the stability a parrot requires should be adequate reason to discourage the acquisition of a companion parrot. During the teen and young adult years, the individual's tasks include acquiring an education or job skills, finding a mate, launching a career and establishing a family. Obviously, such activities are time consuming, and the parrot will suffer as a result. College campuses are full of unwanted cats and dogs left behind by their owners when summer break rolls around. Parrots should not be added to this pathetic list.

Often, young marrieds desire to have a parrot as a companion. They feel they can give a bird the care and stability it requires. In many cases this is possible, and the bird becomes a cherished family friend. However, in more than just a few isolated cases, the parrot becomes a child surrogate. Then when human children begin to arrive, the parrot often reacts with jealousy, creating distress for the adults and potential danger to the human infant. Parrots can learn to adjust to and accept children as they come into the family. However, they must be helped to do this, and new parents frequently do not feel the time and effort required are "worth it." This is sad example of a throwaway attitude about an animal when it becomes an inconvenience.

In a home where there are young children, please consider the following suggestions:

1. The parrot should be the sole responsibility of the adult who acquired it. It is unfair to expect a child to provide the care these birds require without *ongoing* supervision in the adult's presence.

2. *Never* leave a child alone with any parrot, no matter how tame the bird is.

3. If you wish to allow your child to pet the parrot, the bird should be perched on the adult's arm and the adult should have *full control* of the bird's head.

4. Young hand-reared parrots may be allowed to perch on a child's arm, but *only* after the adult has made a decision about safety for both child and bird.

5. Practice good hygiene in handling of bird and child. Do not touch your child after cleaning the cage unless you have first washed your hands. Conversely, do not handle the parrot after changing an infant's diapers unless you have also washed your hands.

Remember that once a child becomes afraid of a parrot, overcoming this fear will be difficult. In the same way, once a parrot becomes afraid of a child, it may be impossible to reverse its fear, not only of the particular child, but of children in general.

One further comment about parrots and children involves allergies. Some children are highly allergic to any kind of animal dander. Parents of such children, not wanting them to miss the experience of growing up with a pet, often purchase a parrot, not realizing birds also produce dander to which the child may be allergic. Consult your child's doctor if this is a potential problem.

PAIR-BONDING: WHAT IS IT AND WHY IS IT IMPORTANT?

The concept of pair-bonding is very important to the parrot/human relationship. It is one of the genetic characteristics that can make a parrot a marvelous companion, but it can also create problems when the bird reaches sexual maturity. As with so many avian traits, the trick is to understand how to emphasize the positive aspects of pair-bonding while minimizing the negative aspects.

The pair-bond is defined as "a non-aggressive, mutually beneficial relationship between a sexually mature male and female bird. This pair-bond may be strong and last as long as both mates are alive" (Coyle 1987). In the bonded relationship, contacts between birds are continually strengthened by behavior that modifies all of the pair's interactions with each other. Such behaviors include mutual preening, feeding, roosting and defense of each other and their mutual territory. The pair-bond also functions to reduce potential aggression between the bonded pair.

The pair-bond is especially important to birds such as parrots, which live long lives and produce relatively few young. Most mammals do not pair-bond in the sense that birds do because mammalian offspring, in general, do not have long infancies in which they are totally helpless and require intensive nurturing for many weeks (Kavenau 1987). Parrot offspring have long infancies and require more parental care than many other birds. It is therefore necessary that the male as well as the female be involved in their care. The pair-bond ensures that the hen will have the necessary help while discharging her parental duties. Some male parrots such as cockatiels and cockatoos actually help with the incubation of eggs, while males of other species feed the hen as she incubates, guard the nest entrance and then actively feed the young after they have hatched.

Although we do not know exactly what determines the nature of the bond between a pair of parrots, there are three components that are probably operative: mutual attachment to common territory, comfortable familiarity with each other and genuine affection. Welty and Baptista (1988) give an account of black ducks that were observed during a fall courtship and pair formation. On two separate occasions, partners of birds shot by local hunters could not be induced to leave their stricken mates.

A similar story was related to one of the authors, this time concerning a pair of mallard ducks (Soucek 1991). Driving home on a narrow country road after dark some years ago, Gayle Soucek and her companion saw a lifeless hen mallard in the center of the road. Her mate was standing on her body and screaming with what Soucek stated sounded very like grief. She had never heard a mallard make such continuous keening cries. Even though they attempted to move the drake out of harm's way, he refused to leave his mate's body. Eventually, Soucek and her friend had to move the hen's body to the verge of the road in order to coax the male away. As they drove away, the male was still next to his mate, keening in the same eerie fashion.

Similar stories are reported from Australia by those who have observed poisoned cockatoos. These birds' mates refuse to leave them, often tugging at the corpses and vocalizing to them in an attempt to get them to move.

The pair-bonding trait in a parrot destined to be a companion confers some very desirable characteristics. Among these are loyalty, affection and, to some extent, diminished aggressive tendencies directed toward its human "mate."

There are, however, some negative aspects of pair-bonding regarding the parrot's attachment to a favored person. The parrot will often, especially at the onset of sexual maturity, bond with one person exclusively. The bird perceives its person as a true mate, and will often attempt to preen, courtship-feed and copulate with the person who is so honored. The parrot will begin to exercise all the prerogatives of a mated bird, including defending its "mate" against all comers, often biting other family members to drive them away. The cage becomes a potential nesting site, again causing the parrot to bite in attempts to defend this important territory from "predators" and unwanted interference. It is not at all uncommon for the bird to bite its human "mate" in an effort to drive her/him away from perceived "danger," most usually another family member the parrot sees as competition. This type of biting is called displacement biting, and although not intended to express aggression to the favored one, can nevertheless be extremely painful. In addition, these bites are often experienced by the human as being unexpected and unprovoked. (When a parrot bites its mate in this fashion in the wild, all that happens is that it gets a mouth full of feathers. The mate gets the point and moves away. When the bird bites its human mate surrogate, a large portion of tender flesh is assaulted by a beak that may be fully capable of cracking a Brazil nut in one crunch!)

Although these potential drawbacks occur with the parrot, which is genetically programmed to pair-bond with a mate, they may never manifest themselves in the parrot/human bond. It depends on how consistently the bird has been socialized and guided into behavior that is appropriate in the domestic setting from the time it was a youngster. It also depends on the consistency with which the parrot's human companion has set and reinforced behavior guidelines relative to behavior that will not be tolerated (e.g., biting for *any* reason). This can be done so successfully that when the parrot reaches sexual maturity, it will remain as loving and docile a pet as when it was a weanling. The mature parrot will exhibit more adult characteristics than those appropriate to infancy and immaturity, just as children do when they grow up. But as with adult children, the relationship with the adult parrot can be just as close and loving.

A good way to ensure that this is the case (in addition to adhering to the guidelines on page 20) is to allow, perhaps even insist, that adult and adolescent family members handle the parrot regularly. Cleaning and feeding chores should also be divided in the same way. The parrot is then forced to relate to several family members as providers of attention and food. It also accepts that the cage is not its sole property. It is helpful as well if the parrot sees as wide a variety of people as possible, if this is at all possible. Most often, parrots that remain outgoing and gentle are the ones that have had a great deal of contact with many people. These birds are much less apt to bond strongly to just one person. Handling by only one person tends to develop a personality that will be at greater risk of developing negative behaviors sometimes associated with extreme bonding.

PARROT PERSONALITY PROFILES

All species have many personality attributes, which we customarily term positive or negative and which are possessed because of their survival value. Such attributes are determined by evolution, to equip them with the maximum ability to survive and pass their genes on to the next generation. They have nothing to do with equipping the parrot to be the "ideal" companion. It is therefore necessary to understand that any personality trait is neither bad nor good; it merely is. The prospective owner must decide for himself what constellation of traits he is willing to tolerate and work with. For example, if you do not like noise, are intimidated by a large beak and live in a small home or apartment, no matter how beautiful and appealing a macaw is, it is not the bird for you. You will enjoy your parrot friend much more if you select a smaller, quieter and gentler bird.

In our discussion of parrot personality characteristics, we will first address the pair-bonding species, both common and uncommon. We will then discuss the nonpair-bonding species in the same order. Less detail will be included for these birds, for many are primarily kept as aviary and breeding specimens by avicultural specialists, rather than as family companions. However, some of these birds can and do make good pets, especially for those who wish a bird that is very undemanding of social interaction with its owners.

In addition, it should be remembered that each parrot is an individual. The traits discussed here are generalizations. The bird's singular personality is the most important factor to consider in deciding which will be a member of your family.

Last, we will discuss parrots that should never be kept as pets. These are the birds that are endangered and should only be in the hands of serious, expert breeders. Some of these parrots are kept as pets, and many make superb companions. However, we hope that the reader will decide against such birds as potential companions. If you do own such a parrot, consider placing it in a breeding program when it becomes sexually mature.

PAIR-BONDING PARROTS: COMMON

African Grey Parrot *(Psittacus erithacus erithacus, subspecies timneh)*

These parrots are highly desired as companions, not only for their outstanding ability to talk, but also because of their incredible intelligence. There is a mystique, an aura about the African Grey that is difficult to describe but is nonetheless undeniably present. For many, the Grey is the ultimate avian companion, the ultimate parrot. Rosemary Low (1980) states that "there can never have been so many cherished pets among parrots as Greys. The Duke of Bedford, in *Parrots and Parrot-Like Birds* (1969), says of the Grey, "Once he has really given you his heart—and very often only one person is so honoured— he is always gentle except under great provocation ..."

African Grey Parrots tend to be very suspicious of new people, objects and environments. They are highly strung, somewhat nervous birds, very sensitive to the emotional content of any situation. It is rare for this parrot to talk in the presence of those it does not know. A frightened Grey will growl, a sound like nothing else on earth. These parrots are also known for their predisposition to feather picking, plucking and mutilation. Such behavior is often (although not always) initiated as an expression of stress or boredom. A Grey that is neglected is a prime candidate for this distressing habit, which, once begun, is very hard to correct, especially without professional help.

Although this parrot has the potential for becoming the best possible psittacine companion, no one should even consider one of these grand birds unless willing to make the commitment to provide the high degree of emotional care they need and deserve.

The African Grey needs much more dietary calcium than most other parrots, and every effort *must* be made to meet this need. Otherwise, the bird may eventually develop hypocalcemic syndrome, suffering convulsions and eventually dying, unless immediate veterinary care is sought.

Amazon Parrots *(Amazona)*

There are many species in this group, some commonly kept as pets and some so rare that to breed them, one must have a permit from the federal government. As a group, Amazon parrots are bundles of contradictions. Some are comical and entertaining, others aloof and sedate. They may be very social, or prone to moodiness. They can be very curious about their people and environment, or largely uninterested. Some are beautiful, and others rather plain. They can be very predictable, but also very unpredictable. They can be very gentle, or very rough; very adaptable, or very inflexible. All of these traits can be exhibited not only from species to species, but also within the same bird throughout the day! Amazon parrots are very special. Most of this group are very noisy, and many are wonderful talkers. They have powerful beaks and many do not hesitate to use them for purposes of resculpting furniture or flesh if the notion takes them. Amazons are not for everyone.

Most Amazons are very intelligent, and with proper handling can make delightful companions. However, they are strong willed and stubborn, liking nothing better than to be the dominant member of any relationship. This can cause serious problems for the person who does not understand how to deal with it.

One characteristic of many of this group is the potential for *serious* aggression upon reaching sexual maturity. The authors *cannot overemphasize* that the person who acquires an Amazon must be fully aware of this possibility and raise the bird in such a way that it does not become a problem in later years. It is a heartbreaking experience to have a dear pet "turn on you." Both of the authors have in their breeding programs Amazon parrots that were given up by their owners because the parrots attacked their faces, requiring trips to the local hospital for suturing.

In spite of all the above, Amazon parrots can be tremendously satisfying companions if given proper guidance and socialization.

As previously stated, it all depends on the amount of care and commitment you are willing to devote to these birds, and your willingness to accept all the traits that make an Amazon what it is.

Three of this group, the Yellow-Naped Amazon (*Amazona ochrocephala auropalliata*), the Yellow-Fronted Amazon (*A. ochrocephala ochrocephala*) and the Double-Yellow-Headed Amazon (*A. ochrocephala tresmariae*) are among the best talkers in the parrot world. Although they may remain sweet and docile all their lives, they have an especially marked potential for aggression if not handled wisely from their youth. The Yellow-Naped Amazon seems to be particularly prone to this behavior.

The Blue-Fronted Amazon (*A. aestiva aestiva*) is an extremely popular parrot. Its attractive plumage, outstanding talking ability and clownlike personality are all pluses. Although it can be aggressive, it tends to be more sedate upon maturity, especially if its humans have taken care to socialize it properly.

Amazon parrots such as the Mexican Red-Headed (or as it is otherwise known, the Green-Cheeked Amazon) (*A. veridiginalis*) is a quiet, docile bird, and is much less aggressive and strong willed than other Amazons discussed thus far. Many of these delightful parrots are kept as companions. However, their numbers have drastically declined in their range country, and they are endangered. Some aviculturists are now giving their attention to captive breeding of this species. The authors would not go so far as to say that this parrot should not be kept as a companion. However, the responsible course would be to place the bird in a breeding situation at maturity, so that its numbers do not decline in captivity as well as in its native habitat.

Another Amazon parrot that is an outstanding companion is the Mealy (*A. farinosa farinosa*), or its subspecies, the Plain-Colored Amazon (*A. farinosa inornata*). There are simply no words to describe the splendid companion characteristics of this bird. A very large parrot, sometimes measuring almost twenty inches in length, it is nevertheless one of the sweetest, most gentle of all Amazons. Very steady, it rarely resorts to nipping. At maturity, it usually becomes sweeter, and serious sexual aggression does not seem to be a part of its nature. Some of these birds talk and sing exceptionally well; others are only moderate talkers. But for sheer delight as an intelligent, devoted friend, they are hard to beat.

The only drawback is that Mealy Amazons of any species are hard to find. Never imported into this country in the huge numbers that other Amazons have been, it is not commonly seen. In addition, it takes many years for it to arrive at sexual maturity, so one must wait a very long time before a breeding pair can produce offspring. Also, not many of these birds have been set up for breeding, an unusual situation given the wonderful quality of this parrot's personality. However, if you can find a hand-reared youngster of this species, you are indeed most fortunate.

Pocket Parrots *(Brotogeris species)*

These are very small parrots, acquiring their name from their fondness for nestling in pockets, under shirt collars, up sleeves and the like. They can be not only loud, having rather harsh, grating voices, but also have the reputation of being indifferent talkers. To make up for this, they are cuddly, affectionate little fellows and very playful. Even the harsh voice does not have the volume and piercing quality of an Amazon, macaw or cockatoo voice. Commonly kept companion species are the Canary-Winged Parakeet (*Brotogeris versicolorus versicolorus*), the Grey-Cheeked Parakeet (*B. pyrrhopterus*) and the Golden-Winged Parakeet (*B. chrysopterus chrysopterus*) and the Orange-Winged Parakeet (*B. jugularis jugularis*).

The Grey-Cheeked Parakeet can sometimes be aggressive and nippy. The authors feel this species *must* be handled every day to keep it tame. Otherwise, it tends to revert to unsociable behavior.

Budgerigar *(Melopsittacus undulatus)*

This little charmer is customarily, though incorrectly, known as the parakeet. More accurately called the budgerigar or budgie, these birds are extremely enjoyable to watch. And they seem to enjoy watching people just as much! They are very acrobatic, full of amusing antics. Budgies seem to have a joie de vivre that is infectious, and they can also develop outstanding vocabularies, albeit in a tiny voice. Budgies are very affectionate and companionable. Small and relatively easy to care for, they are a good choice for those who want a true parrot, but one that is diminutive. Not only is the budgie a great companion, it has also contributed more than its share to avian breeding and veterinary knowledge.

This little bird occurs in many colors because of the efforts of breeders who have plumbed the depths of its genetic heritage. It is also bred in two sizes, although both are small. The American budgie is the smaller of the two, but *very* active. The English budgie has been bred for a large breast and imposing carriage. This variety is much more staid and sedentary than its American counterpart.

Unfortunately, inbreeding used to fix traits of color and size is directly responsible for one serious drawback to this bird as a companion: it does not have a very long life span, for it is genetically predisposed to cancer. The inbreeding that has produced size differences and so many agreeable colors has also fixed the trait that puts the budgie at risk for this lethal disease. Although a budgerigar of the normal, untampered gene makeup should ordinarily live for fourteen to fifteen years, such a bird is now impossible to find. Even should you acquire a normally colored green budgie, it will not have the pure, unmixed genes of its original wild counterpart. For this little bird to live five to seven years is now considered to be "normal." Many never make it this far.

Cockatiel *(Nymphicus hollandicus)*

A member of the cockatoo family, these small parrots exhibit many of the same characteristics. Just take away most of the desire for physical contact and you've got a cockatiel. The adult cockatiel does not even like contact with another cockatiel in the usual way of things. This little bird enjoys some physical contact and cuddling, but on its own terms. It is very social, however, and adores being in the center of household activity. Cockatiels have delightful personalities, and many are able to develop large vocabularies. They are also talented whistlers and many times can learn to whistle several tunes, sometimes from beginning to end, and note-perfect into the bargain!

Although the cockatiel has a proportionately small beak, it can, and sometimes does, use it effectively to express displeasure. It is a peculiar trait of this bird, that when biting, it does not let go immediately as do most parrots. Instead, it hangs on and grinds. Thus, a cockatiel bite, although certainly not producing extensive damage, can be a very unpleasant experience.

Cockatiels, like budgerigars, occur in many different color varieties. Again, inbreeding is used to fix these color traits, and along with desirable results, can also predispose to health problems. Some of the more exotic color mutations have produced birds prone to night frights, jaw weakness and /or paralysis and shortened life spans. The authors, although recognizing the aesthetic appeal of the color mutations, nevertheless recommend the normally colored gray cockatiel. Such a bird probably has a greater chance to live out its fifteen- to twenty-year life span than those of more unusual hue.

One of the challenges of breeding cockatiels, budgerigars or other psittacids such as the Indian Ringneck Parakeet is to produce and fix (or stabilize) traits such as color mutation in a group of birds. Many breeders of such birds will argue that such breeding does not shorten cockatiels' life spans. Nevertheless, avian veterinarians can attest to the health problems that much mutational breeding may cause.

Conures *(Aratinga and Phyrrhura)*

These parrots are small birds (with the exception of the Queen of Bavaria Conure and the Patagonian Conure) that occur in many colors. Some are predominantly green, such as the Dusky-Headed Conure. Others are arrayed in colors of almost blinding brilliance, such as the Sun Conure and to a lesser extent the Nanday Conure. Most of the parrots of this group make wonderful pets, for they are very intelligent, exceptionally playful and affectionate. Though sometimes strong willed and stubborn, they are basically sweet natured and thrive on social interaction with their humans.

One of the chief drawbacks with most conures (pronounced *con-*yers) are their frequently loud, grating voices. Hand-reared youngsters tend to be somewhat quieter than their wild counterparts, but on reaching sexual maturity they, too, may develop voices that will nearly shatter glass. Nevertheless, this characteristic may be somewhat altered to a "livable" level by good behavioral modification technique.

Another problem of concern with conures in general, and the Patagonian Conure specifically, is that they are noted to be carriers of Pacheco's disease. This is a *Herpesvirus* infection of the liver (not communicable to humans) that causes a fast-developing, lethal avian hepatitis. More a problem of wild-caught conures than of the domestically bred, it is still a matter for concern. *Not all conures carry or will carry Pacheco's virus.* Most never do. The rather remote possibility of this disease need not discourage one from acquiring one of these fine little parrots as a companion if care is taken that the bird is purchased from a reputable breeder and comes from healthy stock.

Commonly kept birds of this group include the Dusky-Headed Conure (*Aratinga weddellii*), the Sun Conure (*A. solstitialis solstitialis*), the Jenday Conure (*A. solstitialis janday*) and the Nanday Conure (*Nandayus nenday*). Although all of these make good companions, the Dusky-Headed Conure is outstanding. Very gentle, affectionate and quieter than most of its cousins, it can also learn to talk.

The Nanday Conure requires comment, also. Of all the conures, it is possessed of one of the most unpleasant voices imaginable. This is a shame, for in all other respects it makes an outstanding pet. As mentioned previously, hand-reared birds tend to be quieter, and behavioral modification can further help minimize excessive vocalization. However, it is natural for *all* parrots to indulge in at least morning and evening screeching bouts, just as they would in their natural habitats. If you cannot tolerate particularly loud, harsh shrieking, the Nanday is not for you. In the mid to late 1980s it was common for pet stores to import these parrots by the thousands and sell them at ridiculously low prices as a "genuine, talking parrot for an exceptionally low price, with cage." Tragically, most who succumbed to this bargain basement approach and bought the birds were bitterly disappointed, primarily because of the horrible noise they made. Nearly all of these birds were disposed of in one way or another when their owners could no longer tolerate them, a real tragedy for the parrots and a negative experience for disillusioned owners. One should *never* get a parrot on impulse, especially one that appears to be a bargain you simply can't pass up. You may find, as did the disillusioned Nanday owners, that you will be unable to live with the bird. At worst, the bird may have been illegally smuggled and have serious health problems.

Cockatoos *(Cacatua)*

The birds of this genus are breathtakingly beautiful, outstandingly intelligent and affectionate to the point of being pests (if not properly raised). They are also some of the noisiest creatures in aviculture. Cockatoos have tremendously powerful beaks with which they can reduce almost anything to rubble (even chainlink fences), and if they feel severely threatened, their bite can be very dangerous. Cockatoos need very large cages and a great deal of supervised freedom. In spite of these potential drawbacks (and they *are* only potential), cockatoos can be the most delightful companions imaginable.

Cockatoos have a special feather called a powder down feather. These feathers continually grow, the tips breaking off and creating a fine powder, which the parrot uses to dress its feathers when it preens. Some people are highly allergic to this powder, so if you have respiratory problems, or are highly allergic, you may not want to consider any of the cockatoo group as a family friend.

Cockatoos also have a very high incidence of psitticine beak and feather disease (PBFD). This disease, also known as avian AIDS, is highly contagious to other birds, though not to humans. There is no known cure for it, although great strides have been made in developing a test to detect its presence before symptoms become apparent, and also in the development of a vaccine. *Never buy a cockatoo whose feathers look bedraggled or whose beak appears overgrown and shiny black.* These are two of the major symptoms of PBFD. Do not believe anyone who tells you that the bird is molting, or is just picking its feathers, or that its cagemate has overpreened it. The heartbreak, not to mention veterinary expense, is too dreadful to contemplate, especially in parrots as endearing as cockatoos.

Moluccan Cockatoo (*Cacatua molucensis*) displaying advanced feather damage of psittacine beak and feather disease. Note the abnormality of head feathers. *Scott McDonald, DVM*

Umbrella Cockatoo (*Cacatua alba*) showing beak destruction of psittacine beak and feather disease. *Scott McDonald, DVM*

Naturally gentle and gregarious, these birds are all too easy to spoil until they become little monsters. One needs to exercise a great deal of common sense to prevent the development of this sad state of affairs. Low feels that cockatoos are so demanding that "only those who have the misfortune to be housebound are truly competent to look after a very tame cockatoo which can demand as much time and affection as a child" (1980). The authors do not agree that this extreme amount of devotion and time to the bird is necessary, or even desirable. We do agree that in the demands they make, they *are* very much like an extremely self-centered and emotional child who, unlike the child, never grows up. Keeping a cockatoo as a companion requires the same commitment necessary to raise a child; the same determination to see to it that it grows into a "good citizen" rather than a juvenile delinquent.

Several kinds of cockatoos are commonly kept as pets: the Molluccan Cockatoo (*Cacatua mollucensis*); the Umbrella Cockatoo (*C. alba*), the Sulphur-Crested Cockatoos (*C. galerita galerita, C. Galerita triton, C. galerita elenora* and *C. galerita fitzroyi*); Citron-Crested Cockatoo (*C. sulphurea citrinonocristata*); the Goffin's Cockatoo (*C. goffini*); and the Bare-Eyed Cockatoo (*C. sanguinea sanguinea*). Less commonly kept is the Rose-Breasted Cockatoo (*C. roseicapillus roseicapillus*). This bird is also known as the Galah (pronounced ga-*lah*).

The Molluccan, Umbrella and Greater- and Medium-Crested Sulphur Cockatoos are all large birds. The other species listed are medium to small parrots. Molluccans are often perceived as "sweet and cuddly." They certainly can be. They are also regal, very skilled at manipulating mechanical objects such as padlocks (some are even able to open combination locks) and highly perceptive. Molluccans are endlessly entertaining, and can be very willful and independent.

The Umbrellas are similar in personality to the Molluccans, but tend to be much more active, compared with the stately and more sedentary Molluccan. They may appear skittish or high strung in comparison. Very loving and attention seeking, they can also be stubborn and willful. The authors have noted that the Umbrella may be somewhat spiteful and bullying to birds smaller than itself. If you already have other small companion parrots in your home, you will need to supervise your Umbrella's out-of-cage playtime carefully to avoid injury to your other parrots.

Sulphur-Crested Cockatoos fall somewhere between the Molluccan and Umbrella in terms of activity level. They may also be more aloof and not quite so demanding of attention—maybe! Otherwise, they are very like other cockatoos in personality.

A pair of young Moluccan Cockatoos (*Cacatua moluccensis*) rubbing beaks, an activity demonstrating mutual affection. *Aviculture Breeding and Research Center*

A Galah, or Rose-Breasted Cockatoo (*Cacatua roseicapillus*). Although a common species in its native Australia, domestically bred specimens command high prices in the U.S. because Australia allows no exports of its native wildlife. *Aviculture Breeding and Research Center*

Umbrella Cockatoo (*Cacatua alba*) and Bare-Eyed Cockatoo (*Cacatua sanguinea*) sharing a perch. *Aviculture Breeding and Research Center*

The Goffin's Cockatoo is a much smaller bird, rather close to the medium Amazons in size. It does not have the regal appearance of its larger cousins, but is very active, charming and clownish. If you have acquired a wild-caught bird, gentling it can easily take the place of your daily workout. (But keep those running shoes on your feet—you'll need them!) A hand-reared youngster or a tame wild-caught Goffin's is an excellent choice for those who want a cockatoo but have space limitations. These little birds possess all of the loving, affectionate traits of the larger cockatoos, and make great companions.

The Bare-Eyed Cockatoo is something of an ugly duckling in the cockatoo family. It resembles the Goffin's in size, but has large bare rings around the eyes. This skin is somewhat bluish in color and gives the impression that the bird has been burning the candle at both ends or has been in a terrible brawl. All this aside, this little parrot is delightful, with all of the typical cockatoo traits, plus the ability to talk well, which most other cockatoos lack.

Lovebirds *(Agapornis)*

These little extroverts frequently "get a bad rap." Hand reared properly and allowed to develop through some normal adolescent behavior, they can be truly delightful companions. Some breeders who raise fine-quality companion birds of these species recommend removing lovebird babies from the nest for hand rearing before their eyes open. The babies are housed in separate small brooders, rather than together as clutchmates. After the babies are weaned, it is very important to establish firm guidelines so your lovebird is never allowed to think it controls the relationship. They should not be given the opportunity to spend unlimited time out of the cage without supervision, nor should they ever be allowed to bite or nibble, even in play. The newly weaned lovebird's wing feathers should *always* be clipped, as with all companion birds.

Species commonly kept as companions include the Madagascar Lovebird (*Agapornis cana*), the Peach-Faced Lovebird (*A. roseicollis*), the Masked Lovebird (*A. personata personata*) and Fischer's Lovebird (*A. personata fischeri*). The lovebird is another one in which many color mutations have been developed by breeders. These birds do not have to be kept as pairs. As a matter of fact, their companion traits will be much enhanced if they are the only one of their own species kept in the home.

Macaws *(Ara)*

These parrots are *very* strong willed and will take the inch you give them and stretch it into the longest mile you have ever seen. They can be excellent with people who can keep the upper hand. Macaws have very powerful and potentially dangerous beaks, and if you are easily intimidated by that, the macaw will intelligently manipulate you into a "fear zone" that is not necessary. There are many other birds that may not have the same effect, thereby enabling a much healthier relationship for all involved.

The large macaws most readily available are the Blue and Gold Macaw (*Ara ararauna*), the Scarlet Macaw (*A. macao*) and the Green-Winged Macaw (*A. choloptera*). Less commonly kept is the Military Macaw (*A. militaris militaris*). There is a subspecies of this macaw, the Buffon's Macaw (*A. militaris ambigua*). It is rare, and although it closely resembles the Military Macaw should never be kept as a pet. These birds belong in breeding programs so their numbers can be increased. If you are considering acquiring one of these parrots, do your homework so you will be able to distinguish one from the other. Books such as Forshaw's *Parrots of the World* or Alderton's *The Atlas of Parrots* provide excellent descriptions and color plates for those needing to familiarize themselves with the difference between these two macaws.

A young, newly weaned Blue and Gold Macaw (*ara ararauna*). *Aviculture Breeding and Research Center*

A pair of Scarlet Macaws (*Ara macao*) peacefully preening and sharing each other's company. *Aviculture Breeding and Research Center*

In addition to the large macaws, there are species known as mini-macaws. Not as intimidating or loud, and requiring far smaller housing, they may be the perfect choice for those who are fascinated by macaws but limited in space. Good choices from this group are the Yellow-Collared Macaw (*A. auricollis*), the Hahn's Macaw (*A. nobilis nobilis*) and the Severe Macaw (*A. severa*).

Blue and Gold Macaws are gorgeous, rambunctious, noisy, affectionate, attention-seeking handfuls. They tend to be moderately good talkers, also very good squawkers. They are steady birds, not inclined to bite in an unprovoked way; but as with all large macaws, one should handle even one's best Blue and Gold friend with respect. No large macaw should be trifled with or teased.

The Green-Winged Macaw is, next to the Hyacinth Macaw, the most regal and imposing of the large macaws. Much quieter and more sedentary than the Blue and Gold Macaw, it will still make its presence known, especially morning and evening when it exercises its considerable lung power. This species, too, can be a relatively good talker, especially the hand-reared birds. Like all macaws, the Green-Winged tends to pick a favorite person and be somewhat standoffish with other family members, even to the point of aggression, if the bird is not wisely handled. A Green-Winged that belongs to one of the authors loathes all of humankind but his significant person and has no hesitation about attacking anyone else. Fortunately, this is not a problem, as he is a breeding bird and is not required to relate to people. It is interesting that although very attached to his mate, Eli still relates very gently and affectionately to his special person. For sheer magnificence and loyalty, you can do no better than this species, if macaws are your weakness!

The Scarlet Macaw is an entirely different story. This bird possesses some of the most beautiful plumage in the bird kingdom. However, it is very prone to unprovoked aggression, even toward its favorite human. Some would disagree, but the authors feel that this is one bird that should definitely be in the hands of only experienced macaw owners. Those having had only smaller parrots should not "cut their teeth" with a Scarlet Macaw. In the hands of a knowledgeable and experienced macaw person, however, these birds can be very good pets.

Monk (Quaker) Parakeets *(Myiopsitta monachus)*

These are small parrots. They tend to be noisy, in a scolding sort of way. They are scrappy, strong-willed, curious and affectionate to their favorite people. They can be somewhat aggressive with those they do not know or who have encroached on their territory, and this goes for other birds as well as people.

The Monk Parakeet is unusual in that it is the only nest builder in the parrot family. Not only does it build a nest, but also the nest is communal, constructed from twigs and reaches an immense size. These birds are very hardy, and they have established feral populations in the United States as far north as Chicago. Because authorities fear the Monk Parakeet will take over the ecological niches occupied by our native songbirds, the species has been outlawed as a companion bird in some states, or strictly regulated in others. Check with your state department of agriculture before you decide to purchase a Monk Parakeet.

Pionus Parrots

These wonderful birds are becoming better known as breeders learn how to induce them to nest with greater frequency. They are somewhat smaller than Amazon parrots, but frequently retain the primarily green plumage. One can tell the difference between the two groups by examining the feathers close to the parrot's vent. In *Pionus*, pinkish-red feathers are always present. This trait is absent in Amazons.

Pionus are quiet, sedate birds that can learn to talk well. They tend to retain their gentle nature even at sexual maturity, which is a big plus. Even their morning/evening jungle calls are not offensive or particularly loud compared with most parrots. They do tend to be somewhat nervous and high strung, and as with *all* parrots, thrive on routine and gentle handling. *Pionus* parrots make asthmatic wheezing noises when upset or stressed, and this can be very alarming if the owner is unaware of the trait. The bird sounds as if it were gasping its last, when in fact it is expressing emotional discomfort.

Species of this group that are usually available are the White-Capped *Pionus* (*P. senilis*), the Bronze-Winged *Pionus* (*P. chalcopterus*), the Maximilian's *Pionus* (*P. maximiliana*), the Dusky *Pionus* (*P. fuscus*) and the Blue-Headed *Pionus* (*P. menstruus*). You may have to search for a while before locating parrots of this genus, but they are well worth it. One other interesting characteristic *Pionus* possess is a gorgeous iridescence when their feathers are struck by sunlight. Under artificial light, they may appear somewhat drab compared with other parrots, but in the sunlight their plumage is scintillating.

Poicephalus Parrots

This group of species hails from Africa, and they are often found with African Grey Parrots, roosting and foraging with them in large mixed flocks. These birds are very special, and those who are lucky enough to share their lives with them praise them highly. Most are medium to small. The largest of the group is the Cape Parrot (*Poicephalus robustus robustus*). This bird, however, is not common in aviculture, let alone as a companion bird. Nor do we recommend this parrot as a pet, even if one were able to find an individual of the species. They are difficult to keep alive, probably because of some nutritional need we have not yet been able to discover. Over and above this, the Cape Parrot needs to be well established in breeding programs so as to ensure its survival.

The *Poicephalus* most readily available are the Jardine's Parrot (*P. gulielmi gulielmi*) and the Senegal Parrot (*P. senegalus*).

The Jardine's Parrot is, we believe, as close to the "perfect parrot" as it is possible to come. There appear to be two races, one somewhat larger than the other. The larger of the two is similar in size to a small Amazon. Its plumage is lovely, being predominantly black with a huge scalloping of chartreuse green on each feather. After the bird acquires its adult plumage (at one year of age), it begins to develop the typical poppy-orange areas on the forehead, wing bends and thighs. The Jardine's has one of the loveliest natural calls in parrotdom—very soft and musical, much like the songs of our native songbirds. (The Jardine's can growl when upset, as does the African Grey, but rarely seems to do so—just another indication of its very steady, calm personality.) It can learn to talk quite well, does not scream and remains sweet and gentle at sexual maturity. Its personality is invariably affectionate. Additionally, the Jardine's seems to be exceptionally intelligent. Only recently has this parrot become a little more available; those who are able to find hand-reared parrots of this species are fortunate. The owner of a Jardine's Parrot can look forward to many long years experiencing one of the nicest encounters of the feathered kind.

The Senegal Parrot is another popular member of this group. Its plumage is very attractive, and as with most of the African parrots, it tends to be much quieter than its New World relatives. It is a small bird and does not need the huge cage that all large parrots require. The Senegal is a fairly strong-willed bird and can go through a nippy stage soon after weaning. However, with proper handling, this will not remain a problem.

PAIR-BONDING SPECIES: UNCOMMON

Barraband's Parrot (*Polytelis swainsonii*)

This parrot is from Australia, but any that you may find have been domestically bred, as it has been illegal to import any of Australia's wildlife for many years. The Barraband is brilliantly colored, about sixteen inches in overall length, but slender and elegant.

The Barraband has the reputation of being a gentle, affectionate, docile pet. Pairs bond strongly, which makes them good companions, as are most pair-bonding species. They can sometimes learn to talk, but do have a somewhat piercing natural call. Barraband's Parrots are strong fliers and should have a roomy cage in which they can fully extend and flap their wings. Unlike many parrots, they are not particularly destructive to plants and household furnishings.

Caiques (*Pionites*)

These small parrots are absolutely delightful. Although not as well known as some other parrots, they are becoming more available because of the success of domestic breeding programs. Their popularity will probably increase in the future due to their beautiful colors, playful and curious outlook on life and acute intelligence.

Caiques (pronounced kie-*eeks*) are usually in constant motion and seem to require continuous stimulation. They can be very destructive with their beaks and should have appropriate chewing material. They are usually good eaters, willing to sample just about anything offered them. One breeder who keeps caiques calls them avian garbage cans. The authors have found that to be the case, also.

Caiques are very strong willed and need to have behavioral limits set from an early age. Having great intelligence, high activity levels and natural curiosity, they can easily get out of control unless the owner consistently maintains gentle, firm dominance.

The Black-Headed Caique (*Pionites melanocephala melanocephala*) and the White-Bellied Caique (*P. leucogaster leucogaster*) are the species most commonly available as companion birds. Their personalities are very similar.

Fig Parrots *(Psittaculirostris)*

These tiny parrots look just like jewels. Their plumage is brilliantly iridescent, primarily green, but highlighted with turquoise, red, orange and yellow. One has to see the bird to appreciate just how beautiful it really is. They are very playful, not at all noisy and have the ability to talk.

However, imported birds are very delicate, and all have very specific nutritional needs, which if not met, will speedily result in their death. Fig Parrots need much greater amounts of vitamin K in their diets than other parrots. If they do not receive it, these little birds are unable to clot their blood properly, hemorrhage internally and die. It is now suspected that they also need large amounts of vitamin C, and that without it a scurvy-like condition may develop. One of the symptoms of this disease is also hemorrhage.

Although Fig Parrots make delightful companions, the authors do not recommend them as companions because they are simply too difficult to keep alive for the average person. Further, as they are not yet well established in breeding programs, and most imported birds are no longer available, they belong in breeding programs with those competent to work with them.

Hawk-Headed Parrot
(Deroptyus accipitrinus accipitrinus)

This parrot is one of the most unusual in regard to its plumage. It has the ability to erect the feathers surrounding the neck in a huge ruff, something like an Elizabethan lace collar. The feathers of this ruff are bright and multicolored and contrast strikingly with the rest of the bird's plumage. Its personality is playful, intelligent and affectionate. It tends to be high strung, nervous and prone to feather picking when consistently stressed.

Although it is a very appealing bird, and some are available from breeders, this is another parrot the authors feel should only be kept in a breeding situation. They are not well established in aviculture in this country, and until their numbers grow, it is hard to justify keeping them as companions—a situation in which the bird will never be able to contribute its genes to the captive breeding population.

Lories and Lorikeets

This is a very large group of parrots, with many genus names. This group of birds possesses some of the most magnificent feathering of any of the parrots. Every color of the rainbow is represented, in addition to brown, black and some hues that almost appear to have been invented just for these parrots! They are amazingly intelligent, extremely playful, curious and very social, and some can learn to talk. Their natural calls are often loud, high pitched and piercing. However, this seems a small price to pay for such beauty and intelligence. They can be very affectionate with their human companions, and for the most part are not particularly aggressive.

The beak can be very sharp, its edges being somewhat like a razor, so if the parrot does happen to nip, the damage, although not extensive, can be painful. Unfortunately, these parrots do possess *one very great drawback*. They are primarily fruit and nectar eaters, unlike most other parrots, which consume some seed, animal protein, flower buds, insects and various other foods in their natural habitats. This in itself is not a problem insofar as feeding these birds in captivity, for there are prepared nectar formulas on the market specifically for them. The problem lies in the nature of the birds' droppings. They are *very* liquid. Add to this the fact the bird's habit of hanging on the cage wires and defecating out into the room (and they can easily project their feces three to four feet), and you have a large problem. In addition, nectar formulas contain large amounts of glucose, which is sticky, so therefore these parrots need frequent bathing. The cage also needs meticulous and frequent cleaning.

In recent years, dry diets formulated for these birds have come onto the market. They do dry up the droppings, so that they more closely resemble that of other parrots and are therefore much easier to cope with. However, we do not know, regardless of what manufacturers claim, the long-term effect on the birds' bodies of dry diets. Their bodies have been equipped by nature to utilize a semiliquid diet, and there are particular concerns regarding the effects of a dry diet on their kidneys. Until all the information is in, the authors would recommend keeping lories and lorikeets on a diet more in keeping with the ones they would eat in the wild. This means, of course, that as house companions they are not suitable. They are, however, wonderful aviary subjects for those who have such facilities.

Of this group of parrots, species often available are the Chattering Lory (*Lorius garrulus garrulus*), the Black-Capped Lory (*L. lory lory*), the Dusky Lory (*Pseudeos fuscata*) and the Rainbow Lorikeet (*Trichoglossus haematodus moluccanus*). This last species is also known as the Swainson's or Blue Mountain Lorikeet.

NONBONDING PARROTS: COMMON

Ringneck Parakeets *(Psittacula)*

These are elegantly colored, long-tailed parrots with streamlined bodies. All parrots of this group have large heads in proportion to the rest of their bodies, and very large beaks. Accordingly, they are great chewers and must be supplied with appropriate chewing materials or they will furnish their own from what is available in their surroundings. There are bound to be serious differences between bird and human about what constitutes "appropriate."

Psittacula species, being nonpair-bonders, tend to remain aloof from their human companions. They enjoy attention, but not handling. Many, especially the Alexandrine (*P. eupatria*), become excellent talkers. These birds are sexually dimorphic, meaning that the plumage differs between male and female. Thus when these birds become mature, it is simple to tell the sexes apart. However, feather differences are not apparent in the newly weaned or immature parrot, so if you are especially interested in a companion of a particular sex, surgical or chromosomal (feather or blood) sexing must be done. Generally, it makes no difference in terms of personality whether the parrot is male or female. In this group, the hens tend to be somewhat nippy and aggressive, the males shyer and more docile, as well as more colorful. Indeed, the hen of a breeding pair may be so formidable in behavior toward her mate, that if he is unable to overcome his fear of her, breeding will not take place and re-pairing will be necessary.

The Alexandrine Parakeet, already mentioned, is one of the most popular of this group of hookbills. It is quite large, measuring nearly twenty inches in length. It, like all of this group, is an active bird and needs a spacious cage, not only for exercise, but also to prevent fraying of its magnificent tail. Also popular are the Indian Ringneck (*P. krameri manillensis*), the African Ring-neck (*P. krameri krameri*, the Moustache Parakeet (*P. alexandri fasciata*) and the Plum-Headed Parakeet (*P. cyanocephala cyanocephala*).

Eclectus Parrots

These exquisite birds fall somewhere between pair-bonders and nonpair-bonders. They do tend to form a type of bond with their humans, though not to the degree of an Amazon, macaw, African Grey or cockatoo. *Eclectus* parrots require special attention and gentle handling, as well as a certain amount of tranquility. One must have respect for not only their considerable beauty, but also their peace of mind. Because of their loveliness, it is easy to refrain from setting much needed guidelines and discipline. As with any parrot, the enjoyment of the bird's beauty can quickly be replaced by stress for both bird and owner if such limits are not set and consistently enforced.

Eclectus hen is noted for its red feather-ing and purple "vest." *Aviculture Breed-ing and Research Center*

Eclectus male. Unlike the primarily red hen, the male is predominantly green. *Aviculture Breeding and Research Center*

As with the *Psittacula* group, the color differences between male and female are marked. Likewise, the hen tends to be the more aggressive of the two. Some say the male makes the best companion, but others disagree with this, stating that if properly hand reared and handled correctly subsequent to weaning, the hens make just as good companions. As with all such issues, this is largely a matter of opinion, and much depends on the individual bird, as well as the owner. However, one cannot expect the same closeness to an *Eclectus* as one experiences with true pair-bonding parrots. Again, this is not a plus or minus. It simply is what exists, and whether or not people desire a relationship within the limits set genetically by a bird such as an *Eclectus*.

Author Fred Baver (1990) states that the reputation these parrots have for being unintelligent is not at all deserved. According to him, the flat affect and "lethargy" sometimes seen with *Eclectus* parrots is a reaction to stress and unfamiliar people and situations. Once the perceived threat no longer exists, Baver remarks this bird becomes "highly animated, garrulous, curious, and affectionate" (ibid. 1990). He further states that the hen *Eclectus*'s need to be in control in the breeding situation is an evolutionary imperative that carries over in her behavior to her human companions, but that hens can nevertheless be very affectionate. Even Baver admits, though, that the male *Eclectus* is the "real lover" of the two.

Grass Parakeets

The term *grass parakeets* is used to denote several genera of small hookbills originating in Australia. All now available in this country have been captively bred for generations. They are ideal aviary subjects, as many of them breed readily and produce reasonable numbers of offspring. They do not make good companions for those who wish a very personal relationship with their birds. But if one is looking for a pretty, small parrot that is quiet and makes few demands on its humans for interaction, then grass parakeets are a good choice. They require large cages, for although they are small, they are very active.

The most commonly kept are the Bourke's Parakeet (*Neophema bourkii*), the Red-Rumped Parakeet (*Psephotus haematonotus*) and the Princess of Wales Parakeet (*Polytelis alexandrae*).

Several of this group can only be transported across state lines with a U.S. Fish and Wildlife Service Captive Wildlife Breeding permit. These permits are difficult to obtain, and penalties for violation are severe. Grass parakeets falling into this classification are the Orange-Bellied Parakeet (*Neophema chrysogaster*), the Beautiful Parakeet (*Psephotus pulcherrimus*), the Scarlet-Chested Parakeet (*N. splendida*) and the Turquoisine Parakeet (*N. pulchella*).

Rosellas *(Platycercus)*

These parrots, too, are from Australia, and like the grass parakeets, have been captively bred in this country for many generations. Although they retain all the characteristics of most nonpair-bonders, they can nevertheless be delightful pets on their own terms. These terms include respect for their personal space, and refraining from caresses, which the birds interpret as too familiar. The maxim "Good fences make good neighbors" seems to be a golden rule for rosellas, as well as other nonpair-bonders.

Of this genus, the Crimson Rosella *(Platycercus elegans elegans)*, the Golden-Mantled Rosella *(P. eximius)* and the Western Rosella *(P. icterotis)* are the most readily available.

NONPAIR-BONDERS: UNCOMMON

Great-Billed Parrot
(Tanygnathus megalorhynhos)

This most uncommon bird is from the islands of Indonesia. A very beautiful parrot, with a large head and huge beak that is somewhat disproportionate to the rest of its body, it is not yet being bred in any large numbers. For this reason alone, it should probably not be kept as a companion, but given a chance to produce offspring and help ensure the continuity of its kind. Those who keep this bird have noted that the imported ones tend to mutilate their feathers. This is thought to be due to some type of nutritional deficit we have not yet been able to discover (Desborough 1991).

In personality, it is reported that the Great-Billed Parrot is very similar to the *Eclectus* parrot. This means that personality will vary from individual to individual, and that daily routine, soft voices, patient and gentle handling, are of prime importance (ibid. 1991).

Kakariki *(Cyanoramphus novaezelandiae)*

This is a small parrot, and as the Latin name implies, a New Zealander. Like all parrots from this country and Australia, those available in the U.S. are

45

domestically bred. The Kakariki is an *extremely* active parrot requiring a large cage. It is naturally tame (in the sense that it does not fear humans), and even parent-reared birds exhibit this same fearlessness. Nevertheless, they do not enjoy the close contact that pair-bonding birds do. This parrot is also high strung and susceptible to stress. To paraphrase Rosemary Low (1980), they breed and die with equal enthusiasm. This parrot should only be kept with those who have extensive experience in psittacine husbandry.

THE ENDANGERED ONES: PARROTS THAT SHOULD NEVER BE KEPT AS PETS

There are certain parrots that should not be kept as companion birds, even though they are occasionally sold for this purpose. Parrots such as these should only be in the hands of skilled breeders. Although many of them are of outstanding companion quality, they are nevertheless too rare and/or not well enough established in aviculture to keep singly. When this is done, they are never able to contribute to their species' gene pools to perpetuate their own kind.

In addition to the rare status of some species, the parrots on this list are either officially listed as endangered, or are endangered but not yet officially listed as such. The reason for this is that, as with any bureaucratic governmental process, the placing of a species on CITES Appendix I (an international treaty) or the Endangered Species Act list of protected species (a federal law) is a very slow process.

Species listed on both the CITES Appendix I and the U.S. Endangered Species Act protected list require that both the buyer and seller have federal Captive Wildlife Breeding permits if the birds are to be moved across state lines for *any* reason. To violate this regulation places one at risk of severe civil and/ or criminal penalties.

The following is a list of parrots we feel should under no circumstances be kept as companion birds. Parrots requiring a federal permit are so indicated. The list is by no means all inclusive, but does include the parrots that are more commonly offered as pets. All of these birds are *extremely* costly. If you are approached by any individual offering them for sale at well below the expected cost, *beware*. These parrots are very likely stolen or smuggled.

A Pesquet's Parrot (*Psittrachus fulgidus*). Note the vulturine head and bare facial area. *Aviculture Breeding and Research Center*

The Black Cockatoo Group

These hookbills are native to Australia and are therefore illegal to import for any reason. Some are being domestically bred in this country by *very* few breeders, primarily for use in their own or fellow breeders' programs. If you are considering acquiring one of these birds for a breeding program, *be very careful that the bird is close banded and has all appropriate paperwork to prove its lawful, domestically bred status.* Species included in this group are:

Black Palm Cockatoo (*Probosciger aterrimus*)

Gang-Gang Cockatoo (*Callocephalon fimbriatum*)

Red-Tailed Black Cockatoo (*Calyptorhynchus magnificus*)

Glossy Cockatoo (*Calyptorhynchus lathami*)

White-Tailed Black Cockatoo (*Calyptorhynchus baudinii*)

Yellow-Tailed Black Cockatoo (*Calyptorhynchus funereus*)

Cuban Amazons and Subspecies

Amazona leucephala leucophala, A. plamarum, A. caymanensis, A. hesterna and *A. bahamensis* comprise this group. All of these lovely little Amazons require federal permits.

Hyacinth Macaw
(*Andorhyncus hyacinthinus*)

These spectacular and largest of all macaws are still being kept and sold as pets by many people. This should not be, as there are only an estimated two to four thousand of these birds left in their range country, and all available individuals in this country should be contributing their genes to the next generation. If you already have one of these gentle giants, *please* consider placing it in a breeding program when it becomes mature. The responsible husbandry of these parrots requires no less.

Kea (*Nestor notabilis*)

This parrot inhabits the montane regions of New Zealand and cannot be imported legally into the U.S. It is very large, intelligent, comical and very strong physically. It has had, in the past, a reputation for preying on sheep and at one point was the object of extermination by New Zealand sheep ranchers. Its alleged propensity for live flesh has been disproved, however, and it is partially protected now in its range country.

Keas, unlike most other parrots, are ground breeders. In order to encourage breeding, elaborate and unusual setups must be provided (Peters 1991). Their playful destructiveness is legendary. We have included two excerpts that illustrate this. The first is from Peters:

> *The worst which can happen to you is when Keas are able to unlock their aviaries. I remember one time coming in the feeding corridor in the morning. The Keas sat peacefully in their aviary, but it looked as if a bomb had been thrown. All feeding buckets were turned upside down, paper bags torn, rubber fittings destroyed, lamps screwed out and smashed, the feeding instruction on the doors littered, and a lot of doors of other aviaries opened, which allowed their neighbors to fly out. Keas are able to open water taps, and they obviously like to pull out the stopper in their pool and watch the water going out. Only a 4 ½ pound heavy stone stopped my old cock from doing this. In spite of all this, I can't be mad at them, and enjoy it when they come behind me hopping on both feet like a kangaroo.*

Brykczynski, who experienced these parrots firsthand in their native habitat reports:

> *You can't park for more than a few minutes outside the entrance...without the roof of your car becoming a landing field for*

Keas. At first you may confuse the thump with large rocks which often tumble down in avalanche country. But when a head drops down your windshield to swing like a pendulum…you had better act fast if you want to avert certain disaster. Upon encountering humans, the Kea expects to either be fed or amused and if not immediately satisfied they first scold you. Then they will begin twisting off your wiper blades, ripping rubber moulding out, and slashing your upholstery if you leave a window open…. A Kea temper tantrum is not to be taken lightly. They can open tinned cans with their beaks. They have been observed dragging off four and one-half pound axes, tea kettles, and 35 mm cameras with motor drives to be dropped down cliffs when the burdens become tiresome. Interiors of unsecured buses and helicopters have been demolished and radio antennae crippled from their mischief. (1985)

Pesquet's Parrot (*Psittrichas fulgidus*)

This parrot is thought to be one of the more primitive parrots. Forshaw, in the second edition of *Parrots of the World*, considered the Pesquet's to be closely related to the *Eclectus* parrots. In the third edition, however, he seems to have withdrawn this opinion. (The authors feel that, undoubtedly, familial relationships of parrots with each other and with other bird groups will be elucidated and clarified by the advent of DNA hybridization studies.) This parrot has no feathers on the head, probably an adaptation to prevent soiling of the feathers, as the bird is primarily a consumer of a soft fruit diet. Pesquet's Parrot, like lories and lorikeets, produces liquid droppings.

A pair of Black Palm Cockatoos (*Probosciger aterrimus*) displaying to each other. *Aviculture Breeding and Research Center*

Queen of Bavaria, or Golden, Conure (*Aratinga guarouba*)

This marvelous parrot is like the Hyacinth Macaw, in that both have outstanding personalities and are wonderful companions. Alas, the rarity and severely endangered status of the Queen of Bavaria Conure precludes keeping it as the companion it is so admirably suited to be.

Thick-Billed Parrot (*Rhynchopsitta pachyrhynca*)

This bird has the distinction of being our only native U.S. parrot. It is highly endangered and the object of an intense captive-breeding program jointly administered by the U.S. Fish and Wildlife Service and the Avicultural Breeding and Research Center in Florida. *Thick-Billed Parrots may not be privately owned under any circumstances.* There is *no* permit that is applicable to this species. Penalties for illegal ownership are severe.

Vasa Parrot (*Coracopsis vasa*)

This brownish-black parrot comes in two varieties: the Greater Vasa and the Lesser Vasa. Both are from Madagascar, are avicultural rarities and are poorly established in captive breeding programs at this time. It is hoped that this will change in the near future.

3

How Do Parrots Grow and Develop?

In this chapter we will explore the physical, social, intellectual and language development of parrots. There are striking parallels in many areas of psittacine and human growth and development. There are areas of difference and contrast, also, but the parallels that exist are worth noting. Some research has already commenced in this fascinating field: Irene Pepperberg (1991) in language development of the African Grey Parrot (*Psittacus erithacus erithacus*) and Millie Fink at Northwestern University in cognitve development of Kakariki (*Cyanoramphus novaezelandias*).

...I will bite if I feel threatened... *Diane Schmidt*

51

Although some of the concepts presented in this chapter will be new to many readers, it is our hope as authors that those who are in a position to do serious research concerning these ideas and speculations will do so. There is a vast body of experiential data amassed by breeders worldwide, which indicates that many concepts of human growth and development are applicable to parrots and may be used with good effect in socializing them successfully. They also prove effective in correcting behavior problems.

Although we have divided this parrot growth and development into physical, social, intellectual and language areas, the topics overlap to some degree. For example, it is impossible to talk of a chick's increased ability to explore his environment (an intellectual accomplishment dependent on the learning imperative) without noting that certain physical achievements must first occur (such as control of large muscles, eye-beak-foot coordination, etc.).

PHYSICAL DEVELOPMENT

EMBRYO DEVELOPMENT AND HATCHING

In beginning our discussion of physical development of parrots, psittacid/ human parallels begin even before birth. Just as human infants develop in a head-to-foot manner (craniocaudal development), so does the parrot embryo. This pattern continues after birth as well, with regard to developmental control of all motor functions. This is not surprising, for all living creatures possess the same DNA, the powerful stuff of genes that dictates how every living organism will grow and develop, be it human, parrot or microbe.

The parrot embryo lies protected in its eggshell, nourished by the yolk, just as the human infant is contained in the uterus and nourished by the uterine placenta. The inner surface of the shell is lined with a membrane (the chorioallantois) that contains an intricate network of blood vessels. These supply the embryo with oxygen, which is taken in through millions of pores in the shell itself. Excess carbon dioxide and water produced by the growing embryo's metabolic processes are transported by these same blood vessels from the embryo to the inner shell surface, where they pass through the shell pores to the outside world. These membranous blood vessels are connected to the developing chick by an umbilical cord.

In the human embryo, the placental blood vessels perform the function of gas and water exchange, as well as nourishment. However, just as with the bird, the human is connected to its support system (the uterine placenta) by an umbilical cord.

Let us now look at the embryonic development of a well-known and commonly kept parrot, the cockatiel (Brice, Cutler, and Millam 1992). This process never fails to astonish, for it is so beautifully orchestrated, so perfect in its completion, that it is nothing less than a miracle. The fact that some species weighing no more than two grams (a penny weighs two and a half grams) can hatch and start life in this world with everything it requires to grow and thrive is amazing! All body systems are "up and running," some more efficiently than others. But with time and proper care, that blind, naked, almost featherless creature will emerge as a magnificent and imposing macaw, a regal cockatoo or perhaps a wise, mysterious African Grey.

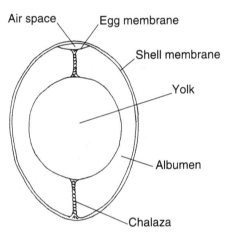

The hatching chick, emerging from the egg, after having made both internal and external pip. *Martha Vogel Lucenti*

Interior view of egg with structures that will support and nourish the embryo. *Martha Vogel Lucenti*

The developing chick, nourished by a network of blood vessels in the eggshell membranes. Note the chick's attachment to these vessels by the umbilical cord in the abdominal area. *Martha Vogel Lucenti*

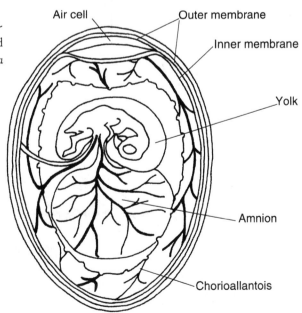

Once the hen's ovum is fertilized by the cock's sperm, a small growing cluster of cells appears on the surface of the egg yolk. This cluster of cells is seen as a small bump at about forty-eight hours of incubation. At about three days, blood vessels are apparent on the surface of the yolk, and at four and a half to five days, the embryo itself can be seen when the egg is candled (or looked at against a very bright, focused light) to ascertain the chick's development and embryonic health). At this stage the embryo is a very strange-looking little creature, seemingly all head. The midbrain (the section of the brain that controls orientation of the bird's eyes, head and body toward sights and sounds) can be detected as a huge bulge on the back of the head. The developing eyes are apparent, and tiny wing and leg buds are also discernible. On the sixth day the midbrain is even more prominent, the eye is larger and one can see the beginnings of digits on the feet and wings. Day seven to seven and a half sees the continued development of the eye, and the egg tooth, so necessary for the hatching process, is forming. The embryo's skeletal structure is changing from soft cartilage to hard bone because calcium is being deposited in it.

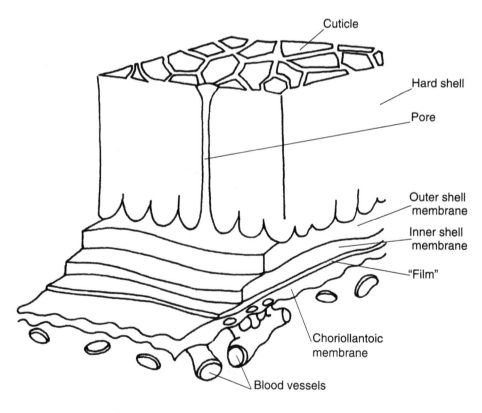

A cross-section of the eggshell. Note the pore (one of millions), which allows the chick to "breathe." *Martha Vogel Lucenti*

Two healthy Umbrella Cockatoo (*Cacatua alba*) chicks in the Late Phase of Stage II (the Preliminary Stage). *Scott McDonald, DVM*

By the ninth day the egg tooth is prominent, the midbrain less so. Little down feathers are beginning to form, and the chick's bones continue to calcify. From day thirteen on the embryo develops very rapidly. Lungs and air sacs mature in preparation for independent respiration. The remaining yolk is absorbed into the abdominal cavity and the umbilicus seals itself off. Finally, the embryo orients itself to the hatching position: head under the right wing with its beak pointing toward the air cell. By the sixteenth day the eyelids have closed over the eyes; the beak has enlarged, and the egg tooth and nails are completely calcified. Yellow skin pigment shows that fat utilization is occurring in the growing chick. On the eighteenth or nineteenth day the chick hatches and becomes a psittacine citizen of the world.

Some interesting things occur at the time the chick is ready to hatch. At this time, even with the efficient gas exchange mechanism of the eggshell, a carbon dioxide buildup has occurred. Most authorities believe that this increase in carbon dioxide content of the blood stream initiates spasms in the enlarged neck muscles, drawing the chick's head up and back so that the egg tooth comes into forceful contact with the shell. The shell cracks (known as the external pip), and the chick is well on its way to emerging into the world.

Before this happens, though, the chick makes what is known as the internal pip. When this happens, it breaks through the membrane that forms the air cell at the large end of the egg. Now the chick is no longer dependent on the air supply provided by the egg membranes, but has become an air-breathing organism.

Another fascinating thing that occurs as the chick is industriously working to emancipate itself from the egg is the beginning of chirping. This is no tiny chirp, either. It can sometimes be heard across the room! In a study reported by Welty and Baptista (1988), it has been observed that young mallard ducks begin to vocalize as soon as they have accomplished their internal pip, nearly two days before they emerge from the egg. As soon as the mother hears her chicks, she begins to cluck to them at frequent intervals. It is thought that this vocal exchange probably helps chicks learn to recognize and imprint on their mother (Welty and Baptista 1988). Imprinting will be discussed in greater detail later in this chapter, for it has great significance for the hand rearing of domestically bred parrots.

Some authorities think that the vocalizations of a hatching chick also act as a stimulus to its clutchmates to begin hatching (Coyle 1987). This has obvious advantages for the chicks themselves, because all will be approximately the same age and size, thus decreasing the risk that a very young chick will not be able to compete with its siblings for food. It is also a boon to hardworking parents as the total time spent rearing a nest of babies will be less, therefore minimizing the stress associated with caring for offspring. Rearing babies is hard work, as any breeder can attest. And parent birds do not have the luxury of food in the refrigerator just a few steps away!

Another interesting thing that occurs with embryo chicks is that even though blind, they respond to light. This is readily seen when an egg is candled, especially after the baby has made its internal pip and is chipping away at the shell. Many times the authors have candled chicks during this phase to find the baby quiet, as if resting or napping, only to have it begin vigorous movement as soon as light penetrates the shell. Baby parrots probably appreciate this necessary process about as much as hospital patients like being awakened in the middle of the night by the nurse's flashlight when medication time has arrived!

When at last the parrot chick emerges from the shell, it often falls into an exhausted sleep. So, too, does the human infant after the tremendous stress to which it has been subjected during the birth process. (Imagine how it must feel to leave a dark, warm, protected environment and be suddenly thrust into a world filled with noise and light; to have been totally dependent on the life support system of the egg or uterus and to have, all at once, to perform all bodily functions independently!) Parrot breeders often, if the chick has been incubator hatched rather than parent hatched, allow several hours to elapse before the chick is fed. The chick needs this recuperation time, during which it is nourished by the last remnant of egg yolk absorbed into its abdomen during incubation.

EARLY INFANCY

The parrot chick is blind and naked (except for sparse down feathers), unable to regulate its own body temperature and totally helpless as a newborn. In this respect it has much less going for it than the human baby, who is able to see and hear at birth, as well as regulate its body temperature much more efficiently (Caplan and Caplan 1984). Nevertheless, both new little creatures are equipped to survive and prosper because of various inborn reflexes. It is these very reflexes that allows both organisms to begin to know and learn to operate in their respective worlds.

Inborn reflexes are primitive. When the parrot chick arrives in the world, most of the reflexes it possesses allow it to eat and maintain an unobstructed airway. The chick has a feeding response that appears when the beak is touched or manipulated in any way. A gag reflex is also present, as is the capacity to cough and sneeze. The chick is also able to lift its head and roll from its back to its stomach if necessary. When hungry, the chick has a feeding cry that is particularly insistent and demanding. The infant bird is able to pant when too hot, and shiver when cold. If startled by touch, jarring or sudden light, its body will twitch, and the chick will attempt to move away from the unpleasant stimulus. As a very young baby, the parrot chick will sleep almost continuously, curled up in a fetal position with legs against the body and wings tightly furled. Occasionally, the baby sleeps in a sprawling, froglike position. There is always one baby that insists on sleeping on its back, although the authors feel every effort should be made to keep the infant on its stomach to prevent accidental aspiration of food. This can be successfully accomplished by placing the baby in a small container filled with wood shavings (no cedar, please) or toweling, in which a depression can be made in which to place the chick in the correct position.

The human infant possesses many of the same reflexes, again designed to allow the optimum chance for survival. A rooting reflex is present; if the baby's cheek is touched he will begin to nuzzle for a breast. The sucking reflex is well developed at birth, and the gag reflex is present, as is the ability to cough and sneeze. Tightly shut eyelids are a response to sudden bright light, and sudden noise or jarring will elicit outraged cries. Human babies also cry to elicit feeding or other comfort-directed care. Interestingly, the human baby also sleeps in a fetal position, or sprawled froglike. During the first week of life, he will need at least ten feedings per day, just as the parrot chick will require ten to twelve. (Many breeders call the busy baby season "brain dead season," for parrot infants must be fed every two hours around the clock, with perhaps one longer stretch during the night. This leaves very little time for their human caretakers to get a full night's sleep.)

We can readily recognize the many arresting similarities between parrot chicks and human babies in the first critical period following birth (known as the neonatal period). However, once this brand-new phase of life is completed, the parrot's growth and development is greatly accelerated compared with that of the human. Naturally, there are also differences in how the two species develop, although parallels continue to manifest. The differences have more to do with the way the growth imperative is manifested, rather than any essential difference in the imperative itself. For example, one of the most important things a human baby learns to do in his first year is to coordinate eye-hand movement. The baby is unable to grasp objects or learn to feed himself until he has mastered the muscular control allowing accuracy when he reaches for something. He must then transfer it to his mouth instead of hitting his cheek or nose. This same task must be accomplished by the parrot chick, but involves the ability to balance on one foot and transfer food or some other object to its beak with the other foot. However, the task of both human and parrot are grounded in the accomplishment of ever-increasing muscular control, although the actions themselves are obviously different.

GROWTH THROUGH THE WEANING PERIOD

The time span from birth to weaning varies tremendously among different species of parrots. A small bird such as a cockatiel will wean between six or seven weeks. Likewise, so will many of the small conures and other parrots of this size. Medium-sized birds such as most Amazons, African Greys, mini-macaws and the like wean at approximately three to three and a half months—while birds such as large cockatoos and macaws wean between four to five months, with some taking as long as six months. Regardless of the species , all progress through the same developmental tasks.

O'Connor, in his book *The Growth and Development of Birds* (1984), cites the work of Nice, who studied the developmental patterns of altricial and precocial nestlings. (Altricial birds, such as parrots, are born totally dependent on parental care for survival. Precocial nestlings are able to feed themselves soon after hatching. Ducks are examples of precocial birds.) Nice's work was done with song sparrows and spotted sandpipers. Coyle (1987) addresses this same subject using finches as his subjects.

Although sparrows and finches are vastly different from parrots, the broad divisions in stages of development are applicable, so we have adapted Nice's framework for use with hand-reared psittacids. (Although Nice included a fifth stage, Socialization, we have found through observation of hand-reared parrots that many of the developmental landmarks placed by Nice in this category begin and evolve during the Transitional and Locomotory stages with psittacine species.)

Stage I (The Post- or Late Embryonic Period) is mainly, and not surprisingly, concerned with **nutrition**. This is the primary and overriding task of any newborn, for without adequate nutrition survival is not possible. When discussing parrot chicks at this stage, we find it convenient to subdivide this period into two phases: Early and Late.

During the Early Post-Embryonic Phase, we begin to see slow, then gradually accelerated weight gain. The beginning of motor control and development of sight and hearing also occur. During this time, the chick can move its head from side to side, roll from back to tummy and cry when hungry. For the first day or two of life, the feeding reflex may be slow or moderate, but once the baby has accustomed itself to being fed, this reflex becomes very vigorous. For the first week to week and a half, the chick will need to be fed every two hours, a result of the baby's minuscule crop capacity. Some breeders feed around the clock and others allow the baby to go for a four- or six-hour stretch at night. (No documented differences in weaning weight or other growth parameters have been detected between the two methods.) Weight gain during the first three to five days of life is slow. Some chicks gain nothing for a day or two, and a few may lose a very small amount before they commence gaining. The chick during the early phase of this first stage has only sparse down and must be kept warm in a brooder because it has absolutely no ability to regulate its own body temperature. Even at this very young age, the chick will jerk and twitch in a startle reflex when disturbed by bright light, the touch of a cold (to it) hand or being jarred. The baby sleeps almost constantly between feedings.

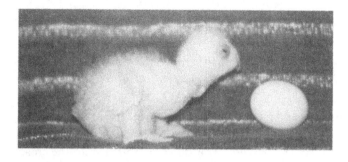

A Senegal chick (*Poicephalus senegalis*), age twelve days. This chick is just entering the Late Phase of the Post-Embryonic Period (Note egg included for size comparison). By now, this Senegal chick's eyes and ears are beginning to open, and it is standing well for very short periods. *Ryan Thompson*

Senegal chick at sixteen days, in Early Phase of Preliminary Period. Note primary down, dark spots on wing indicating feather tracts from which pin feathers will emerge. Also note the chick has been banded. *Ryan Thompson*

Senegal chick at eighteen days, beginning Late Phase of Preliminary Period. Note emergence of pin feathers on wing, darkening of beak tip and overall increase in body size. *Ryan Thompson*

Moving into the Late Phase of Stage I, we find the chick becoming better able to control its body. It can now stand for short periods during feeds and does not need as much support for its head, although it must still be steadied as it pumps down its formula. A stronger cry, often timed to anticipate feeding time is apparent. As the baby's crop capacity enlarges, feeds are reduced to every four hours, with the chick well able to go eight hours at night without a feeding. The baby's eyes and ears are beginning to open, the eyes usually being first. There is much more down, and some babies may show feather tracts under the skin. Weight gain begins to increase rapidly at this time.

Stage II is the Preliminary Stage. According to Nice, this period involves the development of comfort movements such as wing stretching and scratching, and generally accelerated growth toward motor control and independence. Again, we have divided this stage into two phases: Early and Late.

During the Early Phase, the chick exhibits much heavier down and the emergence of pin feathers, first on the wings, then the tail. Because of this the chick can more easily control its body temperature. Although warmth must still be provided, brooder temperatures can be lowered somewhat. At this time, the chick begins to have short periods of wakefulness immediately before and after feedings. By now, its eyes and ears are fully open, and it is beginning to move deliberately about the brooder. The infant's attempts are comical to watch, for it pushes its posterior up into the air, leaving its head on the brooder substrate, and proceeds to plow along like the Queen Mary cleaving the Atlantic!

Feedings are down to four times a day. The chick now takes large volumes of formula relative to its size, and weight gain is astounding. It is literally possible to see the baby increase in size from morning to evening. It is during this time that breeders are careful to watch for the window of time in which a chick can be banded. A chick whose leg band fell off in the morning often retains the band when it is reapplied at night. Sometimes breeders miss the optimum period for banding and then the chick must be fitted with a band that is too loose and may cause injury later in life. Or, the chick remains unbanded, which in this time of ever-more-restrictive legislation, could eventually become a serious legal problem for the breeder or pet owner.

The Late Phase of the Preliminary Stage is a tremendously active one for the chick. Many things happen, and they all seem to happen at once. One of the hallmarks of this period is the development of a fear response, which occurs even in the human surrogate's presence. If the breeder opens the brooder or otherwise disturbs the chick, it crouches at the far back corner, swaying, hissing and acting as if terrified. This response is possible because the chick can now both see and hear, and has the locomotory power to move freely in the nest or

Senegal chick at twenty days, well along in Late Phase of Preliminary Period. Pin feathers very apparent, as is heavy secondary (or adult) down. Body size continues to increase rapidly, and some feathers on leading edge of wing have emerged almost fully. *Ryan Thompson*

Senegal chick at twenty-eight days. Still in Late Phase of Preliminary Period. Wings show increasing feathering and tail pin feathers are emerging. *Ryan Thompson*

Senegal chick at thirty-five days. Body size still increasing. Wings almost fully feathered. Tail feathers emerging. Crop and belly also feathering. *Ryan Thompson*

brooder. The same response can be elicited if the chick is suddenly startled by loud noises or bright lights. This response is likely an inborn survival response to help baby parrots in the wild cope with predator invasions in the nest. O'Connor states that this reaction has been shown to occur at the time when the chick "depends on increasing experience of the parents coupled with a negative reaction to all non-familiar objects" (1984).

It is probable that a domestically bred, hand-reared chick's fear response (which is exhibited with total impartiality to those it knows well and persons who are unfamiliar) has little to do with real fear of its human parent surrogate, and it is simply a reflexive reaction based on species genetics. Certainly chicks that exhibit this reaction, once lifted from the brooder, soothed and fed, show no continuing fear whatsoever.

Human infants also show fear responses at about the seventh or eighth month. This is a result of increased locomotion skills that expose the baby to a bombardment of stimuli before the child has had the chance to adapt (Caplan and Caplan 1983). We feel this may be a factor in the fear/startle reaction of chicks as well. In the case of the parrot infant, not only has it learned to begin moving about, but also its eyes and ears are now fully functional. This has the effect of increasing the amount of stimuli to which it is exposed and with which it must learn to cope.

Also during the Late Phase of Stage II, pinfeathers are emerging and growing at a rapid rate. The chick begins to preen itself and its clutchmates. It is much more skilled at walking, though still wobbly, especially after having been fed. The full crop makes it top heavy, and balance is very difficult to maintain in this state, as is the chick's dignity! The toddler parrot is now standing well in place, holding its head up strongly whether feeding or playing, and can be seen occasionally to sleep in an adult position. The first efforts to accomplish this are always fun to observe. The chick still does not have the balance to tuck its head under its still nearly featherless little wing, and more often than not it falls over onto its side in a heap.

Comfort movements and their skill and frequency are increasing. Wing stretching is much in evidence, as are attempts to scratch the head to remove keratin feather sheaths—another activity that usually winds up in disaster for the chick's balance and dignity! Also at this time the toddler begins to grasp the breeder's fingers as it is lifted from the brooder, rather than lying passively in the palm of the hand. It is very common for chicks of this age to exhibit fear of heights. Unfledged birds are equipped with this instinct to prevent an accidental tumble from the nest. Feedings are often down to three per day, and weight gain continues at an astonishing rate. Usually about this time, the chick begins to demonstrate a marked lack of interest in its formula, once the first hunger pangs have been satisfied. This is the time when chicks are often introduced to their first solid food. Many chicks indicate their readiness for this by picking at wood chips or specks of discarded feather sheaths. Although chicks of this age do not usually ingest more than a tiny amount of the solid food offered (and that usually by accident), this activity prepares them for the later process of weaning. A very successful breeder known to one of the authors years ago stated that she felt that if this "crucial" window were missed, weaning was much delayed in hand-reared chicks. The authors agree with this observation. The urge to start picking at small objects and particles of food in the environment is yet another developmental phase designed by nature to prepare the toddler parrot for eventual weaning and independence. To ignore or overlook it seems somehow to confuse the chick and delay its acceptance of solid food.

One of the "fun things" that happens during this phase is the chick's new interest in toys. It also begins to respond to its persons' voices with vocalizations of its own. Human babies, in contrast show increased interest in human speech around the fifth month. The chick's attention can be captured by music, as his attention span and curiosity develop. Some breeders make deliberate efforts to enrich the environment for their psittacine toddlers, not only to enhance their successful socialization, but also to develop the language and learning capacities of these very intelligent birds. The authors hope that more and more breeders will begin to do this, as we feel there are definite benefits gained by the parrot that will become apparent as the bird integrates into its human family. Every effort should be made to respond to the chick's increased attention by repeating, slowly and clearly, simple words such as "hello." Talking softly while caring for the chick will give it a chance to become more and more familiar with human speech, and this may enhance the bird's capacity to learn human language. Enrichment of the parrot chick's environment will be discussed in depth later in the chapter.

During the Late Phase of the Preliminary Stage, chicks remain awake for long periods between feedings. This time is spent in practicing motor skills, playing with siblings, exploring and carefully observing their surroundings.

Stage III, the Transitional Stage, is concerned with **maturation of basic motor skills**. It, too, is a busy time for the toddler chick. During this period, the chick is perfecting the skills that will make it possible for it to fledge. Motor skills become highly polished. The only remaining skill to be mastered is flight, which is accomplished in the last stage. Balance will be perfected, whether the chick is walking, standing, feeding, preening, scratching, stretching its wings or sleeping in the adult posture. Frequent, vigorous wing flapping is also seen at this time as the chick performs a sort of continuous "dress rehearsal" for flight. Walking has become second nature, and the chick spends much time mastering the art of climbing. A very big step occurs at this time. Because good balance has been achieved, the parrot is now able to perch—in a somewhat wobbly fashion at first, but within days as if it had been born doing it. Also, the feathering is nearly complete, aided by the constant preening that occurs now. As a result of this nearly completed feather coat, the chick is completely able to regulate its body temperature, and supplying external heat is no longer necessary.

Two feeds per day are now the order, with the chicks making it obvious that it would really rather be doing something else. Although by this time the parrot is eating quite a lot on its own, these small supplementary formula feedings remain necessary to ensure an adequate nutritional and fluid intake. By now rapid weight gain has tapered off dramatically, and the chick is actually showing weight loss. This is perfectly normal, for the chick at maximum nestling weight is too heavy to fly. Nature prepares for this event by seeing to it that wing loading is just right for successful flight when the time comes. One might well ask why a chick gains all that weight, only to lose it before fledging. Welty and Baptista (1988) state that this occurs to provide a cushion that will see the chick through periods of food shortage in the wild, as well as providing energy for use in growing feathers and exercising muscles. Indeed, parrot chicks at their maximum nestling weight may weigh more than their parents!

During the Transitional Stage, there is a marked decrease in the fear/startle response to people and objects that are unfamiliar. The nearly weaned parrot is usually very comfortable with his human surrogate's incursion into the cage for any reason. Also, the chick will amuse himself with periods of babbling. If one listens carefully, this babbling frequently has the intonation and cadence of human speech, although usually no distinct words emerge from the bird's utterances. Most chicks will respond to well-known humans with natural vocalization at this time. In addition to these kinds of vocalization, the chick is now making adult sounds appropriate to its species. The Transitional Stage also sees the chick awake and alert for most of the day. Occasional naps are taken, but they are brief, and soon the chick is again running full speed ahead.

Senegal chick at forty-two days, having entered the Transitional Period. At this point, the chick will be perfecting many motor skills needed in adulthood. *Ryan Thompson*

Senegal chick at forty-nine days, well into the Transitional Period. This youngster has learned to balance and climb. Feathering is complete. *Ryan Thompson*

Senegal chick at seventy-three days. The Transitional Period has been completed, and the chick is now officially a youngster, completely weaned with all the motor skills needed for independent functioning. However, the young parrot will continue to develop intellectually, emotionally and socially—tasks for which it will need continued guidance from its owner. *Ryan Thompson*

The fourth stage is termed by Nice the *Locomotory Stage*. As with all birds, the parrot achieves independence during this period. Feathering is complete. The first flight has been accomplished. The parrot is totally self-feeding and has achieved its adult weight, more or less. Although it looks like an adult bird at this time, it may be a little slimmer through the chest than it will be later. In birds with long tails, such as macaws and *Psittacula* parrots, the feathers may not be as long as they will be at the end of the bird's first year. Birds such as the Jardine's parrot (*Poicephalus gulielmi*) and the Sun Conure (*Aratinga solstitialis*) will not have their beautiful fiery color until after the first or second molt. But most parrots, upon fledging, look exactly like adults except for eye color, which in many species remains dark until around the first birthday.

When this period ends, the parrot will have perfect control of its muscular functions, and will rarely exhibit the startle/fear response, especially in familiar surroundings with familiar people (unless it is truly frightened by something).

During this final stage, the young parrot may be repeating its first simple words. Words such as "hello," "good" or other one syllable utterances it has heard repeatedly throughout the hand-rearing process may be among its first human language accomplishments. Other young parrots may take much longer to learn human speech. African Grey Parrots often do not talk until after their first birthdays, then astonish their owners with their verbosity. It as though they have been storing all they have heard and suddenly the "dam bursts."

A word of caution is appropriate here. As mentioned previously, the newly fledged bird *looks* like an adult. However, it is *not* an adult. A highly intelligent creature, the parrot will continue to grow and learn in the areas of social, intellectual and language development. The young bird still has ahead of it the task of learning to integrate into its human "flock," just as its wild counterpart will have to learn the ways of its parrot flock. Indeed, young parrots of many species stay with their parents for a year following fledging, during which time they are taught the fine art of "parrotness." This period of assisted learning helps ensure the youngster's survival in the harsh reality of natural habitat, where many newly fledged birds fail to survive to their first birthdays.

Taking into consideration the above, the owner of a newly weaned parrot must expect to take an active part in molding the personality of his/her new companion so that a mutually rewarding relationship can be nurtured and maintained. In this respect, the parrot owner is very similar to human parents, who must also accomplish the task of socialization of their offspring. An excellent parrot friend does not just happen. It is a result of commitment on the part of the owner. Do not be deluded into thinking that a hand-reared parrot will automatically be a wonderful, responsive companion throughout its life. Nothing could be further from the truth.

ADOLESCENCE

It takes several years for a parrot to reach sexual maturity. Hand-reared domestic birds achieve this at an earlier age than that of their wild counterparts. No one really knows why this is so. As with human children, this can be a very difficult time. With the first surges of sex hormones, the parrot may begin to act somewhat aggressively, a side of the parrot that puzzles people who have never experienced this behavior before. When the bird reaches full maturity, its behavior during the annual breeding season may put a severe strain on the parrot/person relationship. Much of this behavior has its origins in the bird's genetic/hormonal makeup. The purpose of hormonally controlled behavior is to attract a mate, defend a nest and protect offspring. However, bear in mind that although such behavior is common in the sexually mature parrot, especially in species such as Amazons, it is *not* inevitable. Much depends on the manner in which the bird has been socialized into the family to this point. Just as with adolescent children who occasionally act in ways unacceptable to their parents, but for whom reasonable behavior limits have been set and enforced, the parrot that has been properly socialized may cause episodes of consternation and concern on occasion, but remains essentially a loving companion with a positive mental attitude toward its family. Put another way, there may be temporary "bad patches," but not the ongoing, irreparable refusal to relate that permanently fractures the bird's relationship with its human flock. Difficulties that can be experienced with a sexually mature parrot will be discussed in detail elsewhere in the book.

COGNITIVE ETHOLOGY

Before discussing the intellectual development of the parrot, it will be helpful to understand some of the basic concepts of cognitive ethology. *Cognitive* means the act of knowing or perceiving. Ethology is the study of animal behavior. The field of cognitive ethology concerns the study of mental experiences in animals. According to Donald Griffin, it includes the areas of consciousness, awareness, emotion, intentionality and conscious thinking in animals (Yoerg and Kamil, 1991). Research of this kind with primates, dolphins, whales, birds and other species have been done, and they continue to be studied in increasing depth. Among these species being probed for evidence of intelligence are parrots, notably the work of Pepperberg with Alex, the African Grey Parrot, and Fink's work with Kakariki parrots. Researchers such as these are discovering wonderful things about the parrot and its ability to learn and communicate in a meaningful way using language. In the case of Alex, it is very clear through the use of rigorously controlled research that he is able to do much more than mimic human speech, and we will explore this further in the section on language. Fink has found that her subjects are able to perform certain developmental tasks outlined by the famous child psychologist Jean Piaget during approximately the same time in their learning development as do children (Fink 1992).

To derive the greatest benefit from our discussion of parrot intellectual and social development, the reader should suspend or discard any previously held notions that animals do not possess true intelligence. While this concept is deeply ingrained in Western civilization, research is now indicating that it may, however, be incorrect, and is discovering splendid things about the minds of animals and birds. Additionally, our definition of "mind" and "thought" are far too narrow. To explore the world of "another" intelligence is broadening and freeing, an experience we cannot afford to spurn for the sake of clutching narrow egocentrism. In the words of Michel:

> We tend to ignore statistical and abstract information, which may be
> logically compelling…we…twist and distort data to fit the model
> [familiar concept] rather than revise the model. Indeed, we do not
> have to seek evidence that would disconfirm our hypothesis, models,
> and theories, but rather devise tests of them which can only be
> confirmatory…. That is, confidence in our view of reality is more a
> function of simplicity of the view than of its accuracy (1991).

Many would rather hold on to cherished beliefs that animals are "dumb," than to deal with well-researched data that are beginning to prove otherwise. To do this is to deprive oneself of incredible richness and increased understanding of the animals in our lives, and in this particular instance, the parrot.

THE AVIAN BRAIN

The avian brain—the physical organ—that controls the bird's physical, mental and emotional functioning is a marvelous structure. Of all avian brains, that of the parrot is thought to be one of the finest in terms of intelligence (Welty and Baptista 1988; Forsyth 1988; Kavenau 1987). "Birds have demonstrated in test after test that they are capable of highly intelligent behavior, sometimes surpassing the abilities of mammals with greatly superior cortical development" (Stettner and Matyniak 1968).

Parrots have one of the largest brains in the class *Aves*, brain size being significantly correlated with intelligence. According to Dale Russell of the Canadian Museum, "…parrots now have the same brain/body ratios as gorillas" (Gore 1993). Large brain size develops because of the demands placed on the bird by its natural environment. In the case of the parrot, the need to forage effectively for food, and a well-developed social structure are thought to be primary reasons for their large brain volume. Increased intelligence enables such birds to function in a flock setting and to learn from their conspecifics, thereby increasing their chances for survival. An individual in isolation is much less able to acquire experience and knowledge than one surrounded by others of its kind that it can observe and consequently learn from. For both humans and birds, social interactions seem to influence to a great degree what can be learned (Pepperberg 1991).

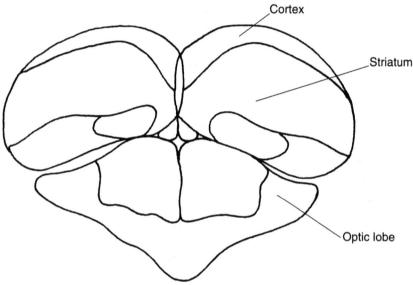

The avian brain in cross-section, showing the relative proportion of striatum to cortex, a condition reversed in mammals. *Martha Vogel Lucenti*

The major differences between the avian and mammalian brain are in the sizes of the cerebral cortex and the striatum. Both these structures are a part of the forebrain (see diagram). The cortex, in humans and other mammals, is the area responsible for intelligent thought, the striatal area being very poorly developed. In the avian brain, however, it is the striatum that is well developed, the cortex being small and insignificant. In birds a specific part of the striatum, called the hyperstriatum, is not even present in some mammals. The striatum in birds is their locus of intelligent thought, and the striatal area is to birds what the cortex is to mammals (Stettner and Matyniak 1968). More recently, researchers are beginning to believe that the neostriatum of the avian striatal area may be the main locus of intelligent thought (Pepperberg 1993). It becomes apparent, based on these facts, that the parrot does indeed have the "hardware" with which to process information and act on it intelligently. The parrot simply uses a different part of the brain than mammals do for this function; mammals utilize the cerebral cortex. The lack of a cortex in avian species does not preclude intelligence, just as in humans the presence of a cortex does not necessarily guarantee it!

SOCIAL/INTELLECTUAL DEVELOPMENT

PIAGET

Jean Piaget was a French psychologist who studied the learning development of early childhood, categorizing and defining intellectual accomplishment by chronological age. Erik Erikson was another who worked in the field of child psychology and studied children from the standpoint of their psychological and social development. Both these men made observations and developed theories that are now classic in the field of childhood growth and development. Their ideas and theories are also fascinatingly apropos to the intellectual and social growth of the parrot. We will be drawing from their work and pointing out parallels between human children and parrots concerning the parrot's maturation in these areas. Although the authors certainly do not claim that human and parrot are identical in their progress through these tasks, there are valuable insights to be gained about the parrot from studying and applying the work of Piaget and Erikson to these highly intelligent creatures. Although the parrot's development in these areas takes place in a relatively short time frame, as opposed to that of the human child, many of the same landmarks are present in both species.

Piaget divided psychosocial development into four stages. The first is the Sensorimotor Stage, which occurs from birth to about two years of age. In this stage, the infant learns how to control the movements of his body and derives all of his knowledge of his world through his five senses. In the parrot, we see these events occurring during the Post-Embryonic, Preliminary and Transitional Stages referred to earlier. For humans the second stage is called the Preoperational Stage, usually from two to seven years. In the first part of this period (the Preconceptual Period), the child begins to understand the use of symbols. For example, words are symbols of concrete objects. He learns to use a word to denote an object that is not present at the time and knows what that word means. In other words, the child is able to use words as symbols with which to *think*. Alex understands words as symbols of objects and places, and uses these words to obtain what he wants. Pepperberg (1992) has been able to document that the parrot has functional use of such phrases as "I want to go X (or Y or Z)," "No," "You tell me," and other such requests and demands. Parrots demonstrate the ability to link words meaningfully to objects or concepts to get their ideas across to us, just as the child does during the Preconceptual Period.

The second phase of the Preoperational Stage is the Intuitive Period. During this time, the child draws conclusions about his environment based on observation rather than fact. For example, if presented with two glasses holding the same volume of liquid—one short and fat, the other tall and skinny—he will indicate that there is more liquid in the short, fat glass. Appearances are everything at this stage of life. One sees this with parrots. If they are able to perch consistently above the heads of their humans, they interpret this as actually being larger, and therefore dominant (Davis). Many behavior problems are created in this way. But the point here is that the bird sees that it is "taller" than the person, and therefore decides that it is "bigger" and able to exercise dominance.

The third stage of human development is that of Concrete Operations. This occurs from about seven to eleven years. At this time the child develops the ability to do in his head what he previously would have had to do through physical action. For example, addition and subtraction skills are gained that allow him to know the answer to a problem without resorting to counting out objects to arrive at a solution. It has been proved that birds do possess a concept for numbers. As a matter of fact, birds handle this intellectual concept with more skill than many mammals do. Ravens and parakeets have demonstrated their ability to recognize quantities up to seven, and African Grey Parrots have also demonstrated this skill (Pepperberg 1993). The "ability to respond to numbers per se, without reference to other properties of the stimulus, seems to be very unusual indeed among animals" (Stettner and Matyniak 1968).

Piaget's fourth stage is that of Formal Operations, from about twelve years on. Now the child is able to think abstractly, and concepts such as responsibility, loyalty, good, bad, and so forth, can be understood and acted on. Again, parrots demonstrate that they are capable and often do learn to understand concepts such as good and bad. There are countless anecdotal records of birds that indicate this understanding. For example, Soucek recounts an experience in which she arrived home, to find that her Molluccan Cockatoo had managed to drag part of her mini-blinds into his cage and destroy them. She scolded the bird in an angry tone of voice, and was interrupted by her Blue-Fronted Amazon, Piper. Piper said to Soucek, "You stop that. Mikey [the cockatoo] is a *good* bird" (Soucek 1992).

One of the most valuable insights that Piaget gained about intellectual growth is that until a certain amount of experience and maturation has taken place, certain types of concepts cannot be understood by children. A child who is not yet old enough cannot act unselfishly because he does not know what selfish means. He acts in his own interest, and therefore takes whatever he wants. This sort of thing is commonly seen in two- or three-year-olds who routinely purloin their playmates' toys with no sense of "wrongness" at all. Parrots, no matter how old, never outgrow this mindset. They remain basically egocentric and will never behave from any sense of altruism. Any desired object is fair game for the parrot, regardless of its rightful ownership. Although a parrot can be trained to leave forbidden objects alone, it will not do this simply because it recognizes that such objects belong to someone else and the parrot has no right to them.

Piaget felt that intellectual development should be stressed over rote learning, that children should be taught how to think and how to learn as opposed to responding in a certain way to a specific cue. Intelligence does not develop as a result of teaching word association with objects (Jacob 1992). Piaget also pointed out that there were four factors important in moving a child through these stages of intellectual development: biological maturation, physical experience with the environment, social transmission and self-regulation.

It is evident that until the nervous system matures, an infant can do very little for himself. Control over voluntary muscles and bodily functions (e.g., elimination) must occur in order for the child to have a basis for building other skills. As we have already pointed out, the first three stages of a parrot's development have to do with biological maturation. The young parrot must achieve balance before it can climb and perch, explore, learn about its world. A parrot's nervous system (like the child's), must be developed enough to allow an adequate attention span before it can, like the child, concentrate on sounds and then try to reproduce them.

Physical experience is interaction with environment that allows any young creature to begin to understand cause and effect. The young child learns quickly that a certain type of chair is unstable and therefore useless for steadying himself as he attempts to pull into an upright position. He learns from experience that certain kinds of food are sweet, and that other foods, particularly vegetables, are not as palatable. The young parrot learns that the beep of a microwave presages feeding time. It learns that when a toy bell is struck with its beak, a pleasant sound ensues, and then learns how to reproduce this fascinating event.

Social transmission includes the young child's interaction with other people. From these people, he learns the customs and mores of his particular culture. He learns the things that are acceptable and bring approval, as well as those things that are unacceptable and bring disapprobation. In the same way young parrots being socialized into a human family learn that to bite or chew on furniture will not be tolerated, but that gentleness with its humans will bring rewards of attention and affection. It learns that to roam the house without supervision will bring disapproval, but to be with his humans in a supervised setting again brings pleasure and the reward of companionship.

Self-regulation refers to the inborn ability that regulates the pace and type of learning. A child crawls before it can walk. The same pattern exists regarding intellectual development. Learning proceeds from the simple to the complex. "Just as a thermostat regulates heat in your house, your baby's regulator adjusts what is already known with what is encountered as a new learning experience. In short, the regulator's role is to make sense of new learning encounters by relating the new to the old, and, where it is impossible to do so, by constructing new categories of knowledge" (Jacob 1992). A weaning parrot in the Transitional Stage exhibits a marked fear of heights. However, when it has learned to fly, this fear disappears. It has learned that after flight has been achieved, heights are no longer threatening. The physical act of flying and what it "means" to the bird must first be experienced before the fear is relinquished.

ERIKSON

Erikson emphasized the importance of the first two years of a child's life as critically important in establishing trust. We see the importance of this in the infant and newly weaned parrot. As with any animal, the way in which it has been handled and spoken to, the firmness and gentleness with which behavioral limits have been set, the respect it is accorded by its people, are of utmost importance in helping it learn to trust of humans. Conversely, the authors see many birds in which this process has somehow gone awry, creating an aggressive, intractable bird whose only goal seems to be to keep all humans at a safe distance. This is tragic, and need never happen. Lack of time or sensitivity on a breeder's part, or unrealistic expectations on an owner's part during the first year of a parrot's life can spell disaster for the bird and heartbreak for the owner.

Erikson categorized ages three to six years as the period of initiative and imagination. During this time, the child explores a host of people, objects and situations. The young parrot also explores and learns about his world through play, trial and error and observation. In this way, it is much like the child. One of the delightful aspects of parrots is that they continue these activities more or less throughout life, and seem to be one of the few animals that continue play into adulthood for its own sake.

In summary, it becomes obvious that in many ways the social and learning development of parrots parallels that of humans. The bird learns by constructing new knowledge based on interaction with its environment. Parrots also learn to expand their knowledge by relating a known object to an unknown one. The bird learns that items presented in a certain cup are good to eat. New items in the food cup will likely be sampled because the bird has learned that the contents of that particular receptacle are always food items. In the same way that children come to "own" knowledge by using it, so does the parrot. In the wild, it "owns" the ability to fly because it has tried it, perfected it and can now do it whenever it wishes. It can then use this newfound skill to further learning about its environment (e.g., where to find food and water, how to avoid predators).

LEARNING PROCESSES IN PARROTS

Learning processes in the bird are naturally somewhat different from those of humans. We have examined some likenesses. Now we will look at learning that is unique to birds, parrots included. Although parrots are genetically programmed to behave in ways we call instinctive, they also have the intelligence to learn from observation and experience. They can be, for example, conditioned to refrain from behaviors such as biting, destruction of furniture and other objects and habitual inappropriate screaming. Because parrots are creatures of habit to a certain degree, when working to change an undesirable behavior, *the owner must be consistent* (Blanchard 1991). As a matter of fact, parrot training is actually owner training (Davis 1989). To achieve such consistency, the owner must learn and then make the hour-to-hour, day-by-day commitment to carry through on the appropriate technique. It is in this sense that we speak of "owner training."

There are two major categories of avian behavior: instinctive and learned. *Instinct* is defined as "the most complex form of innate behavior…it means an inborn characteristic of a given animal species. It is relatively unmodifiable" (Welty and Baptista 1988). Instinctive behaviors include those of breeding, care of nestlings, defense of territory, displacement activities and imprinting. Displacement activities are those which are performed in lieu of an intended, but thwarted, initial behavior. This is well known to parrot owners. At times the bird, perceiving a disliked but out-of-reach human, will then bite its owner, on whose shoulder or arm it is perched.

IMPRINTING

Imprinting is a type of learned behavior that is instinctive. It is instinctive in the sense that such behavior is genetically programmed; it is a learned behavior in that the chick must experience for itself certain criteria before imprinting can occur. Imprinting is the "process of restriction of social preferences to specific classes of objects" (O'Connor 1984). In the case of parrots and other birds, this means that the bird learns the characteristics of its species and relates socially to only those of its own kind, both for companionship and propagation. The purpose of this behavior is to prevent hybridization between species in the wild. Thus, Green-Winged Macaws do not mate with Scarlet Macaws, Sun Conures do not mate with white-capped *Pionus*, and so on. There are two types of imprinting, filial and sexual. Filial imprinting occurs when the newborn chick learns to recognize its own parents and accept their care. It is also known as the "following response" and can be seen when a clutch of young ducklings or goslings trail along behind their mothers wherever they go. The obvious benefits of such imprinting are nurturing and protection before fledging. Sexual imprinting, as mentioned above, prevents "mixed breed" chicks, thereby perpetuating a species rather than diluting and eventually ending its existence as a discrete group of organisms.

Konrad Lorenz, famous animal ethologist, listed four important criteria for imprinting (Welty and Baptista 1988):

1. It usually occurs very quickly and is confined to an extremely short critical or sensitive time in the individual's life.

2. It is a very stable type of learning and is most often irreversible.

3. It involves learning of characteristics of its species as a whole, and not just those of its own individual siblings and parents.

4. It is completed long before adult behavior is achieved or expressed.

Sexual imprinting lasts a lifetime and is different from other types of learning in that it requires reinforcement, not reward, to be achieved. One of the important characteristics of imprinting seems to be the retention of information rather than its acquisition. It depends not only on visual input, but also on auditory input as well. (Earlier, we mentioned the dialogue between unhatched chicks and their mother, as a way of aiding imprinting even before the chick is hatched.) There are distinct changes in the brain that occur during sexual imprinting, as well as changes in blood levels of the sex hormones, testosterone and progesterone (O'Connor 1984; Welty and Baptista 1988). It has been found that protein formation (synthesis) in the forebrain is greater during imprinting than before or after the process. These studies indicate a direct biochemical link with the sexual imprinting process, which would help explain its lifelong effect. Increased blood levels of sex hormones have been found at the beginning and end of sexual imprinting as well.

Sexual imprinting has serious ramifications for the domestically bred, hand-reared parrot. They are important in raising companion birds as well as parrots that will eventually be reintroduced into their range countries. In the case of the bird destined to be a companion, imprinting sexually upon a human parent surrogate means that the bird, at maturity, will select a human to which its breeding urge will be directed. In many cases, the bird will "defend" its human "mate" against other humans, which it comes to view as competition. It may also bite its "mate" to drive it away from people and situations it perceives as threatening. Such behavior often seems to be without provocation and comes as a severe shock to its favored human, as well as to others with whom it shares its life. However, set against the background of the imprinting process and its purpose, it is perfectly reasonable behavior for the parrot. This behavior can be modified to a degree by the kind of socialization it has experienced in the domestic setting up to this point. But it can never be completely erased, and some behavior that we humans view as erratic will probably occur each year during breeding season once the parrot is mature.

The owner's best defense against aggression and unprovoked attack lies in first socializing the bird correctly prior to this period. This means setting firm limits that do not allow biting under any circumstance. (Limit setting and enforcement will be discussed in a later chapter.) Owners also need to learn to respect the bird *as a bird,* with all the accompanying behavioral aspects of its personality. This means that tolerance and compassion should be exercised during breeding season for the mature parrot. Retaliation for aggression should *never* be punitive in the sense of striking or screaming at the bird, ignoring it for weeks on end or locking it in a closet or room by itself. To do these things is extremely cruel, and cannot be understood by the bird as a consequence of its behavior. The parrot is acting on genetic programming millions of years old, which is only in conflict with its flock because that flock happens to be human and not avian.

Owners must learn the types of body language parrots exhibit before aggression and respect these indications that the bird is preparing to attack. By observing these signs, you will not put yourself in the position of being bitten. The parrot will be deprived of the chance do so and will therefore not have the opportunity to begin a bad habit. Additionally, the owner who has not encouraged the bird to "kiss" him, or perch on his shoulder, will not be in danger of potentially serious facial injury if the bird should become aggressive. A bird in breeding condition should *always* be kept on the arm, where the owner has control of its actions. Neither should it be allowed to perch higher than the owner's head.

Sexual imprinting on a human parent surrogate should be avoided at all costs for parrots destined for reintroduction programs, for various reasons indicated in the section on domestication in the following chapter. If it becomes necessary to hand-rear such a parrot, breeders take great precautions to see that this does not happen. A parrot that is imprinted on humans will not be able to relate to its own kind when it should be choosing a mate, and will therefore be unable to contribute to the perpetuation of its species when released into its natural habitat. Additionally, birds that will be used for this purpose must be placed in flights very close to adults of its own species to learn flock and sexual behaviors necessary for survival and breeding in the wild.

LEARNED BEHAVIORS

Learned behaviors have several different levels: habituation, trial and error, insight and conditioning. Learning can only take place when information has been stored in the brain and can be recalled for use in other situations as that information applies.

Habituation means that an animal has learned not to respond to meaningless stimuli. For example, on first hearing a sudden, loud noise on the television, a parrot may react with panic, screaming and attempting to fly away from the disturbance. However, over time, it comes to realize that these sounds pose no threat and no longer reacts to them.

Conditioning is a form of behavior modification and will be discussed in depth in a later chapter.

Trial and error learning is exactly what the term implies: "Try, try again, until at last you succeed." Cockatoos are particularly adept at this kind of learning and apply it with great success in escaping from their cages. One such bird known to the authors is named Houdini, in honor of his extraordinary expertise as an escape artist!

Insight learning requires great intelligence and is basically problem solving in nature. Parrots excel at this. One of the author's cockatoos has learned how to steady a swinging perch while eating by observing how close to the cage bars the perch is, moving it much closer, then wedging it between the bars to achieve stability. Only then does she select a piece of food and climb to this favored perch to eat. Tool use is also a form of insight learning. Mikey, the cockatoo to whom we referred earlier, learned to obtain the key, which was thought to be out of reach by the owner, for the padlock securing his cage. He then inserted it in the padlock, opened the device, climbed out, relocked the lock and proceeded to the top of his cage to await the return of his owner and surprise her when she found him in this liberated situation. He also had the foresight to toss the keys into the bottom of the cage, where they could not be retrieved until the entire unit had been dismantled!

THE ROLE OF PLAY

The role of play is important in learning. In the human child it serves several purposes. Play aids growth and physical development, is investigative, provides a "workshop" for learning by trial and error, is relatively free of the demands and standards of the adult world, provides a way of learning adult roles and is vitalizing. It has been shown that the diversion from routine and work offered by play has important neurophysiological effects on both children and adults (Caplan and Caplan 1984). In summary, play provides the opportunity for children to practice and perfect physical, mental, social and emotional skills. When we look at the importance of play in the young bird's life, as detailed by Welty and Baptista (1988), we find that it serves the same purposes! These authors also believe that play "conceivably provide[s] something akin to the 'fun' children get from skipping rope or playing tag." In addition, play provides the opportunity to polish skills that will be needed later for foraging, learning how to behave in the flock, learning about their environment by trial and error and perfecting physical skills. Additionally, with the parrot tribe, play is carried into adulthood and enjoyed with great relish. (This is possibly a neotenous trait that humans find appealing, thus increasing their bonding to their birds.)

LANGUAGE DEVELOPMENT

Language, in its most basic definition is "simply sounds that have meaning" (Blanchard 1991). The acquisition of a vocabulary of meaningful sounds proceeds in an ordered, sequential way. It has been found that with both parrots and human infants, this pattern is very similar (Pepperberg 1992).

"When a child learns that a particular set of sounds refers to or represents an object, event, or feeling, she has found the single most valuable tool for understanding and predicting what is happening in her environment: language" (Caplan and Caplan 1984). The human infant's first vocalization is crying. This primitive communication indicates some basic need that requires care. At first we see initial inchoate sounds. The use of vowels, followed by consonants and diphthongs, emerges a little later. Use of single syllables follows the recognition that certain of these syllables have meaning and produce consistent results when used (e.g., "ma-ma" brings smiles, attention, etc.). Stringing together of syllables to form primitive sentences that have meaning for the baby and can be used to express wants and needs, and to comment on events, finally emerges. In other words, the beginning of meaningful communication has been achieved. This process is assisted by the ever-increasing neurological maturation that allows increased attention span, control over the muscles used for making sounds and the attachment of significance to certain sounds and combinations of sounds.

Throughout the above process, the human baby experiments in an indiscriminate way with sounds to which he will later attach meaning and use functionally. This same process occurs with parrots. In both species, repetition and imitation of sounds seems to be a reward in itself, thus spurring further mastery of the meaningful use of sound (Pepperberg 1991). Once a sound has been assigned a definite meaning, overgeneralization consistently occurs. Pepperberg cites the example in which a child, having learned the word "doggie," for a time calls all four-legged creatures "doggie." Eventually the child learns more appropriate words to label a variety of animals, and overgeneralization ceases (for that particular category, at any rate).

The process by which language is acquired can be observed readily in the infant parrot. (The same process occurs in the wild, as the young parrot learns the language of its flock. However, as we are dealing with companion birds, it is this situation we will discuss.) During the first few weeks of life, insistent cheeping is the only utterance made. It usually indicates hunger, although a too-warm or too-cool brooder will also produce this sound. Once the baby parrot is capable of brief periods of wakefulness, cheeping may begin to occur immediately after feedings. It seems to be done simply for the pleasure of making sounds and is somewhat less insistent than when used to indicate hunger or other discomfort. By the time the young bird has acquired pinfeathers, it is often beginning to make different sounds. These sounds consist of "cooing" noises, and as with the human infant, vowel sounds predominate at this stage.

During the Transitional Stage, young parrots seem to hold long "conversations" with themselves and clutchmates. A definite pattern of pitch, intonation and varying volume is easily detected, and consonants can be heard as well. It is interesting that the time of day for such utterances seems to be consistent from baby to baby. Some indulge this pastime immediately after the first morning feed, others have a "gabby" period in early afternoon and still others prefer evening for this activity. Whether this pattern becomes established as a result of, and in response to, increased household activity at that particular time, or simply an inborn preference of a particular baby, is not known. The authors have observed, however, that when household activity and noise are at a maximum, babies often choose this time to babble. If this proves to be the case consistently, one might then speculate that such babbling is responsive rather than merely vocalizing for the sake of doing so.

By the time the toddler parrot has weaned and fledged, it may have acquired the use of one or two simple words, such as "hello," "bye-bye," "hi," or other words it has heard often. The bird may very well use these words appropriately. As with human children, language acquisition will continue (given the proper environment) throughout its life.

ENRICHMENT

Because it has been strongly suggested in the research situation, and indicated anecdotally in countless domestic situations, that parrots do use speech intelligently, how then do we encourage this most desirable attribute in our companion parrots? There are three factors to consider in achieving such a result. The first is the care and attention to the overall intellectual and social development of the parrot. The second is the attention that has been given to encourage the use of human speech during infancy and weaning. And the third is the continuing commitment of the bird's owner to develop its use of speech over time, based on the groundwork that has been laid during its early life. These three factors may be spoken of in general terms as enrichment, which is something that most human parents strive for with their children. The authors contend that it is also of primary importance when working with both young and adult parrots. Such activities are not only enjoyable in and of themselves, but also we believe that they provide tools and learning abilities that will lay the foundation for excellent adjustment to family life. A well-socialized parrot is stress free. A stress-free parrot is a happy, healthy bird, and a joy to its human companions as well.

It has been documented experimentally that just as with sexual imprinting, physical changes take place in the brain as organisms interact with their environment and learn from this activity. The key factor in effecting the learning experience is activity (Jacob 1992). With any young creature, such activity takes place primarily as play. The quality of interaction between youngster and caregiver is also of utmost importance.

Professor David Krech of the University of California at Berkeley studied the role of early experience on brain development. He took two groups of young rats from the same litter. One group had an "enriched" environment and one did not. The cages of the enriched group contained exercise wheels, tunnels and objects over which they could climb, run around and manipulate. In all other respects the two groups were treated identically. At the end of three months both groups were sacrificed and their brains examined for any differences. Krech found that the brains of the enriched group weighed more, had more folds on the surface (sulci) and contained an enzyme associated with learning. The brains of the unenriched group did not contain this enzyme (Jacob 1992).

Another, similar experiment was performed, using the same methods of enrichment versus nonenrichment. In this case the rats were not sacrificed at the end of the experiment, but were given an "intelligence test" for rats: a maze through which they had to run to obtain a food reward. The enriched group learned the maze much more quickly. These experiments strongly indicate that interaction with a stimulating environment has a marked impact on actual physical brain development, and that this in turn greatly influences learning ability.

The infant–caregiver relationship also has great impact on future learning ability, for a well-socialized individual is more likely to reach his potential than one without these social skills. A study done by Dr. Mary D. Ainsworth of Johns Hopkins University (Caplan and Caplan 1984) explored the use of discipline (in this case, the frequency of mothers' commands and intervention in their children's activities) on babies' compliance with their mothers' demands. Dr. Ainsworth found that the mother who accepted all facets of her baby's behavior, including his less endearing qualities, and who made the commitment to care for her child even at the expense of her own activities, received much greater cooperation from her offspring in situations requiring her to interfere with his activities. It was also discovered that the accepting mother was very good at "mood setting which helps him [the toddler] to accept her wishes or controls as something congenial to him." At the other end of the scale was the mother who did not willingly accept all of her child's behaviors and needs, and felt a great deal of annoyance at having to sacrifice her own activities to the care of a child. This mother was not able to see her child as a separate person with a distinct personality and needs different from hers. She seemed to feel that she had a perfect right to treat him in any way she felt at the moment, without regard for her child's right to be himself within the limits of safety and reasonable behavior. Such mothers had great difficulty in exacting obedience from their children:

> Motherly qualities—sensitivity to, acceptance of, and cooperation
> with the baby—were especially associated with the baby's obedi-
> ence.... The first and most important step in socializing a human
> being is a baby's willingness to do as he is asked. So the growth of an
> initial, unspecific disposition toward compliance may be critical for all
> later social development and learning [italics added].

The preceding has great application to the process of socializing and encouraging the intellectual and language development of the parrot. The authors have found, for instance, that those individuals who are unable to acknowledge and accept the "birdness" of their parrots have a great deal of difficulty exacting compliance to behavioral limits. They tend to see the parrot as a status symbol, rather than a living being worthy of respect in its own right. Therefore, any unacceptable behavior on the parrot's part is seen as mutiny, or a personal attack, rather than a regrettable but natural parrot behavior in a given circumstance. This is not to say behavior such as biting, unmitigated screaming or destruction of household objects should be tolerated. However, owners such as those being discussed are poor candidates for learning the techniques necessary to correct unwanted behaviors, because motivation to correct undesirable behavior is simply not there. There is no real understanding of the parrot or consideration for its quality of life. More important, the parrot itself will not be inclined to cooperate because congeniality of relationship necessary to foster compliance has not been established and nurtured by the owner.

The above material makes it abundantly clear that those birds which have had an opportunity to interact with a varied and interesting environment, and which have been allowed to develop trust in their humans, may have a much greater chance of fulfilling their potentials, regardless of species. Granted, a parrot is not a human being. However, enrichment will allow it to develop in an optimum way, within the limits of its genetic programming. Because of the parrot's tremendous intellectual capacity, this is something to be strived for. It has been pointed out that young parrots in the wild learn from observing their parents and other flockmates, and that parrot parents encourage exploration by their offspring of their surroundings. However, the point has also been made that too often persons working with infant, toddler and newly fledged parrots do not encourage this behavior, thus creating a situation in which the youngster has virtually no coping skills and is easily frightened by even small changes in his people and surroundings (Blanchard 1991). This can and should be avoided.

PRE- AND POSTHATCH ENRICHMENT

There are many things that can be done to enrich the environment of the parrot. Let us first look at the infant bird, beginning with prehatch, postpip. Although the authors are unaware at the time of this writing of any studies that have been done using tape recordings at the time chicks are hatching, and long-term effects on their socialization and language acquisition, this would seem to be a fruitful area for study. Plans are underway at this time to institute such a study and to publish results at some time in the future. The use of an endless loop audiocasette for several periods during the time in which the chick is hatching, placed in the incubator, should be a simple thing to accomplish. The tape contains the voice of the person who will be the primary caregiver, and the voice of one other person of the opposite sex. We recommend this because often young birds that have been exposed primarily to a female voice exhibit fear when confronted with a louder masculine voice that has a distinctly different pitch and timbre. A small, battery-operated tape recorder would suffice admirably to accomplish the purpose. The authors would welcome hearing from those who wish to participate in this study.

INFANCY AND TODDLERHOOD

After the chick has hatched, the use of the same recording in the brooder two or three times a day, for ten to fifteen minutes each time, is recommended. As the chick grows a little older, recordings of various kinds of music and voices are recommended, especially after feedings, when the baby will be increasingly wakeful for short periods. Music should be quiet and melodious, and of different types, excluding things like rock and heavy metal. The object is to create pleasant sounds and a soothing atmosphere. Taped voices should again include male and female. If you are making the tapes yourself, choose people with soothing, pleasant speaking voices. In addition to music and human speech tapes, environmental tapes are fascinating to growing babies. Avoid those tapes that contain sounds of predators such as wolves, jaguars and the like. Tapes of rain forest sounds, running water, songbirds, frogs and similar material are especially good.

Another type of audiotape that can be used contains fairy tales and nursery rhymes. These can be found in bookstores, record/tape stores and children's toy stores. They serve a dual purpose: human voices *and* the spoken word. They are rhythmic and sometimes dramatic in their rendering, and parrot chicks seem to be very attentive to them.

Another device that will provide pleasant auditory input is the music box. The authors particularly like to use a music box at night after the last feeding and lights are out. In addition to its purpose for the chick, there is something infinitely peaceful about a baby parrot that is warm, full, drowsy and tucked in for the night while a music box tinkles in the quiet darkness.

After the chick's eyes are open, various toys can be used to good effect in encouraging curiosity and play. Colorful crib mobiles, some of which have music boxes, can be attached over the brooder. Chicks may at first be somewhat fearful of such objects, but soon accustom themselves and learn to enjoy them. It is important to note that this process of learning not to be afraid of things that are not harmful (i.e., habituation) is extremely important for the chick. These experiences lay the groundwork for future encounters with new and different objects and situations. The parrot that has learned to take such things in stride will be much less apt to become stressed and upset over new experiences.

Toys should, of course, *always* be chosen with absolute safety in mind, as well as for their usefulness in encouraging exploration and play. The infant toy section in children's toy stores and in large drugstores are excellent sources for toys for toddler parrots. Large sets of plastic keys, used as rattles for human babies, are colorful and can be hung in the brooder or weaning cage. Brass bells made for adult parrots are also a good selection. Wooden blocks that can be rolled, chewed on or otherwise manipulated provide good fun, also. A big favorite with the authors' young parrots are baby bath toys made to chime when they float. Placed on the bottom of brooder or weaning cage, they provide lots of amusement and activity. *Please note:* As chicks become older, their beaks become more powerful. Toys that were appropriate and safe only days ago may suddenly become dangerous, and will need to be removed and replaced with stronger, safer toys.

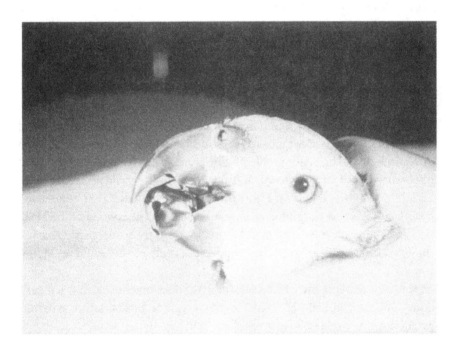

This Amazon parrot has trapped its lower mandible on the slits of a jingle bell. Toys with such small openings are unsafe for *any* bird, no matter what its size or age. *Scott McDonald, DVM*

As chicks grow and are better able to regulate their body temperature, they need the opportunity to explore new surroundings. A large cage set aside for this purpose, and equipped with materials not present in the weaning cage, can be used. It should be placed in a high-activity area where chicks are exposed to family members' comings and goings, along with other stimuli such as television (*Sesame Street* and *The Electric Company* are good choices for viewing), stereo or radio and other family pets. Be sure that pets do not have access to the chicks, so as to avoid accidental harm to them. It is recommended that time in the "playpen" be limited to two sessions per day for thirty to forty-five minutes each, when the young birds are normally awake and alert. An alternative to this method is to bring the chicks into the family living area in the evening to interact with persons other than the primary caregiver. In addition, while chicks are in the weaning cage, speaking to them often and affectionately is a must.

Also, during the time that chicks are still in the brooder, every effort should be made for cuddling and talking to them when care is being given. This is a natural time for these activities because chicks are then awake and able to respond interactively with the human surrogate parent. The more speech and affection they receive during this time, the better the chance that lifelong learning habits will be enhanced.

There is a caveat to the above remarks. Although the authors believe an enriched environment is extremely necessary to enhanced growth and learning development of parrot chicks, *it is very easy to overdo it.* This must be avoided at all costs, the reason being that overdoses of attention create "spoiled brats" that often become imprinted screamers or feather pluckers, or develop other undesirable behavior problems. Enrichment should help the bird fulfill its potential in all areas of growth and development. It should *not* create a bird that thinks it is the center of the universe. Enrichment of the environment and positive interaction with humans must take place in the context of the bird's *total* environment. A balance must be struck so that the young parrot also has the opportunity to learn to be by itself, amuse itself and enjoy these "alone" times.

Achieving this balance may seem difficult, if not impossible, but it can be done. One must basically proceed with the rearing and socialization of parrots as one would with one's own children. All parents know and act on the knowledge that children, in addition to their need for affection, guidance and teaching, must also learn that the world does not revolve about them and their needs to the exclusion of the needs of others. The same principle holds when dealing with parrots. If this is kept in mind, the breeder and/or owner will find that achieving a balance between enriched environment and interactions

This owner certainly has good intentions! However, such a profusion of toys usually results in bewilderment and a parrot that will not play with any of its toys. *Scott McDonald, DVM*

Contrast the cage of this Amazon with the previous photo. There is nothing to capture this parrot's attention or provide mental stimulation. In addition, the circular perch being used by the bird does not provide adequate grasp for its feet. *Scott McDonald, DVM*

with people, and preventing the extreme spoiling that will defeat all one's good intentions, will proceed very naturally The desired balance will result with very little difficulty. However, it seems to be an entrenched notion that parrots, especially hand-reared parrots, must be given attention 150 percent of the time to meet their social and intellectual needs. Not so. Part of any bird's needs includes the need to learn to be alone, to be a bird and to amuse itself. A well-rounded parrot is the desired result, not a bird so dependent on the companionship of humans that it becomes virtually impossible to satisfy (and, eventually, to live with).

ADULTHOOD

Naturally, once the young parrot becomes adult, the owner should continue to provide interesting, stimulating surroundings. Allowing the bird regular, supervised time out of its cage with the family is imperative. Car rides in a safe, appropriate carrier are beloved by many parrots, as are times on a portable perch on a screened in porch during good weather. A few interesting, safe toys in the cage are very important for the parrot. It is wise to use only two or three at a time, and replace these after one or two weeks. Rotation of toys in this manner prevents boredom and keeps the bird's interest engaged.

In the matter of dietary variety, nutrition is always the first consideration. However, there are many good pelleted foods on the market that can be used as the basis of the diet. These may be supplemented with a variety of fresh fruits and vegetables—*in moderation*—for increased visual interest and taste. There are also several balanced food products on the market that consist of a mixture of various dried ingredients that are then cooked in the home. Corn, many different kinds of beans and peas, dried fruit, nuts, rice and other goodies are included. Unused quantities can be frozen and thawed for later use. These products make a nice change in the daily dietary offering, and are yet another way to introduce interest and variety in the adult bird's life. (These products are marketed and sold through various magazines targeted at bird owners.)

LANGUAGE ENRICHMENT

Development of language by parrots is aided by all the preceding techniques. The actual acquisition of speech may at first be spontaneous, but can be enhanced by consistent, deliberate work with the bird by its owner. Although there are various tapes on the market that purport to teach birds to talk, the authors feel that the only effective way to achieve this, especially if one wishes his bird to use speech appropriately, is by personal interaction with the parrot (which, by the way, is a great way to promote mutual bonding). This involves spending at least fifteen minutes twice a day with the parrot in an area free of distractions. During this time, the person repeats over and over the word or phrase the bird is to learn. While this method is very effective, it will probably not help the bird to use what it has learned appropriately and in context. Some birds, such as African Grey Parrots, have an uncanny ability to learn to do this for themselves, as do some other species of parrots such as Amazons of the *ochrocephala* group. However, there is a much better way to help your parrot acquire use of cognitive speech. It is through the Model/Rival method used by Irene Pepperberg with Alex, her research "partner."

Many people are already familiar with what Dr. Pepperberg and Alex, the African Grey Parrot, have accomplished in this area. The list of this bird's achievements is nothing less than astounding to people who are not familiar with the outstanding intelligence of parrots. Further, Alex's achievements have been acquired and documented in the most rigorous scientific way.

Not only can Alex identify fifty objects and five different shapes (ranging from two to six cornered), he can recognize seven colors and identify up to six numbers. Additionally, Alex is able to categorize; so if he is presented with a number of objects and asked which one is *both* six cornered and red, he is able to do so. If presented with a pair of objects, he can indicate what about them is the same or different. Alex also knows the concept of absence. This is a very important concept because theory holds that one does not react to absence unless one is expecting a presence, an example of highly abstract thinking. This concept was tested with Alex by giving him either two identical objects or two totally dissimilar articles and asking what was the same or different. Alex was able to respond "none." The ability to categorize is thought to be a good indicator of intelligence, for it falls in the realm of abstract thinking. The animal must first attend to the object and listen to the question being asked. It must then both understand the question and the concept that color and shape are two separate attributes before it can respond correctly.

Alex is also able to combine phrases to request objects or express demands (e.g., "I want to go shoulder," "Want corn"), or to ask questions ("What's this? "You tell me"). It is important to emphasize that his use of these questions and demands are functional and occur appropriately within the context of the situation in which he finds himself.

The training procedures used to help Alex acquire functional use of human speech are basically simple in concept, but as with any training method, require an understanding of why they are used, coupled with absolute consistency in application. As mentioned earlier, the method used is that of the Model/Rival. With this technique, the parrot is perched near two people, one of whom acts as the teacher, the other as pupil. This creates a situation in which humans demonstrate to the bird the types of interactive responses that are desired. In the following exchange, "I" is Dr. Pepperberg, "B" is one of the secondary trainers. This part of the training session lasted about five minutes and was designed to improve Alex's pronunciation of "five," while at the same time reviewing the number concept "five."

> Irene: (acting as trainer) Bruce, what's this?
>
> Bruce: (acting as model/rival) Five wood.
>
> I: That's right, five wood. Here you are...five wood. (Hands over five wood Popsicle sticks. B begins to break one apart, much as Alex would.)
>
> A: 'ii wood. [Incorrect pronunciation.]
>
> B: (now acting as trainer, quickly replaces broken stick and presents the five sticks to Alex) Better...(briefly turns away then repositions himself in visual contact with Alex)...How many?
>
> A: No!
>
> B: (Turns from Alex to establish visual contact with I.) Irene, what's this?

I: (*Now acting as model/rival*) *'ii wood.*

B: *Better...(turns then resumes eye contact)...How many?*

I: *Five wood (takes wooden sticks)...Five wood. (Now acts as trainer, directs gaze to Alex, and presents sticks to him)...How many wood?*

A: *Fife wood.*

I: *OK, Alex, close enough...fivvvve wood...Here's five wood. (Places one stick in the bird's beak and the others within his reach) (Pepperberg 1991).*

In using this technique, it is important to be aware of several things. The first is that there are no extrinsic rewards. This means that the parrot only receives what it asks for. Doing this enables the bird to attach significant meaning to the label or concept it has learned. This will not occur if the bird is rewarded with food or some other unrelated object. Sunflower seed, for example, has no relationship to the concept "five," or the color "blue." The second thing of which to be aware is that after the bird has learned a new label or concept, it must be presented to the bird in several different ways. This assists him in learning its proper usage:"That's right, this is a *carrot*. Is the carrot good? Yes, this is a good *carrot.*" This technique fixes the pronunciation in the bird's mind. The bird also hears it used in normal speech and learns to reproduce the word "without associating simple word-for-word imitation of the trainers with reward" (Pepperberg 1991). According to Dr. Pepperberg, the first word a parrot learns is easier than the second. This is because the first word, to the bird, basically means "Give me something I want." Learning the second word means that the parrot has to make *different* sounds to get the different reward associated with that particular sound.

Another technique used successfully with Alex is *referential mapping*. This is a very scientific-sounding phrase that really denotes a simple idea: the repetition of a word in context *as if* the bird actually knows what it means. Parents do this all the time with children who are learning to talk. The child says "Wah-wah." The parent says, "Oh, do you want a drink of *water?*" After enough repetitions of this scenario, the child learns to associate the sound he is making with a real object and is then able to use this sound to express his need in an intelligible way. In the same manner, if a parrot makes a gibberish vocalization as you are ready to leave the house, and you consistently answer with "Bye-bye," it will eventually associate that combination of sounds with your activity and begin to use them appropriately and meaningfully whenever you perform this action.

Readers who wish to study Dr. Pepperberg's methods in greater depth are referred to her publications cited in the preceding discussion. In particular, her audiotape *Communication with Alex* (1992) is delightful and very instructive.

Why do parrots talk? For the same reasons people do. They use language (either natural vocalization or learned speech) to communicate. A wild parrot has a large range of natural vocalizations that are used to communicate with mates, siblings and other flock members. Pepperberg notes that since humans become the companion bird's flock, its vocalizations are directed toward establishing itself as a flock member and maintaining that relationship. That the companion bird clearly has the ability to do this with rather astonishing success is becoming abundantly clear. To foster this potential in our companion parrots is well worth the commitment and effort required for our own enjoyment as well as theirs.

Domestication and Discipline

It may seem that pairing domestication and discipline makes for an odd coupling. However, the two subjects have a great deal in common. To be unaware of what domestication is and how it bears on the companion parrot is to invite avoidable behavioral problems. Failing to gain the perspective that a discussion of domestication offers may cripple one's attempts to prevent or correct behavioral difficulties in the psittacid.

Parrot owners too numerous to count suffer from overt or covert guilt about keeping a "wild animal" as a companion, no matter how dearly they love their parrots. The authors have seen countless situations in which this sense of guilt seriously interfered with or actually prevented owners from working effectively with their companion birds. This guilt, coupled with complete lack of understanding of what constitutes discipline, is at the bottom of the great majority of parrot behavioral problems. Thus the scene is set in which such problems incubate and grow to serious proportions. When owners are unable to deal with these concepts the chance of problem resolution is greatly decreased.

How, you may ask? To answer this question, one must understand that domestication is not something Homo sapiens foisted on the unwilling ancestors of our domestic animals tens of thousands of years ago. Rather, domestication is thought by some to be one of nature's evolutionary survival strategies that may help ensure a species' perpetuation over eons of time. Domestication as a strategy has been exploited by certain species for their

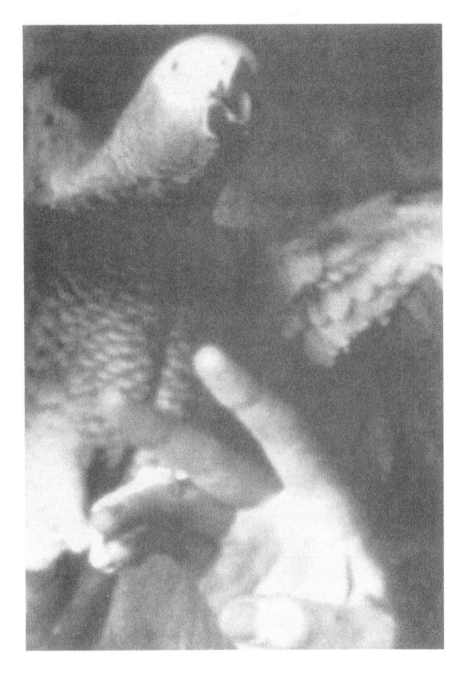

...You see, myself and others like me do not know you...*Diane Schmidt*

survival, albeit unconsciously. (Natural selection always consists of external forces acting on a population of animals, rather than some internal "knowing" on the part of an animal that one strategy is more effective than other alternatives.) It is our premise that parrots are eminently suited to use domestication as a survival mechanism, and that, indeed, they are doing so very effectively. We hope that after having read this chapter, the reader will be able to see that there is no reason to feel guilty about having a parrot as a family companion. Where there is no guilt, there is no overindulgence based on the mistaken notion that the owner must "make up" to the bird what it is "missing" in the wild. Therefore, behavioral problems are much easier to prevent or to correct before they escalate to unmanageable proportions.

Such guilt is skillfully and cleverly exploited by radical animal rights groups with astonishing success. Therefore, it is also our hope that armed with the knowledge in this chapter, parrot owners will be able to judge such tactics for themselves and dismiss the negative feelings they engender. In this way they will become more free to enjoy what can be one of the most delightful interspecies relationships available to the pet owner.

DOMESTICATION

What Is Domestication?

We will first discuss the issue of domestication in a broad general sense, utilizing Stephen Budiansky's hypotheses contained in his excellent book on the subject, *Covenant of the Wild: Why Animals Choose Domestication*. We will then examine what characteristics parrots possess that allow them to exploit this successful survival strategy.

The *Oxford American Dictionary* defines domestication as the act of taming an animal, or of bringing it under control. Radical animal rights groups define the use of any animal for any human purpose as enslavement. Nothing could be further from the truth, as we will soon discover. However, our increasing distance from the true reality that we urbanites call nature has led us into erroneous thinking concerning what nature really is. The truth is far from the cartoon concept of talking animals with endearingly human characteristics, cooperation among all birds and beasts (with the occasional evil character) and happy endings to the story of every animal's life. In this scenario an abundance of food, shelter, safety and the "nobility" of the "free" life in Mother Nature's all-caring, all-providing embrace is the norm.

A hard look at the facts should disabuse all of us of this false picture. Anyone who has had the opportunity to view the PBS documentary, "Mortal Enemies: The Lion and the Hyena" has probably already begun to shed his cartoon concept of nature. Ornithologists and other field biologists give estimates of upwards of 70 percent of the young of most species that never reach a first birthday due to predation, disease and lack of necessary skill in foraging. The cold fact is that nature is brutal and unforgiving. Animals survive in this reality only because of fine evolutionary tuning, which nevertheless fails for many individuals of all species. There is one survival mechanism, however, that has proved splendidly successful in ensuring an animal's continuing presence on this planet: domestication. One has only to consider that there are far more domestic cats and dogs than lions and wolves to understand just how effective domestication is for species perpetuation.

How Is Domestication Achieved?

Regardless of the success of this strategy, most animals have been unable to avail themselves of it. Considering the benefits of protection from predators, regular food supply and shelter of sorts for many domestic animals, why did some animals opt successfully for this evolutionary alternative, and others not?

According to Budiansky, the ancestors of those animals we consider to be domestic had several characteristics that allowed them to exploit this mechanism. First, they were opportunistic in their requirements of habitat and food sources. They were also edge-of-forest dwellers, rather than deep forest inhabitants. In other words, they were generalists in the art of survival, not specialists requiring only certain types of food and habitat.

Second, there existed behavioral traits that these domestic progenitors shared in common with humans and that could be recognized and acted on by both animal and human in an interspecies relationship. One of these traits is that of hierarchy or "pecking" order. In this setting there is a pack leader or alpha breeding pair, to which all others of the group must defer. Submission to this individual or pair is demonstrated by such behaviors as tail wagging, rolling over and exposing the belly, licking, giving place at a pack kill until the leaders have eaten and other such activities. Grooming is another behavior that can not only indicate submission to a recognized leader, but it also enhances both bonding and comfort.

Another of these behavioral traits is the instinct to follow a leader. This is commonly seen in wild horses, bison, wild sheep and other herd animals. This characteristic is seen today in herds of domestic sheep and cattle.

NEOTENY

Given the "raw" material that enabled certain wild animals to live in proximity to man and benefit from it, how then did true domestication come about? Budiansky theorizes that a characteristic called neoteny allowed this to occur. Neoteny means the retention of juvenile characteristics after adulthood has been reached. Physically, such animals exhibit a high, domed forehead, shortened snouts, large eyes and a head large in proportion to the body. These traits tend to be very endearing to humans. Characters like Mickey Mouse and E.T. were deliberately given this appearance to increase their appeal to fans. Additionally, animals that are neotenous also exhibit a willingness to cross species barriers, relating to animals and people as their wild counterparts will not.

These traits seem to "hang together." They can be obtained, not by painstakingly breeding for each characteristic separately, but by selecting for one dominant trait: that of *tameness*. It is plausible to imagine that various groups of wild domestic forebears close to early human encampments or agricultural sites included individuals that demonstrated more docility than others of their species and were therefore tolerated, not driven away. The advantages in food, shelter of a kind and protection from predation that would have existed in such places made it more possible for them to survive and pass on their relative docility than others of their species. Thus, in an unknowing manner, our own early ancestors would have made a very good start at producing a "domestic" animal. For unknowingly, they selected for tameness and all that implies genetically.

Can we prove that selecting for docility, even unwittingly, will eventually produce a domesticated animal? The answer is yes. A Soviet biologist, D. K. Belyaev, in his research for the fur industry, chose to breed foxes, rigorously selecting for docility. He not only succeeded in producing this trait in first generation offspring, but in producing other "domestic" traits at the same time! He found that these offspring exhibited piebald coats in some instances, a trait not found in wild foxes. They approached known persons and licked their hands and faces. They solicited unfamiliar persons for attention by tail wagging. They barked like dogs. Physical characteristics such as the drooping ear of immature wild foxes were carried into adulthood. The vixens' estrus cycles manifested twice a year, like dogs (and unlike their wild counterparts). If such results could be achieved with first generation offspring, it is reasonable to assume that each passing generation will acquire greater numbers of traits associated with domestication, and that these traits will become ever more firmly fixed in the genetic makeup.

THE ISSUE OF SPECIES DEGRADATION

Biologists tend to worry about degradation of species subject to domestication, stating that such animals will be rendered incapable of fending for themselves if reintroduced to native habitat. Indeed, this is one of the foremost criticisms of the technique of captive breeding of psittacids for eventual reintroduction in their range countries. However, if the process of domestication is an evolutionary survival strategy exploited by certain species capable genetically of taking advantage of such a mechanism, then the issue of species "degeneracy" becomes moot. The authors believe that parrots are just such a group of species and that domestication may be a splendid answer to their declining wild numbers. In the instance of those parrots which have always been rare, even in their natural habitat, we tend to agree with Erwin, in his article "An Evolutionary Basis for Conservation Strategies" (1991), in which he states that "forms [of species]...are often unusual or rare, and even interesting to many scientists, but...are predictably on their way to extinction...Conservation of [such species]...is like saving living fossils." He then makes the point that conservationists should include in their efforts the species that show genetic vigor and adaptability, and that are capable of continuing evolution as viable groups. We certainly espouse any efforts that can be made to preserve such rare and unusual parrot species, but we also contend that parrots are creatures tending to domestication and that this obvious tendency to domestication and captive propagation should be reason for rejoicing, rather than outcries of degeneracy and "better dead than bred."

DOMESTICATION AND THE PARROT

Having examined the broad issue of domestication, we will now look at how parrots as a group fit this picture. They are endowed with all of the characteristics that are precursors for domestication. Those birds which have been bred in captivity manifest traits that even in the first generation indicate a dependence on man their wild parents do not exhibit. This is not to say that they are at this point in time, domestic; but they seem to be moving in this direction. In ten or fifteen generations of captive breeding, much psittacine aggression we now see (especially during breeding season) will probably be greatly modified. Over many hundreds of generations, these birds may retain few of the overtly aggressive traits of the wild parrot. We make no judgment as to whether this is bad or good. We merely point out that should this occur, parrots as a group will have succeeded in surviving, where many other species will have succumbed to the tragedy of habitat degradation and resulting extinction.

Wild Parrot Traits That Tend to Domestication

The parrot as a wild creature exhibits several characteristics that provide striking parallels with those possessed by the wild forebears of other domestic animals. They are excellent colonizers under the right conditions (Wiley, Snyder and Gnam 1992), and they do not seem to be "extreme habitat specialists and can be expected to survive even in modified habitats (ibid.). Parrots possess "resilience to human disturbance and habitat changes" (Beissinger and Bucher 1992). Parrots are notorious for exploiting agricultural crops in Africa, Australia and Latin America. These birds possess a sense of curiosity, which allows them to explore and take advantage of new food sources. They also have a powerful beak and flexible foot that enable them to manipulate nontraditional foods. "The expansion of agriculture into previously forested areas is an accelerating process in Latin America and provides an ideal combination of feeding habitat (crop patches) and nesting habitat (forest patches) for many species of parrots" (ibid). Crops used as food sources by parrots in South American countries include corn, sunflower, wheat, sorghum, peaches, pears and other types of fruit. Citrus plantations also receive the attention of hungry parrots, as do tree plantations, in which the leaf and flower buds are consumed.

In the city of Canberra, Australia, the Gang-Gang Cockatoo (*Callocephalon fimbriatum*) is so well known that it appears on the city's official seal (Hohensee 1989). These birds generally inhabit the hills surrounding Canberra, but in the winter they descend into the valley to avail themselves of the food offered by plantings in backyards and city parks. The Yellow-Tailed Black Cockatoo (*Calyptorhynchus funereus funereus*) have moved into softwood and pine plantations to take advantage of the pinecones there. The Galah (*Eolophus roseicapillus*) is often seen drinking from water troughs placed for the use of domestic livestock in Australia. Most species of white cockatoos in this country have become such agricultural pests that they are shot and poisoned by the thousands, although the Australian government prohibits their export for pets and breeding.

In Africa, African Grey Parrots consume maize crops, as well as millet. William Donald Clark reports that the Hyacinth Macaw (*Andorhynchus hyacinthinus*) nests in close proximity to ranch houses in South America's Pantanal. This area has been cleared to a great extent to allow cattle ranching. The Hyacinths on the ranch visited by Clark frequented a grove of trees two hundred yards from the main house, and three pairs actually had nests in the backyard of the hacienda (Clark 1991). Hyacinths, too, avail themselves of water from livestock troughs. One of the authors was told of a field trip into this region to study Hyacinths in their habitat. The birds exhibited great curiosity about the researchers and followed them back to their camp, flying at low levels with great composure. Even when nests were disturbed to remove babies for weighing and observation of other growth parameters, parents did not seem to be unduly disturbed and seemed to accept the whole process with equanimity.

Puerto Rico has at least six species of parrots that are not native to the island, but that nevertheless have established themselves as wild flocks. Interestingly, these birds have chosen not to inhabit niches of the island's native parrot, but the populated urban lowlands and second-growth forest (Wiley, Snyder and Gnam 1992). Conversely, two psittacids that have been domestically bred for hundreds of generations—the cockatiel and the budgerigar—have had great difficulty in establishing themselves as feral flocks. The cockatiel has *never* been able to do this, and the budgie has only achieved this in very warm climates where humans provide food at their backyard bird feeders!

Besides being habitat opportunists with a great deal of curiosity, parrot flocks possess a well-developed hierarchy. Dominance and submission are the dualities by which they lead their lives in the wild. They carry this into the domestic situation, where they both recognize and act on these behaviors within the context of their human "flock." As discussed in Chapter 2, many parrots are pair-bonding, a behavior they transfer to human companions. Parrots preen their owners' hair and eyelashes, bow their heads and ruffle their neck feathers to be preened in return, regurgitate to a favored human and otherwise demonstrate the bonding and comfort-giving behaviors they would in their wild flocks.

In physical appearance, parrots have many characteristics that are endearing to humans. Their faces have many of the characteristics of the neotenous animal, including large eyes and head. And with the beak giving the appearance of a foreshortened snout, the overall impression is rather that of a slightly bucktoothed, lovable child. The clumsy gait of an earthbound parrot is for all the world like a human toddler's, and the tame parrot's obvious enjoyment of the attention of his people has an exuberant, childlike quality as well.

Domestically Bred Parrots and Their Problems "Going Wild"

When one examines the qualities of first-generation offspring of parrots bred in captivity, it becomes obvious that they have developed traits that make them unable to resume a life in the wild unless extraordinary precautions are taken during the rearing process. Munn states that "developmental, physiological, and behavioral traits appear to be very sensitive to founder effects, and many of the traits that accompany domestication have *high heritability*..."(Derrickson and Snyder, 1992; italics added).

Derrickson and Snyder point out that domestically bred wild turkeys, for example, show changes in the endocrine system. The adrenal glands, necessary for the "flight or fight" response to danger, are reduced in size. It has been found in domestically bred parrots that their ability to evade predators has been altered, making it difficult for them to survive in the wild. Domestically bred parrots also have difficulty locating appropriate food sources, interacting with their wild counterparts and selecting suitable mates and nesting sites. Additionally, the domestically bred parrot may continue to center his activities close to areas used by people and may often come to them to beg for food.

To prepare domestically bred parrots for reintroduction to their range habitats, extreme care must be taken to avoid imprinting on humans, to teach effective foraging techniques, to introduce them to food they will find in the wild and other such precautions. All of these characteristics make it apparent to the authors that if such profound changes can be wrought in one generation of captive propagation, that several hundred generations will most certainly produce a true "domestic" parrot from original wild stock having genetic potential to use the domestication strategy for evolutionary survival.

In the words of E. O. Wilson, in his excellent chapter "The Morality of the Gene" in *Sociobiology* (1975), "In the process of natural selection, then, any device that can insert a higher proportion of certain genes into subsequent generations will come to characterize the species. One class of such devices promotes prolonged individual survival. Another promotes superior mating performance and care of the resulting offspring." Domestication, for the parrot, provides both of these advantages. It is known that parrots in captivity live longer, remain healthier and reproduce more effectively in terms of number of offspring and lowered mortality of these offspring.

Therefore, parrot owners and would-be parrot owners, discard your feelings of guilt engendered by keeping a "wild" bird as a companion. If we "use" our birds in this way, they at the same time are "using" us as a survival mechanism.

And although they do this unconsciously, it should be apparent that parrots individually and collectively are much enhanced by their association with mankind.

DISCIPLINE

Discipline and Punishment: The Differences

The subject of discipline is grossly misunderstood when dealing with parrots. Most think of punishment when discipline is mentioned. However, discipline also means to train, coach, drill, instruct, teach, tutor, edify, inform, enlighten, rear, bring up, guide, familiarize (Gordon 1989). These are all positive attributes of discipline, and it is only in this context that we use the word *discipline*. When working with a parrot to socialize it or to correct unwanted habits, punishment (especially physical punishment), is never used.

Punishment means "to cause an individual to suffer for his offenses." It does not work for several important reasons. It provokes and encourages aggression. Violence begets violence. Severe or inappropriate punishment does not, therefore, curb or correct unacceptable behaviors or habits (ibid.). These behaviors, in fact, usually escalate with such harsh tutelage. Because the bird has no evolutionary experience of violence as the reward of inappropriate behavior, it does not understand punishment intellectually in terms of cause and effect. Punishment therefore is seen as life-threatening, and the bird acts to protect itself rather than to change a behavior seen by its humans as "bad."

Parrots, as mentioned previously, are very intelligent creatures, and over the centuries have provided abundant evidence of their ability (indeed, their desire) to cohabit with man on a basis of mutual trust and cooperation. Taking advantage of this ability, when working with a parrot, suggests that a system of teaching and persuasion will produce the best results. This capitalizes on the bird's innate desire to be an integral and accepted part of the "flock," and of its native intelligence. True, genetic limitations must be taken into account when socializing the parrot, but in our opinion, these limitations are far less rigid than most would suppose.

It then follows that, as with children, the use of discipline in the best and truest sense of the word is a necessary part of living with parrots. It helps the bird learn to live happily and harmoniously within the domestic setting. With our children, we have the responsibility to rear them to be responsible, caring individuals capable of fulfilling their potential. So do we have the responsibility to provide our birds with the skills to be happy, healthy, self-actualized creatures. Not to do so will result in a bird that will be impossible to live with. In many such cases, the parrot will be doomed to a life of solitude, or shuffled from one home to the next without any knowledge of why it suffers such a miserable fate. It only knows confusion and bewilderment, which it may act out through aggression, withdrawal, and in the most desperate case, stress, illness and premature death.

We must stop viewing discipline as an unloving element in our relationships with our parrots. Discipline should instead be viewed as ultimate love and respect for a receptive, adaptable, intelligent being that comes from a world of which we know very little, into a world of which the parrot has little knowledge or understanding. Overindulgence and lack of discipline is nothing less than lack of respect for the bird. Moving the parrot from one home to another because we can no longer live with the "monster" that has been created will break its spirit. Lack of love and resulting stress engendered by our reaction to unruly behavior will break its spirit. Being locked in a spare bedroom so we cannot hear incessant screaming (which is a plea for meaningful interaction) will break its spirit. Never being allowed to be what it is, a parrot, will break its spirit. Discipline in the form of guidance and gentle enforcement of behavior limits will not break its spirit. In an atmosphere of properly applied discipline a parrot's spirit will grow and bloom. It is an almost mystical paradox that only in discipline does freedom exist: freedom to fulfill one's potential, freedom to love and be loved. *Discipline is a part of love, and love is a part of commitment.*

Discipline and Its Meaning for Parrots

What then, do we mean by discipline, as applied to the parrot? It means teaching the bird to live happily in the domestic setting. With parrots, this can be accomplished most effectively using the principles and tactics of behavioral modification. Because the parrot is probably not capable intellectually of understanding the reason its behavior is unacceptable, it must therefore be conditioned to expect that if it performs behavior x, effect y will immediately follow. This conditioning is usually accomplished by denying the bird something it wants, such as companionship with its "flock," for a predetermined period. Ostracism from the flock is a concept the bird "knows," because genetically it is a flock animal and depends on its congeners for safety as well as companionship. Deprivation of the company of the "flock" therefore becomes a useful tool with which to set and enforce behavioral limits. This is but one example of a "disciplinary" technique used in behavioral modification work with parrots. There are many others, which will be discussed in a later chapter, along with a fuller exploration of behavioral modification itself.

Self-Discipline and the Owner

Self-discipline on the part of the owner and his or her family is also necessary when working with the parrot! Without the requisite motivation to acquire the knowledge, insight and attitudes needed, the individual(s) will not be able to create the setting in which the successful meshing of the parrot/human systems can happen. Patience, love and respect for the bird, and what it is, are absolutely imperative if mutual trust is to be established and the bird's cooperation gained. Without trust and cooperation, as mentioned in the previous chapter's discussion of Ainsworth's study, very little will be accomplished to help the parrot acquire the necessary skills to coexist happily with its human flock. And that which is accomplished inadvertently will not survive in the long term. This often happens when a parrot reaches sexual maturity. Because of the vastly superior ability of humans to accept, learn, tolerate and experience empathy and compassion, it is the owner who must make the greater effort and travel the farther path, to achieve lasting results in crafting a joyous interrelationship between man and bird.

Useful Disciplinary Guidelines

How then do we acquire the necessary attitudes for success in this adventure? Let us look at the work of Rudolf Dreikurs for our guidelines. Dreikurs is a child psychologist noted for his work in the subject of child discipline. His book *Children: The Challenge* (1964) is a classic in the field. In this book he gives many guidelines for parents who wish to help their children achieve both self-control and useful, responsible adulthood, and several of these guidelines have definite application to the person working with psittacids.

The first we will examine is **"Be firm without dominating."** At first this may seem a contradiction in terms, but this is actually not so. Dreikurs's premise is that children are not comfortable without limits. Lack of limits can result in a feeling of "the sky's the limit" before the child has acquired the maturity and experience to handle such a multitude of choices and their results. This quite naturally causes anxiety. It is rather like giving the car keys to a young person who has had only one driving lesson and who, further, does not yet even know the rules of the road!

So it is with the parrot. Not equipped to live safely and confidently in the world of people, the bird will act in ways that may be inappropriate and unsafe in the family setting. For example, it may wade into a tureen of hot soup at the family table, which is unsanitary, unaesthetic and unsafe for the parrot. It is nice to share one's meal with one's parrot, but only if the bird has been trained to behave in a safe and "sanitary" way. To scream at the bird, punish it for what we consider to be a social gaff or otherwise try to assert punitive dominance will accomplish nothing. It is far better to remove the bird from its predicament, make sure it has not injured itself, then place it on its perch with a treat, close to the table where it feels a part of things but cannot disrupt the meal or hurt itself. Further attempts by the bird should be handled by replacing it on the perch as often as necessary. This does not hurt the bird, respects its desire for company and also respects the family's right to eat peacefully. The key to this and all other behavioral modification techniques is *consistency*. If the parrot is allowed, even once, to rummage about on the table during mealtimes, it will take far longer to produce a well-behaved dinner companion. Out of desperation, the bird may be confined to its cage during mealtimes, and thereby deprived of what could have been an enjoyable social occasion *had limits been set and enforced by the owner*.

Another such example involves getting the bird out of the cage onto one's arm. Even the best-socialized parrot will occasionally balk at doing this. However, with parrots, once a demand has been made, the owner should see to it that the bird follows through. (To fail to do so creates a situation in which the bird will respond only when it wants to. In the event that the bird refuses to come out on one's arm on command, do not yell or gesture angrily at the bird (two methods of showing extreme dominance). Instead, if after two or three attempts, the parrot remains obdurate, towel the bird, remove it from the cage and place it on your arm or its training stand. The bird has not been hurt, you have not punished it in any way. You have merely demonstrated in the most direct way that you mean what you say.

The second of Dreikurs's suggestions is "**Show respect for the child.**" Respect for the dignity and uniqueness of another human being is the cornerstone of any relationship. This is emphatically also the case with the parrot. Respect for all living creatures demands that we take seriously their right to be themselves. They are not extensions of our egos. Their lives have intrinsic meaning for themselves, apart from their relationships with humans. Their ways are not our ways, nor their priorities our priorities. True, many times these areas will mesh in a complimentary way, but often they will not. It requires judgment and empathy with the bird to decide when and under what circumstances to refrain from demanding of it that which it is unable or unwilling to give at the moment. Case in point: A bird that is eating should not be expected to leave its food to indulge the owner's whim for companionship at the moment. A bird that is sleeping, engaged in a thorough preening session or feeling unwell should not be expected to perform for its owner or leave its activity because the owner wants the bird *now*.

Although these things may appear self-evident, it is amazing how often owners behave thoughtlessly toward their parrots because they tend to see the bird as an ego extension, or a possession that must always gratify its owner's desires at the cost of its own emotional comfort. (Would you enjoy being snatched from your meal, rudely awakened from a sound sleep, forced to be bright and witty if you had a cold and felt terrible?) Respect for the parrot that allows it to be a parrot, to indulge in its "parrotly" ways (within reason), creates trust on the part of the bird. A bird that trusts is one whose cooperation is far easier to gain, and more willing to learn and relate to the owner in positive ways.

Dreikurs admonishes parents to "**Eliminate criticism and minimize mistakes.**" There are bound to be times in rearing children that mistakes occur. Mistakes, of course, require correction. However, the best philosophy is that the child, it is hoped, learns from the mistake and will not repeat it in the future. This places the emphasis on the positive aspect of learning and does not humiliate and shame the child, the results of which are disastrous to self-esteem. Regarding the parrot, we cannot say with certainty what, if any, self-esteem it possesses. It has been our experience, however, that most psittacids seem to behave in ways that might indicate a sense of self-worth and self-awareness. It is most certainly evident that they do not enjoy being screamed at, ignored, hit or otherwise mistreated.

With this in mind, how can we take Dreikurs's advice and apply it to a parrot's "misdeeds?" As with children, parrots are bound to make "mistakes." The bird will chew a brand-new compact disc into useless shards, unexpectedly nip or scream during the most important part of a TV program or video. Whatever corrective action has been decided on must be implemented without delay. *But*, once taken, do not obsess on the loss of your property, the damage to your person or the disrupted program. A parrot lives in the here and now and cannot comprehend the consequences of its behavior in terms of your emotions. If you are really angry and upset, leave the room and do not attempt to handle the bird. Parrots are masters at sensing emotions, which may induce your bird to act out further in undesirable ways. This is a bad experience for the parrot, as well as for you, and it is best to avoid such events. Live and let live is the key here. Start over again with a tabla rasa, realizing that your parrot does not view the world as you do, nor is it his business to behave like a mindless toy. Let go of the anger and upset, lest such occurrences accumulate to the point where you can no longer deal with the bird and begin to view it as a nuisance, rather than as a welcome friend and companion.

"**Maintain routine**" is another of Dreikurs's suggestions that has great value for the person living with a parrot. Routine adhered to as much as possible creates a sense of security. The parrot knows what to expect, when to expect it and who it will be relating to most of the time. Parrots (indeed, all birds) are suspicious creatures. This is one of their survival mechanisms in the wild, where the unexpected may presage attack from a predator. This mechanism is genetic and the parrot brings it to the family setting. A parrot that never knows what to expect from one minute to the next, or one day to the next, is in a continuous state of low-level stress that will eventually take its toll in the form of illness and emotional unbalance. With this in mind, changes in diet should be made gradually, and a minimum number of hours of darkness per twenty-four-hour period should be maintained, with bedtime at about the same time most days. New pets and people are a source of stress, and every effort should be made to introduce the parrot to these new creatures gently and gradually. Your own behavior and tone of voice should be gentle, slow moving and consistent. This creates trust on the bird's part, and will allow it to exhibit all the best parts of its personality, decreasing the chance that unwanted behaviors will appear because of stress, fear and insecurity.

"**Avoid giving undue attention**" has application to parrots as well as children. According to Dreikurs, a child who seeks constant attention is an unhappy child, and a child who is unable to amuse himself and must be constantly entertained is unable to learn or fulfill his potential. He is continually in a state of anxiety lest his entertainment sources disappear, for then what will he do? Additionally, the parents of such a child labor under the burden of being a full-time entertainment director, and have no time for themselves, either to accomplish necessary tasks, or to relax and enjoy life.

The same things occur with the demanding parrot. It is absolutely essential that the parrot be allowed time by itself to learn to play and amuse itself and to be simply a bird. Any owner of a continually screaming parrot can attest to the distraction, irritation and desperation of living with such a companion. Such birds demand attention twenty-four hours a day, and may even awaken in the night with unearthly screeches, insisting on attention before the beleaguered owner can go back to bed. Needless to say, such a parrot does not long reside in that household or any other. Parrots are self-centered creatures and learn quickly to manipulate owners toward the goal of servant and pacifier, rather than friend and companion. The trick is never to begin a relationship with a parrot on this basis.

This is particularly a problem with first-time owners. Initially the bird is a novelty, in much the same way that a newborn infant captures its parents' and relatives' attention for a good part of their waking (and sleeping!) hours. Gradually a routine is established, and the entire family can begin to resume a somewhat normal lifestyle, integrating the new baby's needs with their own. New parrot owners, wanting to "do right" by their fascinating new companions, and having heard how intelligent and emotional they can be, bend over backward to provide constant attention and companionship for the parrot. Before the owners realize it, the bird will do almost anything to obtain attention, and its methods of obtaining attention are invariably obnoxious and/or upsetting. Everything from screaming, biting and feather plucking may be included in the repertoire.

It is far better to give a reasonable amount of attention, within the framework of flexible routine, from day one. In this way the bird learns from the beginning that there are times to be together and have fun, and times to be alone to play, preen, eat or snooze. Thus, bird and person come together in mutually enjoyable circumstance. This is a far better situation than that in which the hapless owner feels that unless he gives into the bird's demands for attention, his life will become a living hell. This is not enjoyable, nor is it the basis for any type of meaningful relationship. Remember, even as a doting parrot owner, you have a right to time for your own needs.

Dreikurs warns parents to **"Sidestep the struggle for power."** This is good advice for parrot owners as well as parents. As with children, parrots have an innate drive for domination and ascendancy. In the wild, such behavior allows them the best chance of success at reproduction, at getting their genes into the next generation. Domestically, however (unless the parrot is a breeding bird), these behaviors can be inappropriate and potentially disastrous. Yes, the bird should be allowed to express its personality within reason; and yes, the bird should never be regarded as the subject for subjugation. However, it is *not* a favor to the parrot to let it "get away with" any behavior it chooses to exhibit when it is unsafe or detrimental to itself or its humans.

As with establishing firmness without excess dominance, the misbehaving parrot should be handled calmly and firmly, expected and made to follow through with reasonable requests, then rewarded for doing so. Hitting the bird, screaming at it and otherwise treating it as if extreme coercive activities are understood and can be acted on by the parrot is cruel and counterproductive. It will produce escalated aggression. The parrot sees these responses as life threatening and will react to protect itself. It also fixes the owner, in the bird's mind, as dangerous and to be avoided at all cost. Again, not a prescription for a mutually satisfying relationship. By establishing behavioral limits and enforcing them in nonviolent, nonaggressive ways, the owner sidesteps the power struggle between himself and his bird, and is thereby able to maintain the balance required for happy interaction.

"**Make your requests reasonable and sparse.**" However intelligent, parrots are not able, for the most part, to understand complex rules. A few simple commands, gently and consistently enforced, make life easier and happier for all concerned. Decide on essential rules, enforce them consistently and then leave your parrot to be itself. It is necessary for the parrot to get on its owner's arm on command. The bird must be taught that biting and destruction of property will not be tolerated at all, and limits for times when vocalizations will and will not be tolerated must be decided on. These are probably the most important behavioral guidelines you will want to teach your bird. Then, within these limits, and within reason, the bird should be allowed to be itself.

For example, if the parrot (like most parrots), screams loudly for a few minutes each morning and evening, it and you should feel comfortable with this. If however, the bird extends these periods to times you do not feel are reasonable or bearable, then you must act to limit the behavior. Another example is requiring the bird to come out of its cage on your arm, or the arms of other designated family members. It is not necessary that your bird perform this action with any person who comes into your home. In fact, it is stressful for the bird, and in light of the parrot's naturally suspicious outlook on life, unreasonable to expect it. The parrot is your companion, not a plaything to be exhibited to anyone who happens along.

Dreikurs emphasizes that follow-through on any request should be *consistent*. For the parrot nothing else is so important. If a request is made of the bird that it is then allowed to ignore, it will do so the next time the same request is made. The result is a parrot that is unpredictable, totally in control of the relationship and a prime candidate for the development of serious behavioral problems. The parrot may inflict severe injury on its owner or other family members. A large macaw that is allowed to do as it pleases, indulging whatever aggression it feels, is a very dangerous animal. The authors know of one family that thinks it hilarious when their macaw stalks and nips visitors. The bird has always been played with roughly, and one day it will inflict serious injury on someone. In this time of numerous lawsuits, such a scenario is frightening. It also exhibits total lack of respect for both bird and visitors.

Finally, in Dreikurs's words, "**Have fun together.**" This is what having a parrot is all about. Playing together, sharing a meal or a car ride, sitting quietly together while the parrot preens (himself or you!) as you read, watch television or chat with friends or family, are experiences with great depth of richness. They strengthen the bond between bird and human, adding to the quality of life of both species. The foregoing material has been presented and discussed toward just this end: the best of all possible relationships between parrot and person. When all concerned know the rules and follow them, the relationship is bound to be a sound and satisfying one.

5

How Do Behavioral Problems Develop?

In examining behavioral problems in parrots, it is helpful to understand exactly what a problem is: a set of actions and responses between owner and bird that causes concern to the owner or poses some sort of threat to the bird itself. According to the dictionary, a problem is something that is difficult to deal with.

WHO "OWNS" THE PROBLEM?

An interesting thing about problems is who owns them! A number of behaviors that parrots exhibit are normal to this group of birds and cannot be considered problems in the context of their genetic makeup. For example, morning and evening shrieking, territorial biting and chewing. These are normal components of the parrot's behavior and give rise to concern only within the domestic setting. These characteristics cause the *parrot* no problem whatsoever. It is the *owner* who perceives the behavior as undesirable and has difficulty dealing with it. It is the owner, then, who *owns* the problem.

To live happily with a parrot requires patience and tolerance for behavior that is normal to the bird. Acceptance of a certain amount of mess, noise and destruction of property will go a long way in preventing the development of relationship difficulties between person and parrot. If the parrot has been properly socialized, its natural tendencies to boisterousness and self-expression

...And many of us have been abused or mishandled... *Diane Schmidt*

should not be unpleasant for the owner. Occasionally "accidents" will happen, as they do with small children. But they should be the exception, not the rule. As long as the owner understands that there is no such thing as perfection with a companion parrot (just as there is no such thing with a small child), the parrot/owner relationship should be mutually pleasant and satisfying.

RESPECT THE PARROT FOR WHAT IT IS

Nevertheless, problem behaviors do develop in the companion psittacid. *Many of these arise because the owner is unable to respect the bird for what it is:* an extremely intelligent, adaptable creature that may choose to relate to a human companion on an equal level of mutual respect and tolerance, but never as a submissive dependent. As Chris Davis has so humorously expressed it:

> [Parrots] will not collapse all over humans in gratitude—even the
> mocking gratitude that cats seem to have perfected—if they do not
> feel that it has been earned. If it has been earned, the bird might not
> think that it has, even if its owners differ in opinion. [The parrot's]
> attitude is that it's a free country and it has a copy of the Constitution
> in its file drawer in the cage for proof, if [the owner] wants to see it.

It sees itself as an equal, superior, or subjugated, but never an inferior (1989)

OVERINDULGENCE

A further contributing factor in the development of behavioral difficulties in parrots lies with the owner who overindulges his bird or fails to place reasonable and consistently enforced limits on the parrot. This is most frequently a result of guilt on the owner's part, caused by the notion that keeping a parrot as a companion is somehow "wrong," that he is depriving the bird of a life lived "free" in nature. This erroneous idea has been examined in depth elsewhere, and those readers who have not already done so may wish to read Chapter 4 if they feel this attitude has somehow contributed to their parrots' behavior problems.

STRESS: GOOD AND BAD

There is yet another commonly held belief that may create behavioral problems in the companion parrot: the idea that all stress should be removed from the bird's life. In reality this idea has been inadvertently fostered by many articles and books on parrot care. It is true that sustained, high levels of stress can lead to serious illness in the parrot. However, the creation of an entirely stress-free environment for a bird is not only impossible, it is not desirable, either. A certain amount of stress, no matter what one's lifestyle or the lifestyle of one's parrot, is necessary to the biological functioning of the body. Stress can be both negative *and* positive. For example, loss of a beloved owner will be experienced by the bird as a negative stress. On the other hand, an occasional car ride (if the bird enjoys this activity) will produce excitement and enjoyment, and is actually a positive stress. A healthy lifestyle can be said to be a balance between negative and positive stress, between a certain amount of tension and its relaxation. It has even been found that the stress of predators encourages more efficient breeding in certain animals (Levinton 1992). We certainly do not recommend exposing one's companion animals to predators as a method of introducing excitement into their lives! However, just as we experience the positive effect of a balance between tension and relaxation when we have worked hard then relax, animals also experience the difference between stress (or excitement) and tranquillity. In such situations enjoyment is enhanced. For humans, all work or all play produces a deadening effect; so it is with the parrot. If the owner deliberately sets out to construct a stress-free life for his bird, he will be all too willing to rush to correct any situation that elicits a squawk from his avian friend, however minor and nonthreatening. He therefore unwittingly spoils it. This results in behavior problems.

Contributory Factors in Development of Behavior Problems

Our discussion of specific categories that contribute to the development of behavioral difficulties in the psittacid will include the following:

1. The role of instinct and its inappropriate acting out in the domestic setting.

2. Lack of understanding of parrot psychology by the owner.

3. Sexual maturation of the parrot resulting in aggression.

4. Nutritional causes.

5. Other health problems.

6. Lack of routine in the parrot's life.

7. Family problems that involve the parrot.

Any of the above may be important in causing or contributing in a major way to the development of behavior problems in a bird that began life as a tame, hand-reared bird, or in a wild-caught bird that was once tame. Additionally, these categories may also be significant in the failure to tame a wild-caught bird. Because we now have federal legislation that prohibits the import of exotic birds from their range countries, taming wild parrots is not as common as formerly. However, domestically reared parrots may lose their tameness for many reasons. If one acquires such a bird and wishes to gentle it once again, reading this chapter is highly recommended before beginning to work with the bird.

Before beginning an in-depth examination of the above categories, it should be noted that a reasonable amount of emotional distance between guardian and parrot can be a very good thing. It helps a great deal in the prevention of problems if the owner is able to accept his bird's behavior as not necessarily directed at him personally. Again, a vast amount of acceptance, patience and tolerance for a creature of great intelligence, but of a different order from human intellect, is most necessary. To understand the basic genetic "wiring" of a parrot, to know that although some behaviors are modifiable but not eradicable, will help the owner avoid feelings of rejection and anger when the bird acts in ways that are occasionally inappropriate or disturbing.

Instinct Conflict in the Domestic Setting

GENERAL CONSIDERATIONS

Again, who owns the problem? Is the parrot merely acting normally, or have his natural behaviors escalated to the point of obnoxiousness? Is the owner being intolerant, or is the bird out of control? These are questions we must ask ourselves when dealing with a parrot's instinctive behaviors in the home. As discussed in Chapter 3, instinct is an inborn behavior, or an impulse or tendency to act in certain ways. Many such behaviors are aimed at ensuring the parrot's survival in the harsh reality of the natural setting. It is to some degree modifiable, especially in the intelligent, adaptable parrot. For example, it is instinctive for a parrot to fly away from anything it considers to be a threat to safety. However, the thing *perceived* as a threat is *learned*. In the wild, a parrot will flee human intruders if startled. A tame parrot has learned that humans are not a threat, and even if full flighted (a thing we heartily deplore), will not fly from its perch if a human walks into the room. The parrot has become *habituated* to humans in this situation.

CONFLICT AND THE LEARNING PROCESS

Problems can develop, however, during this learning, or habituation, process. They arise from two sources. One is that learning always involves conflict and a certain amount of discomfort on the learner's part. The other is that the bird's owner senses the parrot's discomfort during the process and may wrongly fear that the bird is being "forced" to do something against its will. If one examines this dilemma, one realizes that false reasoning is at work. Teaching a child to swim may involve a certain amount of persuasion by the parent, especially if the child protests loudly and long. The parent in this case proceeds along course, knowing that not only does the skill of swimming increase the child's safety around water, but that it will become a lifelong source of enjoyment and a good social skill as well.

The same thing applies to teaching a parrot to step on one's arm on command. The bird may shriek, scream or lunge because the activity is new and therefore to be feared. The owner knows, however, that once this skill has been mastered, the bird's life will be greatly enhanced because it will be able to participate more fully in socialization with its people. In addition, safety dictates that the parrot be habituated to this behavior so that if disaster threatens, it can be scooped to safety quickly. So the owner ignores the resistance and proceeds calmly and deliberately. The parrot becomes accustomed and learns the skill. Then, as has been the experience of many, the owner may find the bird has become so enamored of being on his arm that it becomes difficult to get the bird off! He then begins the process of teaching his parrot to step onto a perch or its cage, and of course the parrot protests loudly once more! Does our intrepid owner stop? Of course not. He goes right on, and eventually the parrot acquires this skill and thereby avoids the indignity of being scraped off its owner's arm or shoulder by main force!

ENERGY LEVELS

Another aspect to consider is that in the wild the parrot expends *great* amounts of energy in the mere process of living. Parrots may fly upwards of fifty miles to a feeding site. Finding food and water, flying back to the flock roosting area in late afternoon, playing, climbing, grooming, searching for suitable nests, choosing mates, defending territory and nestlings from other birds and predators—all of these activities occupy the parrot in an endless daily round of activity. Contrast this with the companion parrot whose food and water is supplied daily. Such a bird has no need to expend energy to avoid predation or to return to roost at night. Neither does it need to select a mate and find a nest, or protect both from other parrots and predators. The result is that the companion parrot has a great deal of unused energy, coupled with boundless curiosity and intelligence. It is no wonder that parrots often amuse themselves in unwanted ways, such as chewing furniture or screaming too much. Being aware of this reserve of energy and curiosity can help the owner structure the bird's day so that the instinctive drive for activity is channeled and expended appropriately. More than occasionally, a parrot that is not provided with opportunities for this will develop perservative behaviors (obsessive-compulsive disorder). Such a bird may pick its feathers, mutilate its feet or wing webs, make incessant figure eights upside down in its cage or scream incessantly.

REMOVAL OF OPPORTUNITY AND TEACHING ACCEPTABLE BEHAVIOR

Inappropriate or obsessive-compulsive behaviors are easier to prevent than to correct, and by two simple means: removal of opportunity and teaching the parrot acceptable behavior. These two methods apply to all instinctive behaviors the bird may use to excess, thereby creating problems for itself and its owner. The first is to avoid giving the parrot the opportunity to indulge in an unwanted or excessive instinctual activity. The second is to teach it what is acceptable in the domestic setting in which it finds itself. It cannot be overemphasized how important these two concepts are. Although they appear simple, an inordinate number of parrot owners seem to have great difficulty grasping them. We are reminded of instances in which owners brought birds with feather-picking problems to consultants for help. In several cases, the owners persisted in giving their birds toys that for some reason initiated the picking behavior. When the parrots were not allowed such toys, the picking stopped. Even so, the owners continued to provide these "initiators," apparently feeling the bird's enjoyment of them was more important than stopping feather mutilation. But at the same time these owners continued to bemoan the fact that the parrots still picked!

Teaching parrots alternative and more acceptable behavior involves use of behavioral modification, which will be discussed in depth in Chapters 6, 7 and 8.

INSTINCTS IN THE WILD-CAUGHT VERSUS THE HAND-REARED PARROT

There are also obvious differences among the expression of instincts between hand-reared and wild-caught parrots. The hand-reared bird must be taught how to amuse itself. The imported bird has reached maturity without learning to depend on humans for food, protection and amusement. Overindulgence of hand-reared birds, mentioned so many times, is a constant temptation and can have disastrous results. The wild-caught parrot does not depend on people to nearly the same degree and is less predisposed to the effects of pampering. With wild-caught parrots, the owners have not known them since infancy or toddlerhood. The bird is usually acquired as a young adult, although sometimes such birds are fully mature and may have had mates and reared young in their natural habitats. Because of this, the owners of wild-caughts do not have any real sense of changes that occur with the various life stages of parrots. Their adult wild-caught bird is as they found him: possibly aloof much of the time, disinclined to much tactile stimulation such as petting and handling, noisy (especially during early morning and late afternoon) and more than a little aggressive with those for whom it has not developed a fondness.

Owners of these birds seem to have less trouble accepting their parrots' personalities than those with hand-reared birds. The difficulty for owners of hand-reared parrots arises because they *have* known their birds since infancy or toddlerhood and do not realize that just as human and other animal babies change throughout their lives, very young parrots also change. Parrots experience the same life cycles that all vertebrates do: infancy, toddlerhood, childhood, adolescence, sexual maturity and old age. The drive for mastery and independence during the stages of toddlerhood, childhood, adolescence and sexual maturity is great. The total dependence and docility of the very young

This Moluccan Cockatoo (*Cacatua moluccensis*) was not taught to deal with being alone for even short periods, and has chewed a hole in its breast muscle in a neurotic attempt to occupy its time. *Scott McDonald, DVM*

parrot is natural to that phase, but the bird will not remain in this delightful condition for its entire life. Just as little boys grow to the stage that they would rather be tortured than hugged or kissed by their parents in public, so do most parrots eventually prefer varying degrees of physical and emotional distance from their owners. No longer do they like to be cuddled for hours on end, and may show their displeasure in several ways, including a well-placed nip if the unaware owner does not respond to the parrot's cues of discomfort.

Instinctive behaviors in the parrot that may give rise to concern include flight, biting, screaming, chewing, elimination, regurgitation, preening and sudden mood changes. Every parrot does these things. The owner may perceive the normal level of these activities as a problem, or the behavior may for some reason have escalated to the point where the parrot/person relationship is endangered.

FLIGHT

Flight, although not unique to birds, is certainly one of their foremost characteristics. It allows them to be mobile in a special way. Indeed, the ability of birds to fly has linked them with things spiritual in men's minds from time immemorial. Flight also allows the birds to escape predators or any other situation they find unpleasant.

In the domestic setting, a fully flighted bird runs two risks. One is that of safety. Open windows, mirrors or open pots of hot liquid may result in death or serious injury. The second is that a bird that does not want to relate to its owners for any reason can simply leave, and usually does. Fully flighted parrots are frequently aggressive and aloof. Owners of such parrots complain of these behaviors but resist clipping their birds' wings because they somehow think it unnatural. However, they fail to realize that if the bird is allowed to go wherever it chooses, the entire home becomes its territory, and parrots defend their territories, sometimes violently. By clipping the wing feathers, the bird's territory is dramatically reduced. It is also forced to remain with its owner, which results in the parrot learning that relationships with humans are pleasant and that there is nothing to fear or flee. This positive feedback then encourages the parrot to continue the friendship.

We have encountered many cases in which the owner presents a bird that is biting, dive-bombing family members or generally being obstreperous. When the parrot's wings are then clipped, the owner is amazed at the difference in personality. Former feathered fiend has become affectionate and docile, enjoying people and soliciting their attention. Wing clipping is always the first thing to be done when "problem" parrots are presented for training. In some instances, the improvement is so great that further training may be unnecessary. This is a classic example of removing the opportunity for the parrot to indulge unwanted behaviors.

BITING

There are many reasons why parrots bite. *All* parrots bite occasionally (some more often than others), even hand-reared birds. Removing the opportunity for the parrot to bite is a great part of curtailing the problem. Owners complain that their sexually mature birds have become unpredictably aggressive, and that they have suffered unprovoked bites on the face. The answer is so simple as to seem ludicrous: Do not let the bird near one's face! With such birds, the days of shoulder riding are over for good. This does not mean that the bird will not continue to be an enjoyable companion. What it does mean is that the owner must realize the parrot now has demonstrated the capability to act out unprovoked aggression from time to time, and that the owner must make sure he remains in control of the parrot at all times. This means keeping the bird on one's arm, or on a perch so placed that the parrot is at midchest level. It should be obvious with such a bird that putting one's face close to its beak is foolhardy, dangerous and ultimately destructive to the relationship.

In dogs, the tendency to bite is based on heredity, early experience, the later socialization and training of the animal and *the behavior of the victim* (Wright 1991). The authors concur with this in relation to parrots. Certain parrot species, such as Amazons, are much more prone to biting than many others.

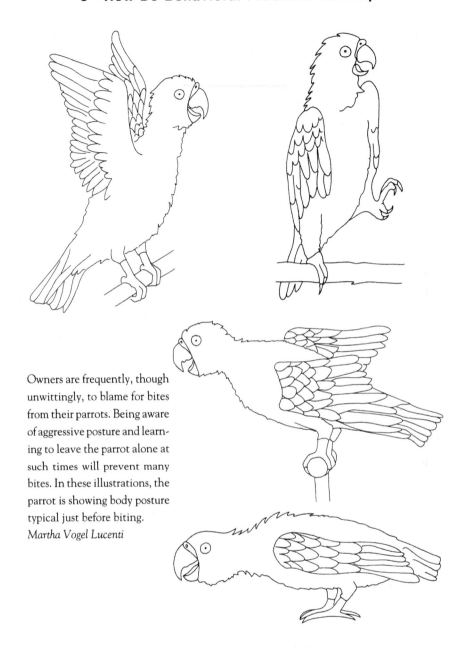

Owners are frequently, though unwittingly, to blame for bites from their parrots. Being aware of aggressive posture and learning to leave the parrot alone at such times will prevent many bites. In these illustrations, the parrot is showing body posture typical just before biting.
Martha Vogel Lucenti

If a parrot has been abused or has not been properly trained to live harmoniously with humans, biting frequently results. That behavior of the owner is a contributing factor in biting cannot be overemphasized. Encouraging the parrot to play roughly, indicating by voice or action that biting is "cute," or consistently avoiding a bird that has once bitten, all reinforce its instinct to bite. Many owners are horrified when they realize their complicity in the problem and work hard to change their attitudes and behaviors. Others, refusing to acknowledge their part in the problem, have no chance of correcting biting behavior.

BITING CAN BE CLASSIFIED INTO SIX GENERAL CATEGORIES:

1. Fear or defense biting.
2. Displacement biting.
3. Biting in reaction to excessive petting or fondling by the owner.
4. Dominance biting.
5. Biting by weanlings who associate fingers with being fed.
6. "Teething" behavior in the newly weaned bird.

Fear or defense biting is found in many species of animals. Its reason is obvious. The parrot perceives a threat, and if it cannot escape, will then stand and fight in what it believes to be a battle for its very survival. Pay attention to body posture, which indicates that the parrot is ready to defend itself and back off. Such warning signs include a horizontal stance on the perch, dilated pupils, flared tail and wings held away from the body. If possible, objects or situations that cause the parrot to react in this way should always be avoided, unless involving medical treatment. The bird must also be taught that a perceived threat is really not a menace. For example, many wild-caught parrots are afraid of hands, and must be taught very slowly to accept touching, petting and care from its owner. Once the bird becomes comfortable with hands, fear/defense biting decrease greatly. A very timid, frightened parrot will probably need the services of a behaviorist who can help the owner learn what approaches will best decrease the bird's sense of threat and therefore its biting behavior. Some parrots react badly to owners who have been drinking. The intake of alcohol often alters the owner's actions, manner and voice, and the bird feels a sense of strangeness and unfamiliarity. This may cause it to feel threatened and bite. The person whose bird reacts in this way should not handle the bird when alcohol has been consumed.

Displacement *biting* is common in many animals. It is actually redirected aggression. This behavior occurs when the animal is aroused but the object of its hostility is inaccessible or no longer present. It then attacks the nearest person or animal. Parrots do this commonly, particularly if a disliked person enters the area but cannot be reached. In this case, the person holding the bird may be bitten. Again, preventing the opportunity for this to occur is the answer. Putting the parrot in its cage or on a perch when a detested person enters the room is a good idea. Removing it from one's shoulder and placing

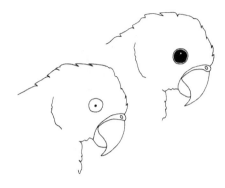

When parrots dilate and contract their pupils, they may be expressing excitement, pleasure or aggresion. Knowing your bird and his reactions to various situations, will help you determine if he is indicating aggression in this way. If he is, to attempt to handle the bird at this point is to almost certainly receive a painful bite. *Martha Vogel Lucenti*

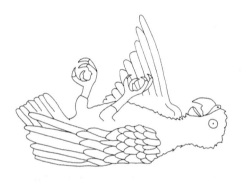

This is the typical "last ditch" defensive posture of the parrot that thinks it will be killed at any moment. Parrots in this posture are very dangerous and should be handled only with a towel, and only if the owner has developed skill and confidence with this technique. After the parrot has been retrieved and returned to its cage, let it rest and recover its sense of security before handling again. *Martha Vogel Lucenti*

it on the arm where more control is possible may also help. Allowing the bird to continue biting in such circumstances will only entrench the behavior, and eventually the parrot will begin biting his favored people in an unprovoked manner.

Overgrooming of the parrot by the owner often initiates biting. Most tame parrots enjoy being petted and stroked. Their mates, siblings and flockmates do this for them in the wild, and it serves to enhance socialization and pair-bonding in birds ready to breed. However, prolonged periods of grooming tend to make the bird restless, and the owner must learn to recognize the signs. Wiggling, snapping the head around to the hand's vicinity or moving away are all indications that the parrot has had enough for the time being. We have noticed a particular intolerance among Blue and Gold Macaws for prolonged petting. Whether this is a species-specific skin sensitivity, or an intolerance to prolonged inactivity (these parrots are usually very active and boisterous), we have not been able to determine. But it does seem that for the adult Blue and Gold a little affection goes a long way.

When petting and stroking one's bird, be considerate. Do not rub feathers the wrong way. The parrot appreciates this no more than a cat. At times of molt, be particularly careful of new pin feathers. These are very sensitive and hurt if handled roughly. There is also the danger of breaking one and causing bleeding. Further, many parrots seem to be rather cranky during a heavy molt. Molting is a physical drain on their bodies, and being stuck full of emerging, prickly new feathers cannot be very comfortable under the best of circumstances. "Gently" and "briefly" are the bywords when petting the molting bird.

Dominance *biting* is very common in parrots. They, being flock animals with an inborn genetic understanding of flock hierarchy and its meaning for their survival, are programmed to attempt dominance in any situation. In the wild, it gives them the best chance at the choicest food in adequate amounts, the most desirable mates and nesting sites, and therefore transmitting their genes to the next generation. Submission to the parrot means a lessened chance of survival and the "good life." Parrots must learn that establishing dominance in the human flock is inappropriate. Nevertheless, a bird that is allowed to remain full flighted, given caging or perches above its owner's head or otherwise allowed to do as it pleases, will interpret all of this as being *numero uno* in the flock. It will fight to retain this position. Perches must be repositioned so that the parrot looks up at humans. Its wings must be clipped. One of the reasons young children are at risk of being bitten by parrots is that no matter where the bird's perch is, it will almost always be positioned above a small child. People with both young children and parrots must be vigilant to ensure that children are not given unsupervised access to parrots.

"Teething" in newly weaned parrots occurs routinely. Young parrots use their mouths to explore their surroundings and are unable to distinguish between an inanimate object and tender flesh. Many owners think this mock biting is cute and encourage it. When the parrot is young its does not have the jaw strength it will develop later. If this behavior is encouraged, the time will most certainly come when it delivers a very painful bite. Such owners are usually all amazement that such a thing could have occurred with their beloved parrot. They do not realize that they themselves have taught the parrot to bite, that the parrot is totally unafraid of them and has every reason to expect biting to remain permissible. By this time the habit is firmly entrenched and will require consistent effort to change. It is far better to distract the youngster with an appropriate toy. By the owner constantly enforcing dominance, the young parrot learns that biting will not be tolerated and the behavior will diminish and fade.

Biting hands and fingers in newly weaned parrots also has another cause. *These youngsters associate hands and fingers with being fed.* They will often seize a finger and shake vigorously, as they did with a spoon or syringe when being hand fed. Although normal behavior for this stage, it should be discouraged consistently for the reasons discussed above. Offering a toy or a small piece of spray millet will serve nicely as a distraction. The object, again, is to remove the opportunity for a bad habit to become established. When this kind of behavior begins, the owner must *learn* to anticipate it and provide distraction *beforehand*. In this way, the parrot will not learn to associate biting with a treat.

Pathophysiological *biting* has its roots in physical illness. Although the authors are unaware of any studies that document organic brain damage in the parrot, this might be considered in the very rare case of intractable biting behavior. Organic brain damage and behavioral epilepsy are documented in dogs and cats. Both these conditions can generate, in some instances, unprovoked biting in these animals (Reisner 1991).

SCREAMING

Morning and evening screaming, with periodic vocalization throughout the day, is normal for the healthy parrot. The owner must accept this or choose another kind of companion animal. However, normal vocalization can intensify and escalate to unacceptable levels. This kind of screaming falls into four general categories: perseverative, fear screaming or growling, imprinted and breeding vocalizations. In addition, there is the boisterous screaming of the healthy, happy parrot, which is prompted by noise in its environment. It is often prompted by vacuum cleaners, music that is loud and rhythmic, running water and other household noises.

Perseverative *screaming* is peculiar in that it is persistent, habitual and uncontrollable, and does not seem to be initiated by anything obvious in the bird's surroundings. In the parrot, problem screaming, as well as some feather disorders and self-mutilation, fall into this category. Perseverative behavior is probably a type of obsessive-compulsive disorder that has its roots in conflict induced by inappropriate environment or management (Luescher et al. 1991). Such behaviors are also labeled *stereotypes* and have been noted in cats and dogs in a variety of behaviors, including rhythmic barking (ibid). Perseverative actions are repetitive and constant, and do not seem to serve any obvious purpose. Regarding vocalization of this type, the owner must carefully examine the bird's environment, handling, husbandry and any life changes that have occurred in the bird's life or that of its family. Medication is occasionally used to diminish stereotypic behavior, but only as a last resort because of possible side effects. All other avenues of remedy should be tried first. Obviously, the prevention of such behavior is much easier to accomplish. A bird that is healthy and well nourished, has had its emotional needs met and for which sensible behavior limits have been set and enforced, should never become the victim of this kind of screaming.

Fear screaming or growling (in African Greys and some other species of African parrots) occurs when the parrot feels threatened and is unable to escape the negative stimulus. When the bird has become accustomed to situations or people it dislikes and learns it has nothing to fear, this kind of vocalization will diminish substantially. If objects or noises in the surroundings initiate the behavior and the bird is unable to habituate itself to them, they should be removed. One of authors has a companion Umbrella Cockatoo hen that regularly makes visits to the upstairs office. For a long time a blowup model of a pteranodon hung from the ceiling. While all the parrots were wary of this object at first, all ignored it after a few days, with the exception of the cockatoo. After months of cowering on the perch, behaving as if she were going to be eaten alive, the offending article was removed and Molly was once again able to enjoy her afternoons in the office.

When habituating a parrot to something toward which it initially exhibits fear (this often happens with new toys), introduce the object, person or sound gradually, if at all possible. Showing your own acceptance and lack of fear in the bird's presence is also helpful. It is instinctual in all birds to be highly suspicious of unexpected noises or anything new in their surroundings. It is a primary survival mechanism. However, they are also intelligent and adaptable and can learn that many things are not necessarily dangerous. Sensitive handling by the owner should help the bird easily overcome its initial fears and preclude screaming or growling on a habitual basis. Occasionally a parrot will scream with fright without obvious reason. We are reminded of a Blue and Gold Macaw who with some regularity screamed for minutes while staring wild-eyed at a point in the owner's kitchen. As there was nothing there for the bird to see, it was a mystery as to what set off the screaming, nor did it happen every day. Reflections from mirrors and windows, shadows and the like were eventually ruled out. The bird behaved as if it were unaware of its owner, and no amount of soothing words and petting could make it stop screaming. Finally, when the cage was relocated so the macaw could no longer see into the kitchen, the terror screaming stopped.

Imprinted screaming is the product of overindulgence and spoiling, and occurs primarily in the hand-reared parrot. Cockatoos are especially prone to this vice. A bird whose every whim is gratified, whose every squeak is soothed, is a bird that quickly learns that it is the center of its owner's universe and behaves accordingly. People would not think of rearing their children this way, yet it is surprisingly common to find them acting in this way toward their parrots. Children are expected to learn to amuse themselves, to integrate into the family and to respect certain limits. A parrot is capable of learning these same things and must be gently and consistently guided to do so. It then rapidly learns that although its owner will not rush to appease every small sign of boredom or emotional discomfort, it will certainly be given more than enough time and attention to meet its needs, and becomes comfortable with this. Time alone to play and simply be a parrot are not then interpreted by it as neglect and abandonment by the owner.

The screaming of sexual maturity and breeding condition is a fact of life with which the parrot owner must learn to live. Parrots in the throes of hormonal surges are naturally much noisier than at other times. A sharp "No," covering the cage for ten minutes or distracting the bird with a new toy or novel treat such as a car ride or time on a favorite playpen, may serve to diminish the screaming somewhat. But until breeding season is over, the parrot will continue to be somewhat more clamorous than usual.

DEALING WITH THE SCREAMING PARROT

There are some very definite don'ts in dealing with a screaming bird. First, yelling back is counterproductive. Parrots have a real love of the dramatic, and a bellowing, gesticulating owner will only spur it on to greater heights of vocal achievement. Second, the bird should never be hit. It does not understand the connection between its screaming and physical abuse. The abuse only creates a parrot that is either terrified of people, shrinking away in fear, or it becomes an aggressive, dangerous one. Neither alternative is humane or acceptable. Third, never shake the parrot's cage, throw the cage across the floor or throw objects at it. This, too, is abuse and serves only to teach a parrot fear and hatred of humans. Fourth, never lock the parrot away in a dark room or closet for lengthy periods. To do so is a cruel deprivation of its emotional need to be with others. Additionally, such actions deprive it of adequate nourishment and is ruinous to the circadian rhythms that regulate all its bodily functions through the twenty-four-hour day/night cycle. Time out in a covered cage or carrier for ten minutes, repeated judiciously and as necessary, is an acceptable method for calming the habitually screaming bird. Total and protracted isolation is not. It may, in fact, have the opposite of the desired result, for the parrot may redouble its shrieks in an effort to reestablish vocal contact with its "flock."

Finally, do learn to tolerate a certain amount of noise. Ignoring a screaming parrot can accomplish wonders when it learns that it will not be given the attention it craves when it roars. Rewarding the bird for being quiet will earn it the notice it covets, thus establishing the basis on which the bird learns an appropriate behavior with which to garner praise and attention.

CHEWING

Chewing various objects is a fact of life for the parrot. It does this for amusement as well as to keep its continuously growing beak trim. Birds in breeding condition often seem to have a heightened urge to chew, probably because in the wild chewing is involved in preparing a suitable nesting cavity. (With few exceptions, parrots nest in hollow tree trunks or limbs, often enlarging openings and fissures already made by natural processes or other birds.)

The difficulty is that the parrot does not distinguish between your brand-new cherrywood television console and its own wooden perch. To avoid systematic demolition of furniture, plants and other valuable personal possessions, the parrot should be trained to stay on top of its cage or on its training stand during "out" time when the owner is not actually holding the bird. An acceptable alternative is a T-stand or playpen on which the bird is expected to remain. The operative word is "expected." For the parrot to learn that he must stay in the designated area, the owner must consistently replace the bird if it climbs down or flies down. And naturally, keeping the parrot's wings clipped is imperative if this behavior is to be accomplished. Under no circumstances should the bird be allowed to roam on the floor at will, for its own safety as well as to prevent destruction in the household.

Teaching the parrot to remain where placed will also prevent the nasty habit of nipping and biting feet, a behavior owners frequently complain about. In some instances, this behavior has become so severe that owners have been chased into other rooms with closed doors to protect themselves from painful bites and a lunging parrot in hot pursuit. Although this may sound comical, indeed it is not. When owners are questioned about how this started, invariably they reply that they had allowed the bird to roam the floor unsupervised in a misguided effort to give it its "freedom." A parrot does not benefit in any way from lack of behavioral limits. Nor do owners. Parrot and people alike are better served by teaching the bird to remain where placed. It is time consuming (at least initially) to pick up the parrot and consistently return it to its space. But it will save much grief in the long run. Remove the opportunity for the parrot to chew inappropriate items. Give it a variety of toys, rotating two or three every week or so. As much as possible, "parrot proof " the bird's immediate surroundings, much as you would for a small child (see Chapter 3). And when the occasional mistake happens, be tolerant. Above all, praise the parrot for remaining in its suitable, designated play area. Unwanted chewing should then rarely occur.

SUDDEN MOOD SWINGS

Parrots often exhibit sudden mood changes, which can be baffling to owners. Many parrots are highly emotional. Further, their attention spans are not as great as those of humans. All these together tend to create a being prone to sudden alteration in humor. Although a mood swing from aloof to affectionate is rarely a problem, the reverse often gives rise to concern. It is sometimes easy to forget that basic physiological needs may contribute to this. For example, a contented parrot that has been enjoying a cuddling session may begin to fidget and wiggle because it has to eliminate. Many birds are somewhat self-"potty trained," in that they prefer to return to the cage or deposit their droppings on the floor rather than on their owners. Owners should be alert to this need. Accidents on furniture and clothing can be avoided, and the bird, being once again comfortable, will be a more attentive and enjoyable companion.

It is not uncommon for a parrot to become suddenly boisterous and cranky if hungry. If this happens return the bird to its cage to eat. It often calms and becomes receptive again to attention after its hunger has been satisfied.

The parrot that is inadequately fed may exhibit depression or abnormal behavior. Although much more extreme, the authors have seen birds presented for behavior problems when they were actually malnourished. This condition will certainly affect behavior. In one severe case, a small species of cockatoo was presented for "flightiness" and unwillingness to relate to its owners. The history revealed that its owners were unaware that the parrot should be fed daily and had only been giving it food every three days. As incredible as it seems, they were shocked to learn that they had been starving their companion. Another case related by an avian veterinarian recounts the dehydration and death of a young hand-reared Amazon because it had been given no water in the three weeks the owners had possessed the parrot. They, too, were chagrined to realize that their lack of knowledge had killed their pet.

Boredom with the present situation can also contribute to sudden mood swings in parrots. Often, the bird has had enough petting and cuddling and wants to do something else. Be alert to this and place the bird on its play area or perch. Failure to heed the warning signs, as with a parrot that is reacting to overstimulation, may well result in a nasty bite. Learning to anticipate times when the parrot will wish to end the petting session and returning it to cage or stand before fidgeting occurs, allows the owner to remain in control of the situation.

Fatigue, as with small children, will bring on extreme crankiness with some parrots. This is especially true if the bird has been exposed to large numbers of people, as at a party in its home. Expecting a parrot to be "on display" at a party,

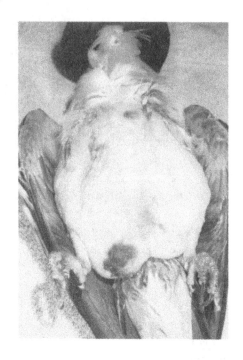

This Rose-Breasted Cockatoo (*Cacatua roseicapillus*) has literally been killed by kindness. Its owners fed it a consistently high-fat diet, which led to cardiac and liver problems, then death. As a result, this bird was never able to react with anything but lethargy and disinterest. *Scott McDonald, DVM*

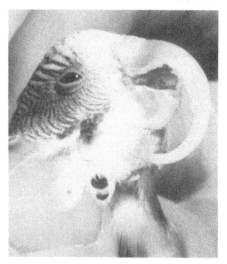

This Budgerigar (*Melopsittus undulatus*) will never bite its owners! Its overgrown beak is a result of a seed-only diet, which has caused irreversible liver damage. *Scott McDonald, DVM*

subject to handling by strangers, is to ask too much. This is usually seen by the bird as an invasion of its territory and it may react with extreme unsociability. Consider moving the bird's cage to a quiet room for the duration.

Crankiness and aggression is also more apt to occur at the end of the day when the bird would normally be going to roost, but is kept up past its accustomed bedtime for some reason. Every effort should be made to avoid this.

Regular bedtime and quiet, dark surroundings in which to sleep are a must for parrots. They require at least ten hours of sleep at night to remain healthy and happy.

REGURGITATION

Regurgitation that is not due to illness is a sign of courtship in the parrot. Cocks feed their hens prior to mating. When the hen is on the nest, the cock will feed her as she incubates the eggs, and then assist with feeding the nestlings after hatch. Young parrots regurgitate also, and they routinely play at mock regurgitation with clutchmates. A mature parrot without a mate of its kind will usually single out a preferred human on which to confer the honor of its regurgitated offerings. Although this is sometimes viewed as unpleasant by the human surrogate, one must realize its significance to the parrot. Reacting in disgust or otherwise violently indicating repugnance will confuse the bird. Calmly returning it to its perch or play area can be done. Distracting it with a favorite toy may also help.

It is most important to refrain in ways that encourage sexual behavior by the parrot. Many people do not realize that prolonged stroking of the bird's back, scratching its abdominal area or flanks, or sometimes even the neck, may arouse the parrot in breeding condition and cause it to regurgitate. It may also initiate masturbatory behavior by the bird, such as rubbing against the chest, arm or furniture in mating attempts. Although the authors do not see this as problem behavior, some individuals are embarrassed by it and wish to avoid such "unseemly" displays by their parrots. Of course, if the parrot becomes aggressive during breeding season, then stimulating behavior on the owner's part, however unwitting, should be recognized and stopped.

One of the authors lives with a Plain Mealy Amazon. Although affectionate in the extreme, this parrot does not seem to be well endowed intellectually, and it is passionately attracted to artichokes as surrogate sexual partners. When first given one as a toy, the bird became nippy, indulged in several amatory advances to its humans and eventually became very aggressive. Until the parrot was seen trying to mate with the artichoke, it was not clear what had precipitated such aggression in a usually docile and loving companion. After having witnessed this peculiar mating attempt, artichokes were permanently eliminated as chew toys and the bird reverted to its customary affectionate personality.

PREENING

Preening is the means by which any bird keeps its feathers in good condition. Absence of preening is nearly always a sign that something is amiss. Many first-time parrot owners do not realize the huge amounts of time a normal, healthy parrot spends grooming and are concerned that it is excessive. Unless the bird is exhibiting bald patches or deliberately pulling out feathers, preening should not cause alarm.

As mentioned previously, some parrots tend to be moody and cranky during molt. Frequent spray baths and gentle handling will make the bird more comfortable and less irritable during this time (Doane 1991). Respecting the bird's possible need for more time to itself (temporarily) will also help avoid irritable nipping. This does not mean that the owner should abandon the bird to its cage for the duration of the molt. It does mean that the parrot should receive the same consideration a person does when feeling slightly under the weather. Unusual stress should be avoided, such as allowing the bird to be handled by strangers, moving its cage or interrupting its daily routine. Because new feathers are made up of protein, be sure the parrot is on a high-quality diet, preferably pelleted. This will ensure that the bird has adequate nutrients to meet its normal needs in addition to increased protein required for new feather growth.

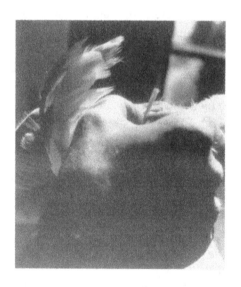

Once the parrot has learned to accept petting, most love help in removing the sheaths from newly formed feathers. The parrot cannot reach its head to do this, so its mate or parrot friend perform this service. It must be done with concentration, as the feather may be tender close to the skin. *Diane Schmidt*

Some parrots, notably cockatoos, have a much greater need for tactile stimulation than do other psittacids. Bonded pairs spend great amounts of time preening each other. A companion cockatoo craves petting and handling by its human companions, and the temptation to overdo this is very great. However, allowing the bird to expect constant attention and handling will lead to the problems of overindulgence, and the owner should take care that in well-meant attempts to meet the cockatoo's emotional needs, he does not create a monster whose needs are never satisfied, no matter how much cuddling it receives.

Lack of Understanding of Parrot Psychology and Its Role in Problem Development

The area of psittacine instinct and psychology overlap a great deal, and it is sometimes difficult to make any real distinction between the two. It is probably fair to speak of instinct and its possible role in problem development as belonging to the bird, although human inability to understand and make reasonable allowances for the parrot's instincts are contributory in a major way, as we have already seen. Lack of understanding of the bird's psychology, however, belongs to the bird's owner, and as such can be rectified. Ignorance creates many difficulties that need not exist and can be avoided with commitment to learn about the parrot's mental and emotional stance toward life.

INTELLIGENCE AND ADAPTABILITY

One of the first areas in which owners tend to lack information is that of the parrot's intelligence and adaptability (see Chapter 3). Parrots often are able to manipulate people and situations to their own advantage, but many owners fail to realize this. For example, a parrot is perfectly capable of obnoxious behavior if it knows such behavior will bring the attention of a favored person. One parrot of our acquaintance, having had an upper respiratory infection some years ago, has learned to fake symptoms to get attention. Although perfectly healthy now, every Monday, when his favorite person leaves for work after a weekend spent with the bird, this parrot sneezes, coughs, droops and generally behaves as if ill. If the wife takes the parrot off his cage, plays with him and talks to him, all the symptoms vanish as if by magic. This parrot is simply missing his favored one and getting attention in a surefire way—by pretending to be ill. Another bird presented for behavioral difficulties faked lameness because that always brought its owner running. Responding to these kinds of behavior once the bird has been pronounced healthy by the avian veterinarian encourages maladaptive attention seeking. Rather, the parrot should be ignored when acting in such ways, much as a small child complaining of a nonexistent tummy ache should be hugged and sent to school anyway.

Parrots are a fiercely independent tribe. However, many owners (often at a subconscious level) see their birds as extensions of themselves. Parrots will certainly never ask "How high?" when the owner says "Jump," nor will they fall in willingly with all their owners' wishes as will many dogs, or even some cats. The parrot's genetic inability to behave in continually submissive ways is a source of great disappointment to many people and leads to diminished feelings of caring, concern and affection for the bird. When this happens, the situation is ripe for development of negative behaviors such as biting, screaming and feather picking as a means of getting attention, even if the attention is negative.

LONG-TERM RELATIONSHIPS

Another area that may create difficulties is the inability of many to understand that a close relationship with a parrot cannot be forged instantly, as with a dog. Genetically the parrot is programmed to react with suspicion, and possibly aggression, in new surroundings and with new people. It is not at all uncommon for the proud owner of a cuddly, affectionate weanling to find that once home the bird reacts to him with withdrawal or hostility. Although parents of newborn babies expect to forge a relationship with the infant over a period of many years, most people do not see the development of firm friendship with their parrots in the same time frame. However, when one examines this, one realizes that the parrot has a very long life span, and that there is all the time in the world to build a lastingly satisfactory relationship. Rushing into things with a parrot is never a good idea. The bird must be given time to adjust to new situations and people. And owners must give themselves time to learn what a parrot is all about, to familiarize themselves with the characteristics, likes and dislikes of their specific avian companion. Even though many personality traits are more or less species specific, each individual bird has its own idiosyncracies, regardless of which species it belongs to. Parrots cannot be treated "generically," any more than can people. The wonderful thing about this is that as each life stage unfolds, there is always something new to learn about the bird, something wonderful to appreciate and cultivate. A sound relationship with a parrot is a dynamically stable one, unlike the more placid, predictable experience of living with a dog or cat.

ROUTINE AND CHANGE

Some parrot species thrive on change and drama. Failure to understand this and provide diversion often results in a bird that becomes so dependent on stagnant routine that any small change may create inordinate stress. This may seem diametrically opposed to our feeling that these creatures need predictability in their lives. However, the secret is to provide change within an established framework. Regular times to eat, to be in the cage, time to play outside the cage by itself, to be with family members and to retire at night are the lynchpins of a regular daily schedule. Within this framework much variety can be supplied. New food items or occasional treats may be given. Tuning in *Sesame Street* or *The Electric Company* on television rather than the usual radio (or vice versa), introducing a new toy or reintroducing an old one are very helpful. An occasional car ride, or placing the cage outdoors in good weather (well secured and out of direct sun) for a time makes a great change of pace. Playing environmental tapes or CDs, especially of moving water, outdoor songbirds or thunderstorms, nearly always elicits enthusiasm from parrots. Accustoming the bird to new people on a selected basis helps habituate it to the fact that there are indeed more humans in the world than those with which it lives. Because the parrot is allowed to become familiar with others besides family members, its stress during social events or trips to the vet is reduced.

Parrots that are so routinized and/or cagebound are victims to needless fear and stress when change comes, as it inevitably will. These birds are frequently afraid of people and unable to act in a free and enjoyable way with family members. They are also at risk of developing physical illness because of their reduced ability to cope with change in their environments.

Another very important aspect of routine for a parrot is that of *consistency* in the way in which it is handled. One's handling of the parrot should always be deliberate, slow and gentle. A calm, pleasant tone of voice soothes and reassures.We have already referred to birds that react negatively to owners whose alcohol intake has altered the way in which they handle their birds. It is also important to realize that parrots are exquisitely attuned to the moods of their owners. Relaxed, cheerful owners generally have relaxed, happy parrots. Depression, anger or hyperactivity in the owner will be noted by the bird and typically create negative moods and behavior. One of the authors has a large macaw that is so adept at picking up on the moods of its human flock members that it almost seems that it predicts their behavior, rather than reacting to it. Human anger and other negative feelings, even if not overtly expressed, generate extremely naughty behavior by the macaw. If, however, owners' moods are recognized and altered, the bird reverts to its usual gentle, benign behavior.

Sudden, jerky movements of children, as well as their frequent changes of vocal pitch, modulation and intonation are threatening to parrots, especially ones who have had no opportunity to accustom themselves to change of any kind. A bird that has not become used to youngsters is often threatened and frightened by them and may react by biting and screaming. Children are often incapable of understanding the psittacid's instinct for territoriality, and if they put their hands and fingers into the bird's cage, they are at risk of being severely bitten. As we have emphasized before, children should never be allowed unsupervised access to a parrot. If there are children in the home, then they and the parrot can be introduced to each other gradually under the strict guidance of an adult. As a result, the parrot will be much less stressed in children's presence and therefore less apt to react negatively.

THE ISSUE OF FREEDOM

Too much freedom for any creature within any system leads to anarchy and chaos. Countless numbers of parrot owners feel that unless the bird is afforded the maximum amount of personal freedom, it is being mistreated. This subject has been covered in depth in Chapter 4, but we reiterate that overindulgence of freedom creates many serious psittacine behavior problems that could have been either mostly or totally avoided. Owners would do well to remember that even in the wild a parrot is subject to the rules that govern flock behavior, as well as the ever-present need to avoid predators, and to find enough food with which to sustain itself. To speak of life in the wild as free and without restriction, regulation or limit of any sort is dangerous fantasy. It prevents humans from recognizing what really exists and how this knowledge may be used both to meet the parrot's physical and emotional needs and to shape its behavior so that it is able to exist harmoniously in another type of demanding environment—that of civilization.

SIGNIFICANCE OF THE CAGE

Its cage means security to the parrot. This is the one place in which the bird can play to its heart's content, chew things, eat, eliminate, sleep and relax without the regulations that circumscribe its life out of the cage. It is rather like being at work all day, fulfilling one's professional and interpersonal commitments, and then coming home, shutting the door, shedding the uncomfortable clothing and settling down for an evening doing what one wants to do, not what others expect one to do. This being the case, the cage serves a number of positive psychological functions for the parrot. It is a place of refuge from family life. (We all enjoy being apart from our families at times, don't we?) The parrot can experience a degree of freedom in its cage that it is not able to indulge on the living room sofa, for example. By habit and custom, the parrot knows that it is protected from any perceived threat in the environment while in its cage.

We suspect that the feeling of security a cage provides has genetic roots. Parrots are prey. (By looking at the placement of eyes in the skull, this would be apparent, even if one knew nothing about parrots. A parrot's eyes are on the

Other parrots in the home may pose safety threats to each other. This Blue and Gold Macaw (*Ara ararauna*) was attacked and seriously injured by the family's Moluccan Cockatoo. *Scott McDonald, DVM*

Parrots and any other pets should never be left to play unsupervised. This Blue and Gold Macaw was bitten by the family's German Shepherd. *Scott McDonald, DVM*

sides of the head, with a visual radius of close to 360 degrees. This allows a perpetual scanning of the environment for detection of anything that might mean danger.) Any bird in the wild is never wholly relaxed: relaxed birds are dead birds. The only place for a wild parrot that provides relative security is the nest hole, an enclosed place to which they take great pains to refrain from drawing undue attention. The cage represents a similar confined space. This is why it is so often recommended that it be placed in a corner or against a wall. A cage open to the room on all sides does not give the same sense of security.

If the owners have done their job properly, the cage should not be seen by the parrot as a prison. Rather, it is appreciated as a comfortable haven. Thus,

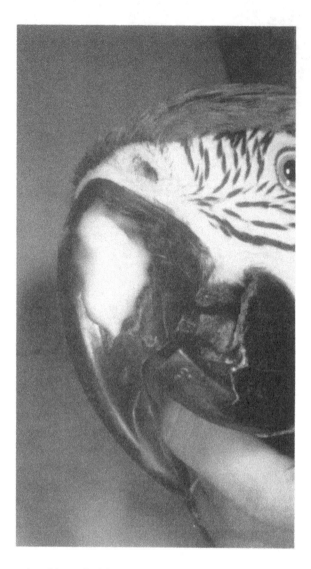

The same Blue and Gold Macaw shown in the previous photo after beak repair with dental acrylic. *Scott McDonald, DVM*

a properly socialized parrot should not feel deprived when spending reasonable amounts of time in the cage, nor should the owners feel guilty about "time in" for their bird. (Because of the sense of security a parrot needs to feel in its cage, the use of a separate cage, or training stand, elsewhere in the house for disciplinary "time-out" is highly recommended.)

OWNER'S LIFESTYLE

This subject is closely allied to the issue of freedom, in that the parrot must and can learn how to live compatibly within the human milieu. Meshing of the parrot/human systems can certainly be achieved. As with any relationship, there must be give and take. Parents of infants and small children learn this in the school of experience, as do the children. Eventually, if the family system is a healthy one, complementarity is achieved and harmonious relationships are the norm. So it is with the parrot and its human family. From the beginning, the bird should know clearly what is expected in terms of behavior, and the limits that are acceptable and tolerated. The bird must also become accustomed to the family's routine and lifestyle (within reason). Practically speaking, this means that if the owners work all day, then it should become used to spending a good part of the day in its cage, amusing itself, with playtime in the evening. If it is more convenient, and results in greater quality time being spent with the bird, to leave it in its cage until after the dinner hour (rather than letting it out as soon as its owners have returned from work), then by all means establish this routine immediately and stick to it. It is actually not recommended that the parrot be removed from its cage immediately on its owners' return. Doing this can lead to negative behaviors such as screaming, if for some reason it is not feasible to allow the bird out at this time. In this way the parrot will know what to expect and will not be confused by being alternately left in its cage and being taken out and fussed over on its owners' return. Confused parrots do not cope well with their surroundings and often respond negatively.

Above all, it is understood that the parrot's owners fulfill their obligations of guardianship by caring for the bird to the best of their ability, bolstered by love and concern, knowledge and understanding. Parrots that know what to expect from their environments and their humans are healthy, happy creatures. They do not pine for what they do not know just as we do not. Any sensible routine that meets its needs will be accepted and appreciated by the parrot.

The case of Holly, a Jardine's Parrot, and her owners, Richard and Elizabeth K, summarize nicely the interplay of parrot instinct, lack of understanding of psittacine psychology by owners, and the effectiveness of approaching a parrot as one would a young child relative to discipline.

Holly was acquired by the Ks four months prior to our first contact with them. The parrot was newly weaned, and the couple were childless. Richard was an expert in early childhood development, and Elizabeth was a kindergarten teacher. They both viewed their relationship with Holly as similar to one with a puppy. They also did not realize that their parrot would not remain a cuddly youngster indefinitely, but would eventually begin to act out its drive for "flock" dominance as it reached maturity.

When Holly first came home, both Richard and Elizabeth played with her on the floor for one to two hours nightly. Eventually, Holly refused to remain in the play area and wandered about the floor, chewing on anything in her path. To avoid this, the couple began to confine her to sitting on the sofa with them, Richard being the one who usually held the bird. Soon Holly became intolerant of Elizabeth, growling when she came near and biting her when she could manage it. The bird was not reprimanded for this behavior, primarily because the couple did not feel good about doing this, nor were any behavior limits set or enforced. Neither Richard or Elizabeth was quite sure how to go about this with a parrot.

After a home visit to the threesome, they were advised of the points made in the preceding pages. It was pointed out that when acquiring a hand-reared parrot, the long-term relationship needs to be encouraged by establishing realistic discipline in accordance with the characteristics of the species. Early in the relationship, time with the bird should have been spent practicing skills fostering the parrots effecive integration into the family and therefore allowing it to relate to each individual in a safe and acceptable way. Such skills included teaching the parrot to come out of its cage when required to do so, stepping up on hand or arm and sitting on a stand. After some discussion, Richard remarked that he had not realized it, but that socializing a parrot seemed to be very like rearing a child! Because of his training in the field of early childhood development, and Elizabeth's experience working with young children in the educational setting, these concepts "clicked." By the end of the session, Holly was once again allowing Elizabeth to pet her, stepping on her arm with no fuss and thoroughly enjoying herself. At the time of this writing, the relationship of the parrot and its guardians remains mutually satisfactory and enjoyable, with the Ks in gentle but firm control of the relationship.

Sexual Maturity and Aggression

We emphasize again: Parrots grow up. They eventually reach adolescence, passing through this stage to full sexual maturity. Many birds that have been properly brought through previous stages never become problems at this point, but parrots that have not experienced the benefits of proper socialization predictably do develop problems. Lack of enforced behavior limits, entrenched bad habits resulting from rough play or handling, or abuse of various kinds, create an animal companion with no impulse control. Aggression toward one or all family members is the usual outcome. Even with well-socialized parrots, nipping during breeding season may occur initially. We say "initially," because the owner's response to such behavior is critical in the determination of whether nipping and biting will remain isolated and infrequent incidents, or escalate to the point at which the parrot becomes dangerous and unsuitable as a companion.

This Budgerigar (*Melopsittacus undulatus*) is reacting to its toy as if it were a mate. Bonding of this kind may precipitate sexual aggression; if so, the toy must be removed. *Scott McDonald, DVM*

DETERMINANTS OF BEHAVIOR IN SEXUALLY MATURE PARROTS

Basically, there are four factors that determine the parrot's future as a companion once sexual maturity has taken place:

1. The owner's recognition that once this stage has been achieved, the parrot will never again (in the majority of cases) be the cuddly, totally responsive bird it used to be.

2. The parrot's habitually learned inner sense of impulse control created by consistent guidance and enforcement in its previous life stages.

3. The owner's response to the almost inevitable attempts to bite or nip during the initial stages of sexual maturity.

4. The type of family system in which the bird finds itself at this time.

In other words, does the bird have a good relationship with all family members, or has it bonded to one person in particular? And if so, how is this exclusive bonding handled by the favored human? This can be critical in the management of the sexually mature parrot.

The owner who realizes that his parrot will mature, and that its behavior will alter correspondingly, has already established the necessary emotional stance to cope with the event. Good parents expect that their children will become responsible and self-sufficient adults who may differ with their parents' lifestyle and philosophy considerably by the time adulthood has been reached. However, to mentally healthy parents this does not mean the end of their relationship with their offspring. It means the beginning of a new adventure as parents. Nor does it spell the end of all intimacy and sharing. There will be greater distance, but the relationship will not disintegrate. There will be flexibility on both sides, and the development of a new mutual respect of adult to adult rather than of caretaker and child. The healthy parent knows this and is prepared for it. Because of this, the transition is a smooth and enriching one.

So it is with the parrot that achieves adulthood (which happens at various times depending on the species). The owner prepared for this event will not be devastated the first time his bird evidences its heightened sense of territoriality through aggression. He will have prepared, and will matter-of-factly handle the situation in a way that will prevent escalation and entrenchment of a very bad and potentially dangerous habit.

How does this occur? First, there is the knowledge that the bird's antisocial behavior is to a large extent genetically programmed. This does not mean that it cannot be modified. It does mean that the first time or two it happens, the parrot will be almost as shocked as the owner. The aggression does not mean a lessening of regard by the parrot for its human companions, but that it has acted out an impulse that has no reason or basis in its previous contact with its family. The impulse merely *is*, and is acted on. Biting of this kind most often occurs when the bird is being taken from its cage or other area it especially regards as its alone. Our well-prepared owner does not back away from the parrot when this occurs, but insists that it follow through. The message has been given that just as in previous life stages, biting in this one will not be tolerated, either. It will not become a way for the parrot to control the situation and avoid relating positively to its humans.

If necessary, the owner is prepared to towel the bird gently and place it on its playpen or T-stand. (Incidentally, it is wise to teach all Amazon parrots to step up on a stick. This will provide a safe, painless way of handling and remaining in control of these notoriously aggressive birds during breeding condition.) The owner is also prepared to go on doing this until it becomes no longer necessary. At the same time, such an owner is able to accept a certain amount of distance during breeding season without feeling hurt or becoming angry with the parrot. This establishes the ground for future amicable interactions rather than fear and avoidance. The owner does not place himself in the position of being bitten in an unprovoked attack fueled by sexual aggression, nor does he attempt to kiss his bird on the beak during breeding season. He sees to it that the parrot is always carried on the arm, not the shoulder, and that perches are kept at a level that forces the parrot to look up, not down, at his human friends. The parrot in breeding condition is not allowed to be handled by strangers or children, and its wings are kept clipped to avoid dive-bombing and facial attacks.

The reader may well say that all of the above are designed to protect the owner and do nothing to terminate the parrot's obnoxious behavior. However, this is not the case. *Always* following through on expected behaviors produces the desired behavior. Approaching and working with the parrot despite its lunging teaches it that you will not be driven away or made submissive to it. Protecting oneself from bites protects oneself from the anger and disappointment that ruptures a friendship irretrievably in the majority of cases. Subsequent breeding seasons are then not so threatening, because both person and bird know what to expect and techniques for handling it positively and humanely are now familiar. There is the added benefit of knowing "This too shall pass," which makes a sometimes difficult and delicate situation more bearable. The owner *knows* that this time, he and the bird will emerge on the other side still friends because this result has been experienced before.

Unfortunately, it is human nature to avoid potentially painful situations, and this is very true of the unprepared owner facing the unexpected aggression of the sexually mature parrot. Once bitten, it becomes difficult to remain in control and insist that the bird step up, or comply with being moved from its cage or otherwise transported. The parrot, being intelligent and capable of manipulating the situation, very soon learns that any biting behavior will drive away the person, permitting the bird to refuse to do what has been asked of it. The biting then becomes expanded to any activity it does not wish to do, in *and* out of breeding season. The owner becomes increasingly frustrated, angry and disappointed, and eventually no further attempts are made to relate to the bird. It becomes feared and avoided, its cage relegated to an unused room, its care gradually occupying less and less of its owner's time and concern. Such parrots are often subject to physical as well as emotional abuse, and are often incapable of reverting to any semblance of tameness without tremendous commitment by its owner—a situation that is very rare. If the bird is sold or traded to new owners, they, too, will have a long, difficult task ahead of them. Placing such parrots in a good breeding situation may be the most viable option and will be explored further in the last chapter.

FOSTERING SEXUAL AGGRESSION

The last area, that of family systems and the dynamics of the relationships of the individuals in that system, can contribute immensely to the parrot's continued position as cherished companion, or at the opposite end of the spectrum, the scenario discussed in the previous paragraph.

It is very common for a parrot to bond almost exclusively to one family member. This person does not necessarily have to be the one who acquired the bird, or cares for, cleans and feeds it. And the bonded parrot may usually tolerate being picked up or cared for by other than its favored person. However, when the parrot becomes sexually mature, its relationship with its surrogate "mate" becomes much more intense and the bird behaves toward this person as it would its parrot mate: it regurgitates to the person, attempts mating with it and defends it against all comers. If the human surrogate mate is of the type who enjoys and encourages this kind of exclusive relationship, seeing it as an ego enhancement or mark of "specialness," great problems can arise.

The most common problem that develops is that the parrot shows overt aggression to the favored person's spouse. The favored person customarily handles this in one of two ways. The first is that although reprimanding the parrot for its behavior, the tone of voice in which the words are spoken are so soft and honeyed as to be interpreted by the bird as approval for its behavior. No real limits are imposed to deal with its aggression, and it continues to act in overtly hostile ways toward the abhorred spouse. The parrot soon learns that this behavior earns it positive attention from its favorite person.

The other way in which the surrogate "mate" often handles such behavior is to put her- or himself in the middle of the situation to mend the damage. The bird may be retrieved, scolded and removed from the vicinity of the disliked person. However, all this amounts to negative reinforcement of the parrot's behavior. It is better to let the bird and the other person work the problem out together, the other person delivering the reprimand or enforcing the limits previously decided on. The favored person should not reward the bird by taking the bird and placing it on his arm or otherwise giving it attention for its aggression. If, as is often the case, the disliked person does not really care to relate to the parrot on other than a casual basis, then the bird's favorite person must be the one to enforce the behavior limits in such a way that the parrot learns that its aggression is disapproved of by its beloved and will lose the attention of that person when it behaves badly. Time out in isolation with *no* attention from any family member, rigidly enforced for aggressive infractions, will help modify such behavior considerably.

Nutritional Causes That Contribute to Problem Development

The old adage that we are what we eat applies to parrots as well as people. It is well documented that various deficiencies in protein, carbohydrate, fat, minerals and vitamins create not only physical illness but also emotional problems. It is evident in humans that when suffering any of a variety of nutritional deficiencies, symptoms ranging from mild irritability to severe depression may manifest themselves, to the person's discomfort as well as that of those with whom he is in frequent contact. Parrots, in our experience, suffer similar reactions. A malnourished bird is often listless and droopy, without interest in life. It lacks the normal parrot boisterousness and enthusiasm. Occasionally, the reverse is true. Hyperexcitability and fear reactions have been noted by the authors in at least one Amazon that apparently was unable to absorb or properly utilize certain necessary vitamins.

PROTEIN AND CALORIES

The literature is replete with studies documenting the effects of protein and calorie deprivation in animals. One study conducted with rats indicates that when these animals were weaned onto a severely protein- and calorie-deficient diet, heightened emotionality resulted as well as poorer performance on maze trials. Prenatally malnourished rats showed less activity and were more emotional. Other studies of malnourished rats demonstrated the same results, as well as increased excitability, decreased ability to cope with frustrating or stressful situations and increased purposeless, random behavior. Nutritional studies of malnourished monkeys consistently show avoidance of new situations, reduced exploratory behavior and disordered social responses. Malnourished dogs, monkeys and rats also demonstrate negativity in response to other animals' overtures; heightened aggression and generally unpredictable behavior (Fitzgerald, Lester and Yogman 1986). These authors also state that animals born of malnourished mothers "are less interested in their physical environments, less capable of appropriate social responding, and less successful at adapting to changes in their environment and making constructive responses in stressful problem-solving situations than better-nourished animals."

Although such studies may never be done with parrots because of their high price and the value of their genetic material, it is possible that the above findings may have some bearing on certain types of psittacine behavioral problems. We have observed personality changes in previously malnourished parrots once placed for a time on a balanced diet. These parrots seem markedly less excitable, and much more calm when approached by people. This has been observed in a variety of species, including cockatoos, Timneh African Greys, Green-Cheeked Amazons and various macaws. Additionally, we suspect that a degree of malnourishment in parents may create subtle behavior problems in hand-reared parrots. Unfortunately, many breeders still use diets heavy in sunflower seed, supplemented with fruits and vegetables. Although this diet is adequate in calories, it is very low in protein, as well as essential vitamins and minerals needed for healthy embryonic development of chicks.

In addition, many breeders still formulate their own hand-rearing formulae. Although weight gain and growth seem to be adequate with the use of such preparations, we speculate that some behavior difficulties in some hand-reared parrots may occur more often than is realized because of the possibility of marginal nutritional adequacy of some of these diets. Although breeders using such concoctions stoutly defend them, in all fairness breeders rarely retain chicks long enough to be able to judge the long-term effects of their hand-feeding diets on these youngsters.

To our knowledge, no studies have attempted to measure the effect on behavior of a protein/calorie-deficient parental diet on behavior characteristics of psittacine offspring. The effect of a nutritionally marginal hand-feeding diet on behavior in chicks has not been explored either. We feel this will be a fruitful area for study, perhaps yielding interesting and surprising results.

VITAMIN B COMPLEX

This group of water-soluble vitamins is essential for proper body functioning (as indeed are all essential vitamins and nutrients). In humans, deficiencies of B complex vitamins can result in mood changes, insomnia, changed appetite, sugar craving, impaired metabolism of drugs and decrease in immune function. All the components of the B complex must be available in the correct amounts for the group as a whole to do their job (Slagle 1992). Depression, irritability, personality changes (including aggression), emotional instability, nervousness, mood swings, confusion, withdrawal, fatigue and hallucinations may also result from varying degrees of B complex deficiency (ibid.). Physical problems such as anemia, roughened skin, dermatitis, diarrhea, sore tongue and polyneuritis (a condition in which inflammation of many nerves occurs, with symptoms of paralysis, pain and wasting of muscles) are also found in humans with deficiencies of B complex vitamins (Gilman and Goodman 1985).

Our concern with the possible correlation of B complex deficiency and behavioral aberrancy rests with several cases (one of which was dramatic), in which treatment with injectable Vitamin B complex, followed by oral B complex preparation, brought about marked decrease in severe behavioral problems. These were parrots in which none of the customary behavioral modification techniques were effective, even after long periods of implementation. All these birds had also been checked by a qualified avian veterinarian and no obvious disease processes were noted.

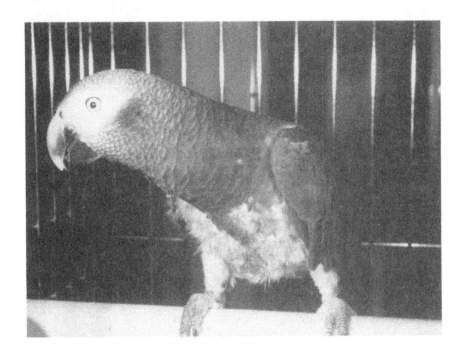

Timneh African Grey Parrot (*Psittacus erithacus timneh*) showing typical feather plucking of breast and abdomen. Such birds may be suffering from a B complex deficiency. *Scott McDonald, DVM*

Because Vitamin B complex is often used as an adjunct to therapy in birds stressed for physical reasons, administration of B complex was tried as a last resort, in the hope that it might alleviate some unknown organic source of psychic discomfort. In at least one bird the effects were so dramatic as to be almost miraculous. It is hypothesized that the parrot for some reason was unable to absorb these vitamins from its diet (which was a high-quality pelleted diet supplemented with fruits and vegetables), and was thus very deficient in B complex. This parrot's case study is presented in Chapter 8.

We realize that our observations are based on a small number of parrots. However, results of B complex administration (under an avian veterinarian's supervision) produced positive results in those birds receiving it. This may prove another fruitful area of research for those qualified to do so.

The authors speculate about the possibility of behavioral problems that may have been initiated or aggravated by subclinical nutritional deficiencies. No studies have been done on the subject at the time of this writing. However, it may prove a profitable area of study for those interested and equipped to examine the question within the research setting.

Other Health Problems That May Contribute to Behavioral Problems

Any organism that is unwell will exhibit personality changes. Some appear suddenly and dramatically. Others develop rather slowly, so that the owner is unaware of the cumulative effect as expressed in his parrot's behavior. Any change in behavior frequently signals the onset of physical illness, and a parrot exhibiting such changes should *always* be taken to an avian veterinarian without delay (Doane 1991).

Nevertheless, there are some conditions for which screening is not routinely done. These conditions can have an effect on the development of psittacine behavior problems. Among these is *Giardia*, a protozoan parasitic infestation of the digestive tract (ibid.). Giardiasis has been associated with feather plucking and screaming in cockatiels. It has become apparent in many parrots seen by us for feather mutilation problems that emotional causes alone were not the sole culprit. Although some of these parrots also had emotional difficulties that aggravated the feather picking and mutilation, the high degree of discomfort they exhibited led us to conclude that some physical cause may also have been at fault. Because of the problems documented in cockatiels with giardiasis, it seemed to us that this might be a possible cause of feather problems in some of the larger parrots that were refractory to behavioral modification. Although *Giardia* is often difficult to diagnose, and tests may give false negative information about the presence of the parasite, it seemed probable that these birds might have undiagnosed giardiasis. After consultation with the parrots' owners and the avian veterinarian in charge, several of these birds were given thorough workups, and all presented for this did test positively for previously undiagnosed *Giardia* infections. When placed on medication these parrots showed a dramatic decrease in their feather mutilation behavior, as well as an increased sense of comfort.

Family Systems and Development of Psittacine Behavioral Problems

FAMILY SYSTEMS

What is a family system? How can it affect the behaviors of our parrots? A family system is a group of people usually related by kinship, in which the whole is greater than the sum of its parts (Bradshaw 1988). A family is an emotional unit. Individually and together, all its members strive for balance in order that emotional needs of all members are met adequately. Its members function reciprocally, acting and reacting to one another continuously. Therefore, the behavior of one individual cannot be understood outside the context of the family in which he or she is a member. All of us residing within families probably have far less independence of action than we like to think, for this reason. In a healthy family, the roles all play are flexible and to some extent interchangeable.

Although generally not recognized, parrots *do* become part of a family system. Their unique characteristics of intelligence, adaptability, capacity for empathy and long life spans especially equip them to become important members of a family. In addition, they are demanding as individuals, and are creatures genetically prepared to function within a social group. These traits may contribute to the position they occupy within the family system and the problems they may develop within that system, or social unit. We have observed that parrots often become pawns, much as minor, dependent children do, in families where members have poor relationships with each other. Parrots can be used by one member to express hostility toward another. In this instance, the triangle portion of family systems theory operates. Triangles will be examined in depth further on.

Parrots can also be used as instruments of denial in less than optimal relationships, a situation termed scapegoating by family systems theorists, and the use of parrots as emotional sinks by those having difficulty relating emotionally to members of their families has also been observed by us. Parrots are also used inappropriately as child surrogates by childless couples, with less than happy results for the bird, as we have mentioned previously. Additionally, parrots fulfilling the role of child surrogate to couples seem to be at risk of overinvolvement with one human in a couple/pet triangle resulting in aggression such as we see when the parrot reaches sexual maturity.

147

There is sound reason for examining parrot behavioral problem development within the context of family systems. According to Kerr and Bowen, pioneers in family systems theory:

Family systems theory is based on the assumptions that the human is a product of evolution and that human behavior is significantly regulated by the same natural processes that regulate the behavior of all other live things ... our preoccupation with the psychic or cognitive manifestations of "mental illness" has probably blinded us to the common denominators between the human and nonhuman emotional dysfunctions. (1988)

These trailblazers also point out further similarities between human family systems and animals and their kinship units. The selfless behavior of an elephant herd toward all its young, regardless of parentage, is one example. Such behavior has also been observed in African wild dogs and chimpanzees (Kerr and Bowen 1988; Wilson 1975). Animals also kill and murder each other. Male gorillas and lions that have achieved alpha (or prime leadership) position within their social group kill offspring that, they themselves have not sired. Lest one be tempted to think that this is an extreme way in which to compare humans and other animals consider the number of children battered and murdered by male companions of mothers whose children were fathered by another individual. What Kerr and Bowen seek to emphasize is the concept that humans and other species share the same basic behavioral potentials and that these are given expression within the social unit.

We have come to believe that parrots and their human guardians share many behavioral potentials, and react to each other and the social units in which both reside, for good or for ill. The parrot with problems, in many instances, cannot be considered as an isolated unit uninfluenced by those humans with which it lives. It is our contention that some behavior problems in parrots are a direct result of family systems that are not functioning well. In these situations family members may be experiencing problems of one degree or another among themselves, and the parrot is an *integral and inseparable* part of the malfunctioning social unit we call the family. In this context, if one examines the entire family unit in which the parrot lives, one sees the meshing of the parrot/human systems in a way that is far from ideal. This is confirmed by numerous experiences with parrots and the individuals or families who come seeking help for the bird's "problem." It often transpires that the parrot is reacting to a family system that itself is not healthy. As a result, the parrot has become the symptom of human relationship difficulties that are far deeper and more serious than the problem for which the parrot is presented.

TRIANGLES

In all families, "triangling" is present. The triangle is a group of three individuals. Triangles are helpful in examining the what, how, when and where of relationships. They "describe the equilibrium of a three-person system" (Kerr and Bowen 1988). It is a normal part of family life, but can become distorted for various reasons. Triangles can create unwanted effects, as the old adage "Two's company, three's a crowd," implies. A relationship involving three persons is inherently less stable than one comprised by an even number of individuals. An example of a triangle is the mother/father/child triad. It is *most* interesting to note that Kerr and Bowen state, "A *live third person is not required for a triangle*. A fantasied relationship, objects, activities, and *pets* can all function as a corner of a triangle" (italics added).

There are several ways in which a third can be pulled into a two-person relationship to create a triangle, but of particular interest to us is the individual who deliberately inserts himself into such a relationship by predictably causing trouble or making himself a problem when tension reaches a certain level between his parents. It is particularly germane to our discussion of problem parrots, in that pets (as mentioned previously) have been documented as able to form the third corner of a triangle. In such instances, the focus is drawn to the "troublemaker," thus reducing the tension between the adult couple. (The couple unite in an effort to help the "problem child," or to defend themselves emotionally against the child's demands.) The third party plays the role of scapegoat, the individual who, if only "normal," would cure all the family's difficulties, in the eyes of family members.

It is important to understand that development of behavior problems in parrots finding themselves in these situations *is not caused by the same dynamic as with children*. Instead, unacceptable behavior escalates as a result of the tension felt in the household. Nevertheless, this behavior may be seen by family members as objectionable enough to permit them to focus on it as the primary cause of interpersonal relationships, rather than as a secondary result of such difficulties. In any case, when this occurs, on a subconscious level it may be to a person's advantage to perpetuate his bird's behavior as a way of deflecting attention from the real problem at hand.

Triangles have been noted in species other than *Homo sapiens*. Data suggests that triangles exist in several species of primates, as well as domestic chickens, mice and lizards (Kerr and Bowen 1988). We have mentioned previously that parrots, with their genetically determined social flock behavior, intelligence and ability to key in on human emotions, can become enmeshed in triangles where the other parties are human.

It is beyond the scope of this book to present a detailed review of family systems theory. Rather, we have tried to present those more obvious areas that apply to the "problem" parrot and its "problem" family in a brief but understandable way, so that the reader may more easily grasp the material following. For those who wish to pursue family systems theory and how it may apply to their particular situation, the references in the bibliography will be most helpful, particularly Bradshaw, Kerr and Bowen, and Toman.

"PROBLEM" PARROTS AND FAMILY PROBLEMS

Couples without children often purchase parrots, seeing them primarily as child surrogates, not as unique creatures with their own specific traits and behaviors. We speculate that in many cases seen by us, that as with couples who decide to have a baby hoping the child will strengthen and bolster a tottering relationship, parrots may be acquired for the same reasons, albeit unconsciously. While the bird is still young (and often still being hand fed by its new owners), the couple's joint interest in the parrot's physical growth, emergence of its personality and beginning attempts at use of human speech can be intensely engrossing. The couple enjoys sharing the accomplishments and progress of their bird, and initially this can enhance their relationship with each other. However, later on, undesirable behaviors acquired by the parrot because of lack of discipline and limit setting can place a strain on a couple's relationship. Usually the parrot has bonded more strongly to one person, and the "left-out" spouse exhibits disappointment, dismay and sometimes jealousy. The favored spouse is then blamed for the parrot's screaming or biting behavior, or its destruction of household items. At this point, the parrot has become a destabilizing factor in the spousal relationship, unlike the stabilizing influence it conferred when still very young and needed more care and attention.

The fate of parrots in such situations is often unfortunate. Many times we have seen couple/parrot triangles such as this dissolve with the birth of the first real child. The bird is then no longer wanted and is sold because it is now seen as a nuisance, rather than an emotional asset to the couple. We speculate that the parrot, with its distinctive and unusual combination of personality traits, is seen by such couples (if on an unconscious level) as needed for the "parental" qualities it confers and enhances in its owners. It seems doubtful that parrots are appreciated for themselves alone in these situations. We have also observed instances in which divorce or dissolution of the relationship occurred, and the parrot then became the object of a "custody" struggle.

We have seen cases in which the parrot has become the family scapegoat. The reasoning goes something like this: "If this parrot were not such a screamer, biter, so destructive, our lives would be much better." In one case, several parrots resided in the same family. One was the particular companion of one spouse. The other two related primarily to the other spouse. Although all the birds made a certain amount of noise, the blame for any commotion was routinely placed on the birds belonging to the husband. The wife did not feel her parrot contributed to the noise and confusion she bitterly expressed as being almost beyond bearing. Episodes of unacceptable noise seemed uncannily to occur when tension was high between husband and wife. This lady felt that if only her husband's birds would "shut up and give them some peace, life would be a lot more bearable."

It transpired that this woman had undergone several major and unfortunate life experiences within the past eighteen months, some of which involved unpleasant treatment by her husband. However, she was dependent on him financially, and feared alienating him further if she confronted him with his behavior. Clients who present parrots for this reason tend to see difficulties as aggravated or caused by the bird, when in fact the bird has become the safe, nonthreatening focus for relationship difficulties they are unable to acknowledge and confront in a constructive way.

The heightened vocalization of this couple's parrots was *not* caused by a deliberate collective decision of the birds to diffuse an anxiety-producing situation by attracting attention to themselves (as is the case with children when parents are at loggerheads with each other). Rather, it was undoubtedly caused by their reactions to the tension felt in the household, a subject previously discussed. However, the net result is the same: the parrot is seen as the problem source (scapegoat), not the couple's unhappiness with each other.

Some individuals use parrots as inappropriate emotional sinks when they feel unable to have fulfilling relationships with members of their families. An example was a large macaw that was brought for help because it screamed incessantly. The parrot was seen primarily as the woman's pet. It was newly weaned when acquired and was a gift from the woman's children. In working with this lady and her macaw, it became apparent that Mrs. P had difficulty in allowing her children to grow up and develop their own independence. Further, her marriage was a second one, to a man both much younger and more youthful in appearance. There also appeared to be a degree of emotional distance between the couple. Mr. P traveled a great deal, and the children of the first marriage were in high school and college, leaving her alone much of the time. The circumstances were ripe for her overinvolvement with her parrot. This led to overindulgence and complete lack of any attempt to set behavioral guidelines for the bird.

However, with parrot to focus on, Mrs. P's loneliness and "empty nest" problems did not seem so immediately overwhelming to her. Because she equated love and caring with overindulgence, it was difficult for her to learn to set much-needed guidelines for her bird. It is interesting that she had previously owned another parrot, which she sold, for the same reasons she had sought help with her present companion bird.

In this and similar cases, the parrot is treated much as a youngest child that the mother overprotects and smothers because so much of her identity is linked to the caretaking activities of motherhood, an identity she fears she will lose when her last child leaves the parental home.

Use of parrots as instruments of hostility against another individual seems to be distressingly common. One example involved a Yellow-Naped Amazon, brought in by a seemingly concerned husband and his wife. In this case, the parrot was being used by the husband to act out his hostility toward his wife. This tactic allowed him to appear concerned and caring and place the blame on the parrot. Mr. M stated he was heartbroken because the bird would not allow his wife to handle it and was very aggressive with her. He expressed a desire for her to feel comfortable with "his" bird, and to have the parrot enjoy being with his wife. Mrs. M said that although she was not as fond of the bird as her husband, if it would make him happy she would try to learn to handle Bandit without being bitten.

As work with the parrot and the couple progressed, it became obvious that there were difficulties between husband and wife. Regardless of guidance and instruction given that would have facilitated a better relationship between the bird and Mrs. M, the husband constantly undermined his wife's ability to handle the Yellow-Nape. In both subtle and overt ways, Mr. M made her feel inadequate and stupid when she attempted to get the parrot on her arm or pet it. This increased her feelings of fear and timidity around the bird. Bandit sensed this and exploited her fear and hesitation, with the husband's tacit approval. In this instance the wife was never able to develop the skills to handle the parrot comfortably, and needless to say, never learned to enjoy the Amazon's company. Mr. M professed disappointment at this outcome, but said he supposed that the Yellow-Nape was just his bird and was totally unable to be any other way.

Another instance in which a parrot became the third in a triangle in which a husband and wife had relationship problems is Slugger's case. Although this case study is presented in depth in Chapter 8, we mention certain aspects here because the parrot's behavior toward the wife was strongly encouraged by her husband. When Slugger chased Ann into the bedroom, lunging and biting her heels, David made no attempt to stop the bird or discipline it in any way. On getting to know the couple better, it became apparent that there was considerable difference in education and professional background between David and Ann, and a great deal of unacknowledged and unspoken friction about this, creating a situation in which it was safer for David to let his parrot be the "bad guy," rather than taking responsibility for his own feelings and the health of his relationship with Ann.

A third instance in which a companion psittacid became involved in a situation of dysfunctional family dynamics involves a Meyer's Parrot (*Poicephalus meyeri*). This small bird was purchased by the family as a pet. The husband was an aggressive person and presented himself as an expert on any topic that arose. He was also a person for whom being right in every situation was very important, and actively sought dominance over all with whom he came in contact. Mrs. A was a timid, quiet lady who never seemed to be able to assert herself, especially with her husband. Mr. A treated her in an offhand, condescending manner rather than according her the respect of an adult equal. Mr. A rapidly became the favorite of the parrot, even though Mrs. A was responsible for the bird's care. Given the husband's dominant personality and the wife's timidity, the Meyer's came to see Mr. A as the alpha male of the flock, and itself as the beta flock member or "second in command." Muffin began to chase Mrs. A when out of its cage, biting her severely several times. When this occurred, Mr. A retrieved the parrot, hugged it and kissed it and told it, in dulcet tones, what a naughty bird it was. This positively rewarded the parrot for its aggressive behavior and also provided a way for the husband to act out his hostility and contempt for the wife he considered to be so far beneath him intellectually.

Mr. A sees the parrot's behavior as acceptable and excuses it by stating that it is only a "dumb" animal and cannot help itself. He feels he is the only person in the family who is equipped emotionally and intellectually to cope success-fully with "the feathered demon," as he somewhat proudly expressed it. His attitude is similar to a father with a teenage son whose outrageous escapades are denounced on the surface, but secretly admired and covertly encouraged because the father sees the son as "just a chip off the old block."

In our society, aggression and winning in the business arena are seen as positive attributes by some individuals, who often prize these qualities in their pets. For example, there is a tendency to keep large, aggressive dogs and actively develop such traits in the animals.

IN SUMMARY

When parrots such as Muffin, Slugger or Bandit are perceived by owners as ego extensions (consciously or unconsciously) and used as weapons against other family members, or if their parrots are used inappropriately to fulfill emotional needs that should properly be met by healthy family relationships, there is little chance that these parrots' unacceptable behaviors can be changed.

Although the authors do not imply that all, or even the majority, of parrot behavior problems are the result of poorly functioning family systems, this situation is seen often enough to merit consideration. It is particularly likely to be a cause when lack of remedial progress is made, regardless of all effort expended. When human relationship problems seem to have created, either in part or in whole, the parrot's problem, it is unlikely that any real and lasting progress can be made until the individuals involved can solve their own problems first. As we will see in the next chapter, *a united and consistent approach by all who live with the bird* is necessary for permanent changes to occur. It is doubtful that this atmosphere can be created by persons who are invested in maintaining unhealthy relationships. We strongly feel that in situations such as these, until the humans change, the parrot will not, for the individuals in any system function reciprocally. Only when the family context changes, can the parrot be effectively helped to change also.

6

Behavioral Modification: What Is It and How Does It Work?

Basic Concepts

Behavioral modification is a learning process in which the behavior of a person or animal is changed in some way. Learning is considered to have taken place when a relatively permanent change in behavior or knowledge occurs as a result of experience. The learning process in behavioral modification is one of association. The individual is habituated to a *consistently* predictable response to a particular behavior.

CONSEQUENCES OF BEHAVIOR

When working with a parrot to effect behavior change, positive and negative consequences always follow a specific behavior, and they follow immediately. Subsequently, the subject of modification learns a desirable behavior or abandons an unwanted one. Negative consequences do *not* consist of physical punishment. Rather, they may include withholding some desired object, activity or interaction.

Confusion often arises about how positive and negative consequences are used. Consider the example of the screaming bird. The most common response by the owner is to yell at the parrot when it screams. The owner usually

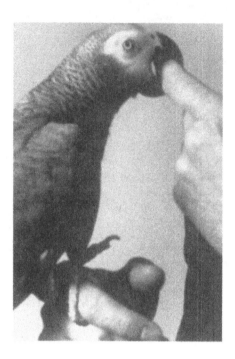

...we can forgive you for that... *Diane Schmidt*

considers this to be a negative consequence that will decrease the parrot's screaming. In reality, the drama of shouting only encourages the parrot to scream more vociferously. For the bird, it is perceived as an enjoyable and positive consequence of its behavior. An appropriate negative consequence by the owner would be to place the parrot in a covered carrier for ten minutes, thereby depriving it of an audience or any other interaction that brings it attention, and to do this *every time* the bird screams inappropriately. In this way, screaming will diminish and eventually stop, except for brief morning and evening periods of vocalization, which are natural and normal for parrots. Positive consequences that encourage the parrot to remain quiet are praise and attention given when it is sitting or playing quietly without shrieking.

CLASSICAL CONDITIONING

Classical conditioning consists of pairing a conditioned stimulus with an unconditioned stimulus to obtain a desired response. As an example, consider Pavlov's famous experiment with salivating dogs. In his experiment, food was the unconditioned stimulus that caused the dog to salivate, salivation being the unconditioned (or spontaneous) response to the food. Pavlov found that if he always presented a certain musical tone at the same time food was presented, eventually the dog would salivate in anticipation of being fed when only hearing the tone. This kind of conditioning has more value in the behavioral science laboratory than practical application to animals exhibiting unwanted behavior.

However, there is one area where classical conditioning can be used to good effect: desensitization to allay fear. Many fears are learned by the process of classical conditioning. A painful experience at the dentist can create a fear of dentists, although in the normal course of events the dentist himself is not a fear-producing figure. Having been a victim of a mugging in a dark street will create fear of dark streets, although the dark street, in and of itself, is neutral. Learned fears are often long lasting and can have both mental and physiological effects. A situation in which a person experiences severe stress because of his treatment by another person in a work setting, can elevate blood pressure. Eventually, even if the unpleasant individual is removed, the victim will experience a rise in blood pressure when he or she enters the workplace (Roediger et al. 1984).

Learned fears, with their emotional and bodily effects, are of great concern to parrot owners. It is reasonable to assume that if the lingering effects of fear/stress remain with humans, even after the initial stimulus that caused them has been removed, the same probably holds true for parrots. Desensitization, which teaches the subject to make a different and healthier response to situations that cause anxiety, will enhance the parrot's quality of life and remove inappropriate stress responses that could eventually produce disease and death. It is a gradual process over time, carefully designed to allow mastery in small stages. A wild-caught parrot that fears humans must be conditioned first to accept their presence in its vicinity, then to become more comfortable with the presence of humans in ever greater proximity. The parrot is then taught to accustom itself to being removed from its cage. In consequence, it begins to learn that being close to humans is not harmful and can actually be pleasant. Next the bird learns to sit on arm or hand, then to accept petting or scratching on its chest, cheeks and back. All of this is done in a gradual manner over time so that the bird achieves comfort on each level before going to the next. Each step is designed to require a little more contact than the previous one, but not enough more to raise anxiety to levels that are intolerable and trigger regression.

OPERANT CONDITIONING

Operant conditioning (or instrumental conditioning) is the behavioral modification technique most commonly used when working with parrots to instill desired behavior or diminish unacceptable behavior. With this technique, positive and negative consequences *always* follow after the specific behavior that is being learned or abolished. Very simply, if the subject performs as desired, rewards such as praise, food or a treat of some other kind is given immediately by the behaviorist. If the subject does not perform as desired, corrective (aversive) consequences follow immediately. Positive consequences tend to effect desirable behavior because organisms tend to repeat that which is pleasurable to them. Negative consequences are experienced by the organism as unpleasant, and they tend to suppress unwanted behavior; organisms naturally tend to avoid that which causes emotional and/or physical discomfort.

Take as an example the parrot that picks its feathers. If this bird is the subject of behavioral modification using operant conditioning methods, it will be given attention and praise when it is *not* picking or otherwise mutilating its feathers. When the parrot is engaged in these activities, *no* attention is given whatsoever. The bird is not scolded, its owner makes no eye contact with it or indicates by facial expression that he has noticed the behavior. Feather butchery is totally and completely ignored. (The owner must be very dedicated and committed to this course of action, since it will not "feel" right to him at the time.) Because the parrot desires attention and seeks it by means of feather mutilation, being ignored for this behavior becomes a negative consequence. It can only gain the attention it seeks by refraining from the behavior, with the result that it receives the attention it craves. This attention becomes the reward for desired behavior—not picking or plucking. It becomes linked in the bird's mind with leaving its feathers alone. To reiterate: Ignoring the parrot when it picks becomes the negative consequence. Praising and giving the bird attention when it does not destroy its plumage becomes the positive desired consequence.

Another example of operant conditioning can be seen with the biting parrot. The bird's reward is to interact with its human flock, to receive attention and affection when it remains on hand or arm without biting, or allows its family to pet it without aggression. The corrective action could consist of tapping the beak and issuing a loud "No," then isolating the parrot in its covered cage or carrier for ten or fifteen minutes. This is experienced by the bird as deprivation of something it desires very much: positive flock interaction. Further, the parrot has realized that its bid for dominance has failed and that the owner is determined to maintain his position as "alpha leader."

We emphasize again that the use of positive and negative consequences to modify behavior must be absolutely consistent, for reasons that will be discussed in the following section.

ADDITIONAL CONCEPTS IN BEHAVIORAL MODIFICA-TION: EXTINCTION, SPONTANEOUS RECOVERY AND INTERMITTENT REINFORCEMENT

Extinction is a phenomenon that occurs after a conditioned response has been formed, in which this response tends to weaken or disappear if certain stimuli are abandoned. For example, a biting parrot that has been conditioned to come on hand or arm without biting for the reward of "time-out" of its cage to be with its owner may revert to biting if this reward is eliminated. A screaming parrot that has learned to refrain from this activity for the reward of praise and attention may revert to screaming if its good behavior becomes taken for granted by the owner and attention is greatly diminished as a result.

Spontaneous recovery is the event in which a conditioned response is resurrected when stimuli used to condition the subject are resumed. If, for instance, the biting bird is once again presented with the accustomed positive and negative consequences of its behavior, aggression will probably lessen or disappear once more.

We wish to emphasize that we do not recommend food treats to condition desirable behavior in the parrot. For one thing, the use of a food treat presupposes that the bird is hungry and will perform to satisfy its hunger. Allowing a parrot to go hungry for any reason is cruel and harmful to its health. Further, it is very inconvenient for the owner to carry on his person an adequate amount of food at all times and in all circumstances so that desired behavior can be reinforced consistently by this method. Inevitably, the time comes when there are no peanuts or sunflower seeds in the pocket and the training protocol becomes impossible to execute. This encourages the parrot to refuse to do what is requested. (And in all fairness, why should it if the expected reward is not forthcoming?) It is far more effective to use praise, attention or nonfood treats to modify a parrot's behavior. Examples of nonfood treats are "out time" on cage top or T-stand, being on the owner's hand for some "flock" activity such as playtime with its people or some other activity that the parrot enjoys, the deprivation of which will cause a sense of loss.

Intermittent reinforcement of behavior is reinforcement that occurs at irregular intervals. This creates serious problems when attempting to modify unwanted behavior in the parrot. It is the opposite of the constancy of approach that is absolutely essential if success is to be obtained. Intermittent use of rewards and corrective action leave the parrot confused and not knowing what is really expected of it. If the parrot is allowed to "get away with" a particular behavior with one person, and always corrected by another, it will usually continue to behave badly with the lenient one. If both parties correct behavior one time and let it go by the next, the parrot will be inclined to continue the unwanted behavior because, very often, no unpleasant consequences follow and the behavior is something the bird enjoys doing. The parrot is encouraged to try just one more time, because, after all, the last time it bit, screamed, pulled out its feathers, nothing "bad" happened. *The positive consequence of good behavior must always be given. Unwanted behavior must always be followed by the negative consequence.* Inconsistency in delivery of these consequences is particularly a problem when more than one person is working with the bird.

We are reminded of a large cockatoo, owned by a young couple, with which we worked. Meg was wild caught and shy with her owners. Although she was very gentle and did not bite, she would not step on their arms or come out of her cage when requested to do so, unless she felt like it (which was not often). Nor would she allow any kind of petting unless she particularly wished it. Joan and Ted wanted a much closer relationship with Meg, and felt that this could be achieved, but did not know how to go about it. Because Meg dictated the tone and terms of her relationship with the couple, one of the first things to be done was to remove this control and give it to Ted and Joan, to whom it rightfully belonged. Further, without this control of the relationship, they would be unable to teach Meg how to live comfortably and happily with them. (A parallel situation occurs with parents, who by reason of age and experience are equipped for the responsibility of socializing their children. All of us are probably familiar with parents who have abdicated their role of control and responsibility and have relinquished it to their offspring, with results ranging from the mildly amusing to outright tragedy.)

Meg was no longer allowed to spend time on top of her cage when and if she pleased, but was required to leave her cage and to remain on a T-stand when her owners desired this behavior. She was not allowed to leave the stand and run about on the floor. She was taught to come out of the cage on her owners' arms, and if she refused, she was gently grasped about the shoulder and neck and supported while she stepped up and was removed from her cage and placed on her stand.

Things went very well, and eventually Meg was discharged to her home. Not long after, however, Meg began to revert to her old ways. On questioning Joan and Ted, it was discovered that Ted was not as involved with Meg as was Joan, and was therefore not as motivated to follow the program at home with the same attention and consistency of approach. Meg was receiving mixed messages. Because she did not understand what was expected now, her behavior lapsed to its original aloofness and refusal to comply with her owners' requests. After some discussion, Ted and Joan agreed that only Joan would work with the bird, and that Ted would not interfere by approaching Meg and then withdrawing if she were initially hesitant about complying with his requests. Prior to this, Ted just walked away if Meg did not immediately come on his arm when it was presented. Joan understood that Meg must be made to follow through *every time* a behavior was required, and saw to it that this happened. Ted agreed that his lack of motivation had encouraged Meg's setback.

Once the nature of the setback had been identified, and the couple had agreed that Joan would be the primary "trainer" for Meg until the cockatoo's behavior had changed consistently for a long period, the bird began to progress again. Mixed messages were eliminated, and Joan's devoted discipline allowed Meg to learn not only to obey commands, but also to enjoy being with both of them.

WEAKENING AN UNWANTED BEHAVIOR

When working with a parrot to diminish or extinguish objectionable behavior, one must make every effort to eliminate any response to that behavior that tends to reinforce it. This must be the first goal. The second goal is to decide on a positive consequence of the desired behavior, and a negative consequence of the unwanted behavior. The third goal is to use these consequences *each time* the parrot's behavior warrants it. This is where the owner's understanding of behavioral modification and his commitment to the process become absolutely essential if desired results are to occur. The owner *must* remember that intermittent reinforcement of a desired behavior will at best produce erratic results, and that the same applied to inappropriate behavior will ensure that undesirable actions persist.

Let us take a newly weaned Amazon parrot through this process. This will be a youngster newly acquired and in the midst of exploring its new environment and testing limits with its new owners. Because it is genetically programmed to use its mouth for exploration activities and to push for dominance in its flock, and because it has only recently given up hand feeding and the urge to grab anything it thinks will provide food, this young bird will be predisposed to nip. At first the nips will be relatively painless, but this behavior will be persistent. As the parrot grows, the nips will become serious bites. The bird will learn that it can control any situation with aggression, and the inevitable result will be a parrot that is no longer controllable or an integrated part of the family. Nor will it be a source of enjoyment and companionship to those with whom it lives.

The owners have determined that this scenario will not occur with their young parrot. In deciding on a program of behavioral modification that will eliminate nipping, the owners first discover what factors encourage it, and then eliminate them. They notice that if they play roughly with the youngster, it tends to become excitable and nippy. They further notice that when the parrot becomes hungry, it bobs and whines, soliciting feeding, then grabs their fingers. Additionally, when the parrot is on their shoulders, it nibbles in an exploratory manner on their ears, sometimes pinching painfully in its enthusiasm for this fascinating "toy." So—no more rough-and-tumble play sessions. Instead, the bird is spoken to softly, stroked and petted, but no longer treated like a Saint Bernard puppy playing tug-of-war. Second, they are alert for indications that the parrot is hungry, and place it in its cage to eat if this is the case. Third, the parrot is not allowed on the shoulder, but firmly encouraged to remain on hand or arm. Doing these things *removes the opportunity* for the bird to develop entrenched nipping behavior.

Third, the owners decide that positive consequence of nonbiting behavior will be consistently used to reward the youngster for good behavior. They determine that as long as their parrot does not nip or bite, he may remain on their arm while they read, watch television and so on. In addition to this, they ensure that their bird's cage is provided with two or three appropriate chew toys that it can mutilate to its heart's content, thus providing an outlet for its natural urge to chew. They also decide what negative consequence will be used when the parrot nips. They determine that when this occurs, the parrot will be reprimanded with a tap on the beak and a stern "No," and placed in an empty cage by itself in another room away from family activities for ten minutes.

This program is implemented rigorously, no matter how time consuming, and no matter how inconvenient it may be. As a result, the parrot learns quickly that nipping/biting for any reason will not be tolerated. It further learns that when it performs this behavior, social deprivation *always* occurs, something the parrot dislikes and will avoid if at all possible. The owners' mental attitude is focused on reality because they recognize that in conditioning the parrot to refrain from biting/nipping, they are preparing it to assume a trusted position in the family, with all the privilege and freedom appropriate to an animal companion in the domestic setting. They have enhanced the parrot's life, rather than constricting it, because they understand the multitude of benefits that will accrue to the bird when it behaves appropriately.

MAKING POSITIVE AND NEGATIVE CONSEQUENCES WORK EFFECTIVELY

THREE CONDITIONS MUST ALWAYS BE MET TO MAKE POSITIVE CONSEQUENCES USED IN BEHAVIOR MODIFICATION WORK PROPERLY (GORDON 1989).

1. The parrot must want something that only the owner can provide (e.g., time out of the cage, attention, affection), and it must want it badly enough to submit to the owner's informed control.

2. The positive consequence offered by the owner must be perceived by the parrot as need-satisfying in some important way.

3. The parrot must be unable to supply the positive consequence itself, and must be dependent on the owner to supply it.

Owners must be prepared at all times to supply the positive consequence immediately whenever the situation demands it. Parrots are unable to see into the future, therefore withholding the reward until it is convenient for the owner to supply it will have no effect whatsoever. In fact, if positive consequences are withheld, the condition of intermittent reinforcement comes into effect, producing erratic and unpredictable results.

For negative consequences to have effect, the following conditions must be met (ibid.):

1. Once a behavior has been "punished" with a pre-determined negative consequence, it should ALWAYS be followed with the same negative consequence.

2. The owner must be careful to ensure that the unwanted behavior is never rewarded. (For example, in our newly-weaned Amazon, if a visitor should be the recipient of nipping/biting, the parrot should experience the same negative consequences it customarily does, even if the visitor says, "Oh, don't put him all by himself. He really didn't hurt me, poor little guy.")

3. The negative consequence should fit the behavior. It should not be inappropriately severe, nor should it *ever* be physically abusive.

In using the operant technique of behavior modification, one must realize that the owner is in possession of the means to meet the parrot's needs and to use this resource intelligently to mold desirable behavior. (We have already seen that the parrot is abundantly well equipped to learn appropriate social skills.) This method uses the simple concepts of need fulfillment and need deprivation. The owner, without question, has control and mastery of the relationship, something the parrot is prepared to accept because of its inborn familiarity with the flock dominance system. We hasten to add that in speaking of control and mastery of the human/parrot system or relationship, we do not imply that this mastery is obtained and upheld by brute force. Rather, it is a matter of exercising what Sally Blanchard terms *nurturing dominance*, and what we call "devoted discipline."

NEGATIVE CONSEQUENCES THAT ARE TOO SEVERE

It is relevant to address the danger inherent in negative consequences that are too harsh. If the negative consequence (or deprivation) is too severe, continues for too long a time each time it is administered or interferes in any material way with the parrot's health, predictable results will most certainly occur. First, need deprivation always results in some kind of frustration. A common result of frustration is aggression. In our example of the Amazon parrot given above, to continue its isolation in another room for longer than ten minutes for each infraction will ultimately deprive it of the social contact it needs to remain friendly and amiable with people. Severe deprivation of any kind of social contact for extended periods usually results in a parrot that bites anyway, for it has been allowed to forget its other social skills.

Physical abuse of the parrot generates extreme aggression on the bird's part in most cases. It has no other choice but to protect itself from what is truly a life-threatening situation. Occasionally one sees a parrot that has become inordinately timid as a result of such treatment, but this is rare. It is far more common to find birds that have developed a true loathing of all humans and have become incorrigibly aggressive. Parrots such as these are dangerous and often succeed in inflicting serious injury. Although smaller parrots can certainly cause painful bites, it is the large psittacids that can unquestionably cause serious injury. Even small parrots, while leaving fingers attached to hands, can cause copious amounts of blood to flow.

Another aspect of too-harsh punishment is the risk of escalating the amount of deprivation when owners feels the initial negative consequence did not produce desired results fast enough. The risk is ever present of making the next negative consequence more severe. As we have pointed out above, this is dangerous to the parrot and eventually to those who live with it. Additionally, this tendency to escalation is counterproductive, because the essence of operant conditioning is *consistent use of the* same *positive and negative consequence* over time *until desired results occur.* It requires patience and commitment by the owner, and any other way of attempting to use this technique will fail. It is a gentle, nonphysical way of humanely changing behavior. If not executed properly, it metamorphoses into something that all too frequently deserves to be labeled cruelty. The use of operant conditioning is designed to avoid abuse, not to foster it.

Finally, depriving the parrot of any thing essential to its physical health (such as withholding food or water, disturbing its sleep patterns, etc.) will cause serious health problems, possible death and certainly long-standing emotional problems. Operant conditioning does not include or condone any of these practices, for again it is a gentle method to be used humanely for the parrot's ultimate benefit, not to "break its spirit," or any other such nonsense.

PARROT RESPONSIVE TECHNIQUES

For convenience we will refer to professional trainers/behaviorists as simply trainers, although they are actually teachers and facilitators. Great care should be given to the selection of a reputable trainer; the best approach to locating one is through your avian veterinarian. Having located one, make sure you are comfortable with the trainer's techniques and philosophy before embarking on what may be a very long journey together. Remember that techniques and methods will vary according to who is giving the instruction.

We will primarily discuss the philosophy and techniques used at Parrot Responsive. Most of the case studies in this book took place at Parrot Responsive's facility, rather than the owner's home (see Chapter 8). Parrot Responsive, in this context, may serve as a model for those seeking criteria concerning a local professional.

Parrot Responsive Responsibility

At Parrot Responsive our primary goal is to relieve stress as quickly as possible. Stress kills parrots just as it does humans. Stressed parrots and stressed owners create a volatile situation that may result in harm to both. Since most of our parrots stay with us for the duration of training, stress is relieved for the owner very quickly.

Generally, by the time we become involved, the owner and parrot have tried numerous techniques and followed all kinds of advice. The result is a shared, elevated stress level for both bird and owner. We are immediately halfway to our goal by temporarily removing the parrot from the problem situation. Since we've also relieved stress for the owner, he has time to regroup his thoughts.

On entry the parrot is quarantined until taken to our avian veterinarian for a complete exam, which includes lab work. The quarantine process allows time for observation before the parrot is allowed in the training area with the other birds.

We have a preliminary discussion of the owner's expectations and degree of commitment, and a complete history is taken. At this point the owner is aware of the learning environment provided at Parrot Responsive, and knows this is not a "quick fix" program. He also realizes that the parrot's problem did not develop in a vacuum. We often find that the entire family may have contributed to problem development and must be involved with behavior modification as well. In some instances, the parrot's unacceptable behavior is a mirror that reflects less than ideal family relationships.

Parrot Responsive's philosophy includes no abuse or deprivation of any kind. Building trust and confidence is the basis for all the work that we do. Using food as a reward should be reserved for trick training. Otherwise we have a parrot that responds for the sunflower seed in our pocket instead of a companion that relates to us on a give-and-take basis as a friend would.

Discipline is practiced. Punishment is not. Discipline allows us to make it clear to the parrot and owner what each can realistically expect of each other.

PARROTS ARE NOT PEOPLE

Parrots are more than intelligent enough to understand that they are not human. A parrot that thinks it is a person rarely remains for its lifetime in one household but generally goes from home to home, with the reputation of a "spoiled brat" following it. It is not easy to teach a parrot that it *is* a parrot once it believes it is not.

When we find ourselves with that task at hand, other parrots become an invaluable resource. Surrounding such a bird with other parrots of its own species can sometimes provide valuable role models in this respect, helping to reduce stress dramatically at the same time. Other parrots may be able to help in the effort to teach the bird that it is, in fact, a parrot. Placing the parrot in a group of like species on the same play gym or other such structure (not on any of the bird's cages) can help teach the bird that there is a pecking order and that it has its place in that hierarchy.

Parrots need close supervision in such situations, but not constant intervention, since this only serves to confirm to the parrot what it originally thought: that it isn't like "those other creatures." We have practiced with this technique with good success in many cases. (Given our unique situation, it has worked. We do not suggest that the novice attempt this, as real harm could befall the birds in such a grouping.)

People are also intelligent enough to understand that parrots are not human. It is very important to let your parrot be a parrot. This goes back to the

When parrots are placed in a group situation, one will generally achieve the dominant position. *Thom Qualkinbush*

Surrounding a stressed parrot by other parrots of its species can sometimes reduce stress dramatically. For the "spoiled" parrot, group interaction may help it learn there *is* a pecking order. *Diane Schmidt*

owners' expectations. Enjoy your bird's "parrotness" instead of trying to create a surrogate human. The rewards are far greater and much longer lasting. A lifetime of companionship is much more likely if you allow your parrot to *be* a parrot.

We cannot emphasize enough that the goal should be that of parrots and people coexisting happily—each being allowed to function as who and what it is. Behavior modification enters the picture when the situation or circumstances have grown out of control. (Constant screaming, biting and feather picking are situations that have grown out of control.) By striving to understand what it really means for our parrot to be a parrot, we can circumvent most problem behavior.

COMMON SENSE

Parrot Responsive philosophy is based heavily on common sense. For example, one commonsense approach is that if you don't want to be bitten by your parrot, don't put your finger in its mouth. Removal of the opportunity to indulge in unacceptable behavior will go far in prevention of these behaviors. In removing the chance to bite, is such a parrot an ideal pet? No. But it will be able to realize a degree of socialization with people and other parrots that would not be possible if allowed to indulge in negative behavior.

NUTRITION

After discipline, nutrition and a well-balanced diet are of prime importance. Teaching owners the importance of this, and providing sound nutrition not only during training, but also for the rest of its life, is essential when trying to reduce stress for the bird. On receiving positive results from the veterinary exam, we begin converting the parrot to a well-balanced diet if it is not already on one. It is amazing that in this day of knowledge many parrots still live (and die) on an all-seed diet. Begin here if your parrot's diet consists of seed only. The parrot cannot have the strength and stamina to endure any kind of behavior modification without the proper nutrition. In some instances, such as in behavioral feather picking or constant screaming, the problem may disappear after simply improving the bird's diet.

THE IN-HOUSE APROACH

This approach is one not commonly seen. It offers unique opportunities when working with problem parrots. The use of other parrots as role models becomes

Healthy diets create healthy parrots. Fresh fruits and vegetables combined with a high-quality pelleted diet and other fresh grains will contribute to improved physical and emotional health. *Diane Schmidt*

Parrot Responsive utilizes a unique, in-house approach that offers opportunities for parrots and people to mend troubled relationships or strengthen good ones. Distractions usually present in the parrot's home are eliminated in this setting, and stress levels and progress are monitored closely. *Diane Schmidt*

possible. Distractions that might normally exist in the home environment are eliminated. It has been a successful alternative to the home (or "out programs") normally seen.

We do have an "out program," in which the trainer visits the home and works with owner and bird on an hourly basis. This practice, which is reserved mainly for newly acquired hand-raised birds and their owners, allows us to counsel for prevention of future problems by educating people and getting them off to a proper start. We will also go to the home for former clients experiencing temporary minor problems.

The majority of parrots are in-house clients. The parrot is brought to our facility for the duration of the program, which we usually try to limit to five weeks. The owner comes in and works with us and his parrot at least once a week. We teach owners what we have learned about their parrots since their last visits. Many people ask, "How do you do this? You bring birds in, mix them with other birds, stress them by moving them to a new location, change their diet and they don't get sick." This is possible because we are, in addition to keeping things scrupulously clean, relieving them of, not exposing them to, stress; we are improving their diet, exposing the parrots to other, "like" birds and teaching them to trust. And every precaution is taken to prevent any disease that might potentially be present. This should not be practiced by the average parrot owner.

The in-house environment enables us to monitor progress and problems. We can really get to know the individual parrot through daily encounters with it. We also get to know owners thoroughly during their weekly visits and through phone consultations between visits. We can monitor and control the birds' diet.

Recommendations to modify behavior will only work if the owner complies. When we have the parrot at our facility the program *will be executed,* so the results are often seen much faster. This contributes to quick relief of stress for all involved. For those who say they had a qualified trainer come into their home without results, take a look at your follow-through. Did you execute the program as advised? Were you careful to be extremely consistent?

Enrollment in our in-house program instills a sense of commitment in the participating owners and makes it easier for them to follow through. The pleasant learning atmosphere is psychologically motivating for both bird and owner, and it gives owners the opportunity to observe excellent care, which is of special interest to new or inexperienced bird owners. It also creates a much-needed break in a behavior pattern for the parrot.

BUILDING TRUST AND CONFIDENCE

Not only does the parrot need to learn to trust its owner, the owner needs to learn to trust the parrot. There's only one sure way to accomplish this. Do it. Start work as soon as possible. If the parrot is always approached with empathy and respect, it will begin to trust. Each time you bring the parrot out for a working session, it learns to trust more. If not, you are practicing negative behavior and need to rethink your approach. As trust is gained, so will be confidence. Each encounter will also increase the owner's trust and confidence as a parrot handler. As the owner becomes more confident and trusting, so will the parrot, and on and on.

PHASES OF TRAINING

We established in Chapter 1 that there are no set formulas for training the parrot. Every individual parrot and person are different. The following represents a general order of processes we go through with each parrot at Parrot

Specialized housing, the box perch, helps eliminate negative interaction between parrots and people while the bird is in training. It also provides a sense of security for the parrot. The box perch is not recommended as permanent housing. Parrots like an unobstructed view of their surroundings. The box perch is used as an aid in the training process, only.
Thom Qualkinbush

Parrot Responsive clients, Sheila and Igor Pollack, begin to reap the benefits of their commitment and consistent efforts to develop a lifelong relationship with their parrot. This photo illustrates the respect that has grown between them. *Thom Qualkinbush*

Responsive, whatever the reason for enrollment. The order or sequence may vary depending on individual circumstances, allowing the general sequence to serve as flexible guidelines to our approach.

First the parrot is enrolled. It is quarantined until the avian veterinarian informs us that the bird is healthy, then is transferred to the training area. It will be kept in specialized housing, a box with clear Plexiglas doors on the front, called a box perch. (This prevents struggles when removing the parrot, allowing us to move on to more important matters. The other advantages of the box perch are a better environment for monitoring droppings and ease of disinfection.) A period of behavioral diagnostics follows. Then specific goals are formulated and a strategy devised to meet them. The owner is involved in all phases of the behavioral modification program each time he comes to visit his parrot. When goals have been satisfactorily accomplished, and both bird and owner feel comfortable in continuing the program at home, the parrot is discharged.

This is the broad process that most birds go through at Parrot Responsive. The specific steps of training are covered in Chapter 7, and the reader is urged to read that section. The degree of emphasis on any given phase depends on the individual parrot and owner. The owner working with his bird at home need not set any specific time frame to reach the end of any particular training phase. Steady progress, however slow, is all that is necessary. Proceed at the rate with which you and your parrot feel comfortable. The business of training parrots can be a complex one. The role of the behavior modification professional should be to help simplify the process for you, not do it for you. The professional should be a facilitator of the relationship between you and your parrot. The rest is up to you.

7

How Do I Work with My Bird?

Owners' Attitudes Are Very Important

"No one ever told me that. Do you really think it's that intelligent?" "I don't want to do anything wrong to stress it out or ruin it." "This bird is a bronco...a maverick...just plain crazy." "I'd like my parrot to be the perfect parrot." "I'm sweating all over" (while trying to pet a parrot for the first time).

These are some of the comments we hear most often from our clients as we begin our relationship. They represent different attitudes or mind-sets that need to be examined and reformulated before you begin working with your parrot. Mind-set or attitude is simply your feelings about what you are doing or are about to do. It is your attitude, positive or negative, about your bird. An affectionate concern for the well-being of the parrot is the basis of a positive attitude.

We must believe that we are doing the best thing we can for the parrot and our relationship with it. The better our relationship is, the happier and healthier the parrot will be. The parrot will sense your discomfort with what you are doing. It will also sense your fear, if this is what you feel. Additionally, the parrot's intelligence is fully capable of exploiting misplaced sympathy or its owner's feelings of hesitancy—which the parrot will interpret as carte

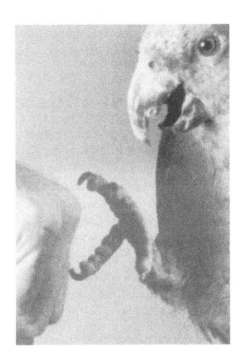

...We just don't want it to happen again... *Diane Schmidt*

blanche to establish its own dominance. Too, if the owner has concerns about stressing the parrot during training sessions, the parrot will obligingly appear stressed.

We need to approach training the parrot with a clear mind, to be definite in our actions and comfortable with what we are doing. By the process of behavioral modification and the training sessions used to reach goals, we are showing the parrot how to function as a part of the family, and to mesh its way of being with that of its human companions, so that mutually satisfying relationships and quality of life are enhanced for all involved.

Some critical detrimental factors to a positive attitude toward the parrot and its training are anxiety, impatience, carelessness, fear, lack of focus, lack of empathy or too much sympathy. In addition, overindulgence, an inappropriate desire to keep the parrot as it was as a baby, lack of knowledge and impulsive acquisition of the parrot will further engender owner attitudes that interfere with successful behavioral modification of his bird.

When speaking of owner attitudes, it is important for the reader to understand we are not just talking about relaxing before sitting down to work with your parrot. We are referring to feelings and underlying reasons for actions, and the results of our actions in the relationships with our parrots. Undetected negative feelings and actions can prevent us from achieving goals. If you doubt the intelligence and capacity of the parrot to sense these feelings, it will be difficult for you to gain control of a negative situation that may exist between you and your parrot.

The Parrot's History

History and current situation must be examined when determining the possible causes of behavioral problems. This involves gathering whatever information available about the parrot's present and previous situation(s). Very important areas to examine include how long the parrot has resided with current owner(s); how many people are in the household; the sex of the primary caretaker; preferences the parrot exhibits among family members; previous owner's personality; whether the parrot was wild caught or bred domestically; length of residence with previous owner(s); type of cage used; how much time spent per day in cage; whether or not the parrot is allowed to come and go from the cage as it pleases; the parrot's diet and level of nutrition; presence and nature of health problems—past or present.

Other questions that yield important information and insights are:

1. Where was the parrot obtained?
2. Was it taken to an avian veterinarian for a physical examination upon initial purchase?
3. If the owner finished the weaning process, was an extraordinary degree of attention focused on the baby?
4. During the weaning process, did the owner moderate the amount of attention given the parrot, realizing he didn't want to give it more attention early on than would be routinely possible in the future?
5. If the parrot was known to have problems when first acquired, what were they, and what were the owner's reasons for taking on such problems?
6. What is the parrot's age?
7. In the owner's opinion, does the parrot look "mean" or "friendly?"
8. Did the owner realize the amount of responsibility parrot ownership entailed when he first obtained the bird?
9. Does the owner think his bird is pretty or does he prefer the way most other parrots look?
10. Is the owner happy with his selection of this particular parrot species?
11. Did the owner research different types of parrots before deciding on the one for him?

12. Does the parrot bite, and if so, when?

13. What is occurring in the room when the parrot bites?

14. Is the owner able to establish any correlation between biting behavior and other activities in the environment?

15. How does the owner physically and mentally approach the parrot?

16. Is the parrot the dominant one in the relationship, or is the owner in control, the parrot following his cues?

17. Is the owner's spouse jealous of the time he/she spends with the parrot?

18. Does the parrot pick its feathers or pluck them out?

19. Does the parrot mutilate its flesh?

20. If feather picking or other self-mutilation problems exist, when and under what circumstances does the behavior occur? Is the behavior associated with consumption of certain foods?

21. If there are children in the household, do they tease the bird?

22. Does the husband or wife like the parrot better than the spouse?

Questions such as these are essential when trying to find reasons for behavioral problems. Searching for contributory causes will most likely involve some soul searching by owners and other family members alike. One client, several weeks into the program at Parrot Responsive, stated she was beginning to realize that not only was she allowing her cockatoo to manipulate and control her, but was also allowing people at work, as well as family and friends, to do the same. In other words, her behavior with her bird was habitual with her in all areas of her life. This realization helped her with her bird, and also allowed her to institute changes in her human relationships that were beneficial to her.

Developing the Behavioral Modification Program

Before embarking on this process, it will be help to know that this process is essentially the same problem-solving technique used in all other areas of life. In setting goals and planning strategies to solve problems, one must realize that the process is dynamic and ongoing. This requires frequent reviews of progress, and making changes in the program that will achieve results in the desired direction. It is critical to be patient and persevering. Sometimes plateaus are reached beyond which it seems difficult to move, so at these times it is important to stand back and take stock of how far you and your parrot have come, and how far you have yet to go. Plan to work on one goal at a time. We find many times that multiproblem situations are tightly intertwined, and that working toward one goal frequently solves more than one problem. However, the focus should remain on one goal at a time.

For the purpose of this book, it is necessary to present the entire process as if all were clear at the outset. In fact, as much as possible is done initially, and the rest is discovered as we go along. This involves revised planning and implementation, and yet more planning, change and implementation. Each day is a new one, and training your parrot is not something you do once and then consider forever complete. The process can be compared to raising a child, requiring ongoing involvement to maintain a dynamic, mutually satisfying relationship and helping to build social skills.

First, then, in constructing a workable behavioral modification program is to find what caused the problem. In addition to asking the questions posed in the previous section, the reader is strongly urged to review Chapter 5. It is not possible to deduce possible causes of unacceptable behavior without a working knowledge of common causes.

Second, decide what goals you will be working to achieve with your bird. They should be very specific. For example: "My bird will not bite me when I remove him from his cage," or "My bird will not scream when I leave the room."

Third, develop the plan, or strategy, for reaching goals you have set. This plan, called the protocol, is simply the way you will go from point A to point Z in the most efficient, stress-free way possible. It is extremely important that all family members understand the plan and that its execution is uniform in application by *all*.

Fourth, continuous evaluation of progress, or lack of it, must be carried out. This allows appropriate changes to be made in a timely way. It also gives the owner(s) the opportunity to appreciate progress that has already been made, thereby providing positive feedback and incentive to continue.

Fifth, put your plan into action. This is the hands-on part, and must be done consistently. The following section, "Implementing the Protocol," will be of great assistance, as it gives practical, step-by-step advice on precisely how implementation is successfully achieved.

IMPLEMENTING THE PROTOCOL

In this section we will discuss the basic phases of training implemented at Parrot Responsive. PRPT (Parrot Responsive Phases of Training) is a modular system, and the amount of time spent on each phase will vary with the individual parrot and the owner's skill and commitment working with his bird.

The sequence is carried out in order. As each phase is successfully accomplished, the next one is begun, but only after all previous phases have been reviewed at the beginning of each session. In some cases you may be able to bypass certain phases that you and your parrot have already mastered. But before doing this, be absolutely certain that they have indeed been mastered.

The length of a session should be determined by monitoring your own and the parrot's stress levels and the bird's attention span. Sometimes you may be able to work for an hour. Other times you may only be able to work for fifteen minutes. What you consistently do with the time is much more important than how much time you spend doing it.

When you begin, be sure you are ready. Frequently the owner stands in front of the parrot trying to psych himself into making the first move. The longer he stands there trying to build courage to begin, the more nervous the parrot will become. If you need to prepare yourself mentally, do it in another room before you enter the training area. Parrots sense fear and respond negatively to it, making progress difficult or impossible. If you suddenly become nervous or frightened while in the middle of an exercise, just stop and walk away, returning when you are again in control of your feelings.

Parrot Responsive Phases of Training (PRPT)

1. Take the bird to the vet for an exam and wing clipping.
2. Learn to pick the parrot up in a towel correctly.
3. Bring the parrot out of its cage (with towel, if necessary).
4. Place the parrot on a T-stand.
5. Work on biting on the T-stand.
6. Work on petting on the T-stand.
7. Work on "stepping up" from the T-stand.
8. Work on returning to the T-stand.
9. Work on petting while the parrot is on your arm.
10. Step up from the T-stand to return to the cage.
11. Step up in the cage to come out to the T-stand.

We will begin with step 2, assuming that the reader has previously taken his parrot to the avian veterinarian to rule out physical causes of behavior problems.

The Mealy Amazon (*Amazona farinosa farinosa*) demonstrates an appropriate, effective wing clip, the first six primary feathers on *each wing* having been clipped. The number of feathers trimmed per wing varies with each parrot's weight and body build. *Diane Schmidt*

2. Learn to pick the parrot up in a towel correctly. This is called toweling. Your avian veterinarian can teach you how to do it. The photograph included here will help, but it is not like having an experienced person show you. The method used is the same avian veterinarians use to restrain parrots for examination. Get comfortable with this. Even with the tamest parrots you may need to use restraint in case of emergency.

In our experience, most people are afraid of hurting the parrot when first learning to towel their birds. It's actually quite easy to do and is a safe, humane way to pick up a parrot that has not yet learned to step up.

3. Bring the parrot out of its cage. If the parrot will come out on your hand, you are that much ahead. If not, towel the bird to remove it from the cage and transport it to the training stand. You may need to alter the cage interior before you begin. It may be necessary to reduce the number of toys or remove them all temporarily. If the parrot is a clever escape artist, you may also need to remove the perches when attempting to remove him from the cage. The more uncluttered the cage, the easier this will be. Keep it uncluttered, so that each time you set out to bring the parrot out you don't have to spend ten minutes removing things from the cage. The parrot will learn after the first time what's going on, so when you approach the next time it will have more time to build to a frenzy while waiting for you to unclutter the cage.

Utilizing the towel, we teach parrots to step up in the cage to come out to their training stands. At Parrot Responsive this phase follows petting and arm training phases. *Diane Schmidt*

Parrot owners need to be able to towel their parrots correctly. It is an essential part of training any parrot. Even hand-raised birds should become accustomed to this procedure. *Diane Schmidt*

The first few times you remove the parrot from its cage can be unsettling for both you and your bird. It will become easier and less frightening each time. Remember to stay calm. Your panic will frighten the parrot more than the towel.

Once you put the towel into the cage to bring the parrot out, you must follow through. If not, you will have sent a distinct message to your parrot that he can control this situation. By toweling and bringing the bird out to the T-stand you will have shown the parrot and yourself that you can do it. If you are not successful, try again, until you succeed.

4. Place the parrot on a T-stand. The T-stand should be in a safe location for the parrot. We prefer not to use the bathroom because of all the hard protruding surfaces. The stand should be located where few obstacles are present for the parrot to run under, hide behind or injure itself on if it jumps off the stand. Place dogs and cats in another room. Other people should not be present in the training area when you are working with the parrot. (Other parrots nearby may help to calm the parrot you are working with or they may upset it. You will need to make this determination based on your individual situation.)

The training T-stand is an invaluable tool in training any parrot. At Parrot Responsive we prefer a very simple stand. We view it as the student's desk in school: the location that represents learning and inter-relating. *Thom Qualkinbush*

The height of the stand should be no more than forty-two inches. This will keep the parrot well below eye level. If your parrot jumps down frequently you may want to consider an even lower stand, around thirty inches. We prefer a very simple stand, without a tray or food cups to get in your way. (The stands seen in the photographs are manufactured by Ryan Parrot Products, P.O. Box 66, Riverside, IL 60546.) It will be necessary to pad the floor with old towels or blankets if the parrot is prone to falling.

Bring the parrot to the T-stand. Gently allow it to climb out of the towel and onto the stand. If it ends up on the floor, immediately pick it up with the towel and try again. Do this as many times as it takes until the parrot stays on the stand long enough for you to move away. Remain away for a few moments or longer. Gather your thoughts and allow the parrot to calm down.

If the parrot jumps down when you return to the stand, pick it up and return it to the stand immediately. Do not allow it to roam about on the floor. Repeat this procedure until the parrot stays on the stand. *Remember, this is a gentle procedure. Do not get rough with the parrot.* If you become impatient or tired, end the session immediately and begin again later.

5. Work on biting on the T-stand. Biting may not be a problem for your bird, so you can omit this phase. If your bird is a biter and you feel the least hesitant about executing this phase, *you must engage a professional trainer.* Do not place yourself in a potentially dangerous situation.

Parrots should not be allowed to bite. A parrot will stop biting once it realizes you are not afraid. When the parrot is comfortable enough to stay on the stand without jumping to the floor as you approach, look the parrot in the eye and raise the back of your hand to his beak. To do this bend the wrist downward and fold the fingers into the palm of your hand (see photo). This stretches the skin very tightly across the back of your hand, giving the parrot nothing to grasp if it tries to bite. You must keep the tightly stretched back of your hand facing its beak; if it can reach around to one side or the other to bite, it will.

When approaching a biting parrot the "back of hand" technique allows the trainer to gauge the degree of aggression the parrot exhibits. It may also be the first step in allowing the parrot to become familiar with hands, as well as the first step for the owner-trainer to become comfortable this close to the beak. *Diane Schmidt*

This Yellow-Naped Amazon (*Amazona ochrocephela auropalliata*) is in the process of learning that his attempts to bite will be to no avail. He has always controlled people by biting, and he just can't figure out why it's not working now. Frequently we see this posture immediately following a failed attempt to bite. [Please note: This photo illustrates the hand in a slightly higher position than it should be when working on biting. The back of the hand should be in more vertical position.] *Diane Schmidt*

This technique allows the trainer to determine if the parrot will bite and how aggressively it may lunge. It may also be the first step in allowing the parrot to become familiar with hands, as well as the first step in permitting the trainer to become familiar with the parrot's beak. Additionally, it also builds trainer confidence when working with a biting parrot. When the parrot realizes that its attempts at biting are to no avail, you are then moving in a positive direction.

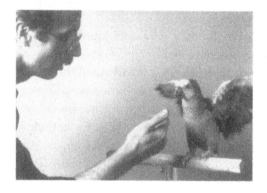

The goal in the first attempts at petting is to find the spot where the parrot is most comfortable and receptive to being touched. *Diane Schmidt*

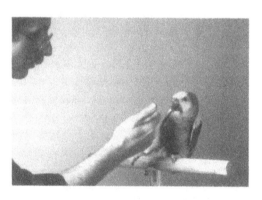

It may appear that this Blue-Fronted Amazon (*amazona aestiva aestiva*) is about to fall off his perch. At the time this photo was taken, this wild-caught Amazon had only been touched lightly on the tummy a few times. He has already given up on biting and actually is beginning to enjoy being petted. He still maintains his resistance until the trainer actually makes contact. *Diane Schmidt*

Persistence and sensitivity will enable you to accomplish your goal. *Diane Schmidt*

When the parrot is no longer trying to bite, you may rest the back of your hand on its beak. Leave it there for a few moments. Let the parrot look at it and become comfortable with it. Keep movement of the hand to a minimum at first.

Once you are both more comfortable (this could be after one session or many sessions), try to move your hand a little, possibly downward toward the parrot's chest. See if you can ever so lightly rub your knuckles on its chest. If the parrot reacts strongly, bring the back of your hand back to its beak, where you are both comfortable. At this point, some parrots will simply lower their heads for a scratch.

If at any point the parrot does succeed at biting, a stern "No!" will often get the idea across that this is not an acceptable behavior. Be aware of your tone of voice, and make certain that the parrot understands it. A low, sweet tone of voice will be interpreted as a sign that biting is acceptable behavior. In training, tone of voice is crucial. Make it easy for the parrot to differentiate between ordinary speech and a reprimand.

Some parrots will require a louder "No" than others, and occasionally a parrot may react very negatively, so be aware of the effect of your verbal reprimands.

Another technique is to combine a sharp "No!" with a tap on the beak. This is not to be misconstrued as hitting the parrot. This tap on the beak lets the parrot know exactly why you changed the tone of your voice (gave the stern "No!"). Although effective with some parrots, however, it is not effective for all. If the reprimand is to work, you must be face to face with the parrot, with the bird on the T-stand, you as the trainer standing directly in front. It must be done immediately, blood dripping from the finger or not! The tap on the beak in combination with the stern "No!" helps the trainer let the parrot know exactly what the reprimand is for.

While working with the bird, you must remain aware of the parrot's actions and reactions at all times. If you are tiring and thinking about ending the session, try not to stop just when the parrot decides to try to nip. End on a positive rather than a negitive note.

6. Work on petting on the T-stand. The transition from the back of the hand at the beak to petting can be an anxious time for the trainer, but one that must be made. The goal is to find the spot the parrot will most like to be touched/ scratched. For some it's the top of the head, others the chest, others the side of the head, others the back. It is at this stage we may inadvertently allow the parrot to start controlling us by attempting to bite. If the parrot turns its head, looking as if it might bite as we try to pet it, and the hand is jerked away, we reinforce the parrot's perception that biting will allow it to refuse anything with which it does not feel comfortable. It is natural to pull away from threat of biting, but the owner must make every effort to pull his hand back only far enough to avoid being bitten. Then he must repeat the attempt to pet in the same or a different spot. Or he may bring the back of his hand back up to the beak—where both are comfortable.

Another technique is to approach the parrot with both hands—one on each side, just above the parrot's eye level. Keep at least twelve inches between each hand and the parrot. Try to touch the parrot with one hand. If it turns its head toward the touching hand, use the other hand to distract it. How you do this will depend on what works with that individual parrot. For some it may only take a slight wiggle of a finger. For others you may need to try to duplicate what you did with the first hand. Repetition of the petting technique can create enough distraction to allow you to touch the parrot successfully.

Once you've touched the parrot, keep repeating, with breaks in between, until you are actually scratching the parrot. It will not take long for the parrot to decide that petting feels good. There will probably be reversions to attempted biting at times, but eventually the parrot will become comfortable and you will be able to begin exploring different areas to pet. Some parrots may have lived a long time having never been touched. Be aware of this and do not overstress such a bird.

It is best to move the hands with slow, fluid movements. Sudden jerking movements may intimidate the parrot. It may appear as though you are lurching at it, which may frighten the parrot or cause a defensive response.

Always keep your eyes on the parrot's eyes when first making attempts to pet. This will be the best indicator of what the parrot will do. Do not be distracted and glance across the room or your attention may be forcefully brought back to your training partner. Parrots have a way of helping us learn to stay focused!

Keep in mind that the parrot may be fighting instincts, and to overcome them can take time. You, too, are fighting instincts when you are trying to learn not to jerk your hand from the parrot when it tries to bite. Knowing that both of you are struggling with the same basic issue will help the trainer to empathize with his parrot.

7 and 8. Work on "stepping up" from and returning to the T- stand. At Parrot Responsive we rarely stick-train a parrot before arm training. We prefer to begin with arm or hand training. In some instances we will begin with the stick, but only if the parrot is really aggressive or has an extraordinary fear of hands. Generally you will know the right moment to begin this phase. You should feel the trust between the two of you. You will feel that you are ready and the parrot is ready.

Don't let the parrot manipulate you into stepping up when you are trying to work on another phase (e.g., biting or petting). Your being unaware of the parrot's history makes it difficult to know what its social skills were with a previous owner. The bird may try to step up when you want to work on biting or petting. Do not allow this. Let the parrot know that you are determined to master the other phase. If you realize that the parrot wants to step up, use this skill to bring the parrot to and from the training area instead of toweling it. (We substitute stick or hand transportation for toweling when the parrot is already stick or arm trained on entry to Parrot Responsive.)

The parrot may not have wanted to step up before. Now that it realizes you are trying to pet it, stepping up becomes the lesser of two evils. If you do give in and allow this, you are allowing the parrot control of the situation: letting it do what it wants to do instead of what you want it to do. This is the opposite of what you are trying to accomplish. Some parrots may be extremely persistent about this. You need to be equally persistent.

When you are ready to teach the parrot to step up, begin warming up by practicing all previous steps mastered. After the parrot has relaxed, place your hand or a stick in front of the parrot, two to three inches above the perch of the T-stand. Parrots prefer to step up, not down. Move your hand in a definite motion straight back toward the parrot and give the command "Step up." If it does, immediately say, "G-o-o-o-d b-i-r-d." It is important that the parrot not be kept off the stand for too long. Tell it "good bird" and place it right back on the stand. To place the parrot back on the stand, slowly move your hand up over the perch. Then lower it behind the perch and bring it forward again so the parrot is more or less forced to step back on the perch. Remember the parrot will step up, not down. As you practice/repeat this, observe the parrot to determine how long to increase the time on your hand before you return it to the stand. Be careful not to fall into the routine of allowing the parrot to jump back to the stand before you put it back. If you find this habit starting, put the parrot back before it starts fidgeting.

For the parrot that is extremely comfortable with being petted but less comfortable about stepping up, it may feel more comfortable if you pet or rest your hand on its back to steady it while you use your other hand to have it step up.

If you are starting with a stick, use the same information above, and use the stick as long as you feel the need. The first time you decide to try your hand instead, have the parrot step up and back to the stand several times using the stick. Develop a slow, smooth flow or rhythm: step up...back to stand...step up…back to stand…step up…back to stand. Without changing the rhythm, switch to your hand…step up…back to stand.

It is best to decide on a command for returning to the T-stand. It makes it clearer to the parrot if you use a command that is different from the one you used when the parrot stepped up to the stand. At Parrot Responsive we say "Okay." Others say "Down" or "Back." It doesn't matter what the command is. Just be consistent in using it.

9. Work on petting while the parrot is on your arm. Once the parrot is comfortable being petted and stepping up, we begin working on petting it while on our arm. You should already be familiar with its favorite spots to be petted. Work in the same way you did on the stand, the only difference being that now the parrot is on your arm.

A parrot that steps up on your hand to come out of its cage is a pleasure. *Diane Schmidt*

Devoted discipline includes teaching your parrot to step up to come out of its cage. Young parrots may be taught this very simple, positive behavior with ease. It is one basic routine that may help prevent future problems between parrot and owner. *Diane Schmidt*

You will be rewarded many times over for teaching your parrot this important discipline. *Diane Schmidt*

If the parrot tries to climb to your shoulder instead of letting you pet it, roll on the floor if you have to, but don't let the parrot get to your shoulder. This can be a difficult habit to break once started.

10. Step up from the T-stand to return to the cage. Once you have progressed to the point that the parrot is comfortable staying on your arm while you take a few steps around the room, try to return it to its cage from your arm at the end of your session. If it jumps down midway, either have it step up off the floor onto your hand or use the towel (if necessary) to return it to the stand. Then try again. Be sure to open the door of the cage before you begin so you don't have to fumble with the door and risk having the parrot fly onto the cage.

11. Step up in the cage to come out to the T-stand. Before you begin trying to get the parrot to step up inside its cage, it should be readily stepping up outside the cage. If the parrot refuses to step up in the cage, don't spend a long time coaxing or chasing. Give the command several times, and if the parrot doesn't step up and come out, grab the towel that you previously concealed in your hip pocket and reach in and bring the parrot out. *Do not close the door and walk away.* Once you start you must bring it out if you want to teach it to come out of its cage on your hand. After you have it on the stand (whether by hand, stick or towel), just go on with your normal routine. Try it again the next session. It won't be long before the parrot realizes that it might as well step up on your hand and come out because it's coming out anyway. Once you get the parrot to the stand, go back and close the cage door in case it tries to fly or run back.

MAINTENANCE TRAINING

At Parrot Responsive, PRPT is a basic plan that most parrots go through. It is used effectively with tame birds that have a dominance or control problem. People with well-trained dogs and horses acknowledge the value of training and practice long after the initial training. We call it maintenance training. It's fun, and the well-trained parrot generally enjoys showing its affectionate owner that it still knows the routine.

Maintenance training is an important aspect of your parrot's care. Most encounters with the parrot should include some devoted discipline. It is necessary to keep reminding the parrot who is in charge—the dominant one, the parent, the teacher.

Supplementary Techniques for Specific Problems

These techniques are used *in conjunction with* PRPT for specific problems such as screaming and feather picking, which PRPT alone may not solve.

PARROT BITES ONLY STRANGERS

Do not allow individuals unfamiliar to the bird to approach it. Persons who will be relating to the bird on a regular basis should be taught the principles of PRPT and go through the process with the parrot. Additionally, lowering the cage and not allowing the parrot to sit on top will reduce dominance and territoriality-engendered aggression.

PARROT BITES EVERYONE EXCEPT ONE PERSON

Those the owner feels are qualified may practice PRPT with the parrot under your supervision. The owner should use great caution, as it is his responsibility alone to prevent injury to others by his bird. Implementation should be consistent among all those working with the bird, including the "favored one." It may be beneficial for those family members not favored by the parrot to work with the bird alone in a room the parrot is not accustomed to being in. Do not allow the parrot to sit on top of the cage. Lowering the cage and changing its location is also helpful in this situation.

PARROT BITES FAVORED PERSON WHEN OTHERS APPROACH

This behavior is displaced aggression and will respond favorably when PRPT is practiced by all family members. In addition, lower the cage and prevent the parrot from perching on top of it. When the bird is on the arm, be very aware of its state of mind. If it attempts to bite, distract it by suddenly dropping your arm one to five inches. This causes the bird to lose its balance long enough to prevent the completion of the bite. It also sends the signal that when it attempts to bite, this might happen again. The favored person needs to be alert to others entering the room if he is to implement corrective measures immediately and appropriately. Once the parrot has been disoriented by the arm movement, look it directly in the eye and talk to it firmly about anything while you return it to the stand. Use several changes of vocal tone enroute. This maneuver further distracts the parrot from biting.

SCREAMING

The reader is urged to review causes of screaming in Chapter 5. Methods used for different types of screaming problems are similar. Knowing the cause for screaming is of great importance in effecting positive change. The following suggestions should help the reader develop strategies to reduce or eliminate inappropriate screaming.

Generally, lowering the cage (all the way to the floor if necessary) and not allowing perching on top of the cage will reduce screaming dramatically. The parrot isn't as inclined to exert its dominance by screaming if it's not in a dominant frame of mind. Height, especially of the cage top (the parrot's domain), allows the bird to feel dominant.

Problem screaming, like biting, usually can be attributed to a lack of control by the owner, resulting in the parrot's domination of the household. *Diane Schmidt*

Leaving the room will sometimes cause the parrot to stop screaming. If after a few moments the screaming does not cease, reenter the room and quickly cover the cage for ten minutes.

After this time, remove the cover.

If covering does not work, place the parrot in a carrier or small cage in a dark area and cover the cage/carrier with a dark sheet or blanket for ten minutes. This technique works for some birds. In other situations it may take too long to accomplish the procedure, and the parrot may forget what the "time-out" is for.

It is important to avoid rewarding the parrot by conversing with it while you are covering it. We have found that for some parrots, conversing when removing the cover becomes a reward. The parrot is able to realize after the cover is taken off that it still will get the attention it was seeking, even if somewhat delayed.

If the situation is such that the parrot doesn't scream every time you leave the room, but only when you are in another room with other people or parrots, it may be desirable to bring the bird into the other room on occasion. Do this *before* the parrot begins to scream.

Finally, do not allow the bird to perch on your shoulder, as this, too, enhances its feeling of dominance and may cause screaming. Be sure to have sufficient toys to prevent boredom.

In some instances the parrot may not be receiving enough attention. Setting aside time each day to spend with that parrot will often work wonders. Use part of this time for practicing PRPT.

PARROT CLIMBS TO SHOULDER

In addition to regularly practicing PRPT, the following suggestions will be of help. If the parrot has progressed and is comfortable with hands, use your other hand to block the parrot's effort to climb. If the parrot bites when you try to block it, work close to the floor on a soft surface and drop the parrot to the floor. Stand on your head, if necessary, to prevent it from climbing to the shoulder!

This is a good case in point for working on petting before arm training. If the parrot is comfortable with touching hands, you stand a much better chance of keeping it off the shoulder without undue contortion.

Many parrots are encouraged to climb to the shoulder by the position in which the owner holds his arm. Parrots innately climb to the highest perch. By keeping the forearm level and the elbow tucked fairly close to your side, you reduce the parrot's inclination to climb. This is an easy preventive measure. If the parrot is already accustomed to climbing to the shoulder at will, then the above techniques should be implemented.

Feather Picking, Plucking and Mutilation

In this section we will deal primarily with the implementation of protocols to reduce or stop feather mutilation. We at Parrot Responsive are by no means convinced that psychological causes are the only causes for this distressing constellation of behaviors. They may indeed be contributory, and much of our strategy is based on correcting such causes. However, we have become

Two African Grey Parrots (*Psittacus erithacus erithacus*) and a Red-Lored Amazon (*Amazona autumnalis autumnalis*) demonstrating Elizabethan and tube collars. These devices are sometimes used to discourage feather mutilation with varying degrees of success. *Scott McDonald, DVM*

increasingly aware of possible underlying physiological causes that may have created, or helped to create, feather- and self-mutilation problems. There is the question of which came first. Does the parrot act as it does as a result of a psychological cause, or does it act in what appears to be psychologically maladaptive ways because of an underlying physical problem? It is not easy to separate mind and body in the parrot any more than it is in humans. There is much we do not know about feather and self-mutilation, and we wish to emphasize that it is not good enough to assume psychological causes. This should prove a fruitful area of investigation for veterinary researchers.

In most instances, regardless of picking, plucking or mutilation of the flesh, PRPT may help. It has proven effective for us especially with those problems caused by overindulgence, neglect, stress and boredom. In addition to PRPT, solutions vary depending on the causes we have been able to discover. Usually a combination of causes are at work.

STRESS

Stress is a complex issue. Because of this we will divide stress into two categories: complex stress and simple stress.

Complex stress refers to those instances of stress resulting from a combination of long-term negative circumstances: overindulgence, neglect and poor nutrition, for example. It may be very difficult to undo behavior developed in response to such a combination of factors operating over long periods. In its severest form, the parrot may resort to mutilation of not only feathers, but also its flesh.

At Parrot Responsive, the parrot with feather and/or mutilation problems is taken through PRPT. However, we have experienced a growing degree of success using complementary medicine in combination with PRPT. Complementary medicine is normally referred to as alternative medicine. We prefer the term *complementary* because it really does complement traditional medical approaches sometimes used with these problems.

Our use of complementary modes of approach has been focused on Annedda (pycnogenol), an over-the-counter drug, and its benefits to the self-mutilator. It is a plant derived-substance, and its versatile action appears to result from its potent antioxidant properties and the fact that it seems to penetrate the brain/blood barrier. We have witnessed dramatically improved skin and feather conditions with its use. In some instances picking has stopped and feathers have regrown. We have also noted dramatically improved moods and lessened depression.

Our experience with Annedda (pycnogenol) and other complementary medicine is in the preliminary stages at the time of this writing. We are optimistic about potentials of this approach in our work with self-mutilating parrots and those in need of a boost in general well-being.

Simple stress, isolated stress as a result of isolated causes, is usually related to a short-term change of some kind. Examples of simple stresses implicated in feather- and self-mutilation behavior include temporary overindulgence, lack of rest, temporary neglect, lack of ambient moisture, temporary drop in nutritional level, boredom, move to a new home, a new plant or other object near the parrot's cage, a new owner, a new baby in the family, a new parrot or other pet in the house, a death in the family, the owner's absence/vacation.

These kinds of stresses tend to be less problematic, and indeed often are. However, they may also be an initial indication of underlying complex stress beginning to surface. Imagine this scenario. You have a three-year-old African Grey Parrot that has never picked or given other indications of problems. While you're at work, unscheduled workmen come to hang new shutters outside the window where the bird has its cage. Normally you would have closed the draperies or blinds and moved the bird into another room, but were unable to do this because you didn't know workmen were coming that day. You come home and find a pile of feathers at the bottom of the cage. It does not stop there. It continues for the next six months.

Now, the results of erratic overindulgence coupled with the parrot's perception of neglect during periods of less attention in relation to the overindulgence, too many late nights, an all-seed diet and lack of intellectual stimulation combine to create a parrot with little emotional resilience. Complex stress has finally produced a situation in which simple stress (the workman) has pushed the parrot over the edge, resulting in feather plucking.

For well-adjusted parrots with deep reserves of emotional resilience, an isolated (simple) stress may only be a temporary factor. A continued course of normal activity, or PRPT in combination with targeted modification activity, will generally halt destructive feather behavior.

STRATEGIES FOR OVERCOMING FEATHER-DESTRUCTIVE BEHAVIOR

Complex stress involves combinations of many interrelated causes and correspondingly more complex strategies. With simple stress the focus is on resolving a short-term problem, and a relatively simple strategy.

The parrot that mutilates is communicating his displeasure of a situation it perceives to be unacceptable, and at the same time making a very successful bid for attention. It may pick/pluck if it's hungry, wants out or wants to be petted. This is the bird that has never been taught to amuse itself or to expect that for some periods during each day it will be without the attention of its owner.

In addition to practicing PRPT, "benign neglect" is the single most helpful technique in working with pickers/pluckers. It involves refusing to respond to the behavior while at the same time instituting positive responses and activities that will eliminate picking/plucking. This can be very difficult, because initially the owner will feel guilty when he refuses to perform an action that he knows in the past has at least temporarily gotten the parrot to stop damaging its plumage. We are *not* suggesting that you neglect your parrot in the usual sense of the word. Benign neglect is a set of responses the owner uses to effect modification of the parrot's feather-destructive tendencies. An example will serve to illustrate what we mean. On your arrival home from work, the parrot begins to pick because it wants to come out of its cage. You bring it out, but now you'd like to make dinner. The parrot starts picking again because it wants attention from you, so you stop what you are doing, pick up the parrot and start petting it. Now the phone rings, and with the parrot sitting on your arm you answer the phone. Your attention is engaged with the conversation and your parrot again starts to pick because you stopped petting it. The variations on this theme are endless, and the parrot's single-minded pursuit of its maladaptive behavior is truly astounding.

Utilizing the concept of benign neglect, the above situation would be handled in this manner. The owner comes through the door, greets the parrot and goes on about his business until the specified time for the PRPT session. The parrot will doubtless begin to pick, but the owner does not acknowledge this in any way. It sounds hard to do, and it is. Guilt feelings will probably flourish. This is when the time you invested in your attitude restructuring will pay off. The owner *knows* what he is doing is correct and that it will have the positive result of a parrot that no longer denudes itself at the "drop of a hat."

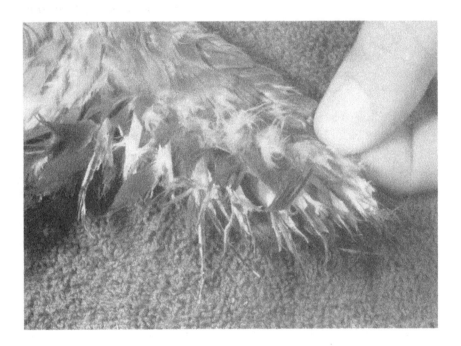

Amazon parrot showing feather self-amputation and chewing of remaining quill stumps. *Scott McDonald, DVM*

Auto-mutilation of foot by Amazon parrot. *Scott McDonald, DVM*

PRPT will enable you to structure quality time to spend with the parrot on a much healthier and more constructive basis. The reader might ask, "Why do I need to implement PRPT when the problem is that the parrot is too tame already?" PRPT will teach the parrot that it has a specified time to spend with you, which it can count on and which is its alone. It will also learn that at other times it will be learning to do without inappropriately constant attention. Be sure to provide varied toys to occupy the parrot's attention during what it will perceive to be a lonely time at first. Be creative in providing other options for the parrot in your absence. Some possibilities to consider: change cage location; move closer to a window; play the radio one day and not the next (remember loud volume equals loud birds); vary the diet; rotate favored toys; rearrange the room; provide an avian companion in a separate cage. After weeks or months, when the picking/plucking behavior has been eliminated, you will once again be able to increase gradually the amount of extra time together.

When feather-destructive behavior is temporary and minor, it may be of benefit to reduce time spent inappropriately with the parrot in a more gradual manner. PRPT in this case should still remain a part of the bird's routine. Again, provide interesting, safe toys and other stimulation for the parrot as it learns to amuse itself without its owner's company.

Other areas of the parrot's life may need correction or alteration in combination with benign neglect. The parrot's diet should be excellent, and it must have at least eight to ten hours of sleep in a dark, quiet room. If ambient moisture is lacking in the home, use a humidifier to correct the situation. Likewise, frequent bathing or misting will also add moisture to the bird's skin and feathers. Dry skin alone may cause some parrots to pluck. If your bird is unaccustomed to bathing, go slowly in order not to stress the bird further.

Parrots sometimes lunge at the water being sprayed when bathing. *Diane Schmidt*

Many parrots' reactions are misinterpreted by their concerned owners when teaching their birds to bathe. Intense flapping to the point…

…of leaving the stand may be interpreted as fleeing the bath. It may just be extreme enthusiasm. This can be especially true of parrots that have not bathed in a long time. Study your parrot carefully when interpreting its actions. *Diane Schmidt*

True neglect is occasionally a cause of plucking/picking/mutilation. If you find that you are unable to give the care your parrot needs, or are unwilling to do so, please find the parrot a home where its physical and emotional needs can be met. See Chapter 9 for a discussion of this topic.

Once the parrot is comfortable with the bath, you may witness an enjoyable display of delight. *Diane Schmidt*

This parrot is using his wing to help work the water into the feathers on his head. Many people interpret this as the parrot trying to hide from the spray. *Diane Schmidt*

Varying degrees of exuberance may be seen during the bathing experience. Do not dismay if your parrot doesn't get this excited with its bath. Most important, *Do not stop* bathing your bird because of lack of enthusiasm. *Diane Schmidt*

Parrot Body Language

Body language, also called kinesics, is the study of body movements, gestures and postures as a means of communication. There are several reasons to become familiar with parrot body language: to recognize stress and reduce it; to interpret what our parrots are telling us; to prevent injury to ourselves; to prevent miscommunication; to grow in our relationships with our parrots.

Reading our parrots' actions is not always easy, but some basic knowledge will help. We have learned that the more we learn about parrot body language the more individual to each bird it becomes. Many body movements, gestures and postures can be interpreted in several ways. An Amazon parrot with dilated (pinning) eyes may be excited to see you—or it may be preparing to bite. It is best to survey the entire situation to determine what a particular signal may mean. For example, we have read that when a cockatoo stamps its foot it should be interpreted as a warning. It has been apparent in many instances that a cockatoo stamping its foot is requesting our presence or attention. Some clients have said that their parrots do not like to be sprayed with a mister to receive a bath. When they were guided to observe and correctly interpret the bird's body language, they found that the parrot was so excited to be getting a bath it could not control itself, fluttering its wings so enthusiastically it lifted off the stand and onto the floor. The misinterpretation was that the parrot flew away in fear or defense. These examples indicate the necessity for becoming familiar with *your* parrot's body language. In this situation, another parrot may well have been attempting to flee. Parrots that have never been exposed to bathing might indeed be expressing fear. The body language the owner observes must be placed in context before correct interpretation is possible.

While it is important to acknowledge and react appropriately to the parrot's body language, it is important to not allow oneself to be manipulated by it. For example, the newly acquired, older African Grey Parrot may never progress to a good relationship with its owner if the owner allows the bird to use its threatening growl to prevent socialization. And the cockatoo that displays dramatically may never learn to be petted if we flee this dramatic display. PRPT allows us to proceed, acknowledging the messages given by the bird's body language, and reacting suitably. The accompanying photographs offer some of the common postures, gestures and body movements you might encounter during PRPT.

This Moluccan Cockatoo (*Cacatua moluccensis*) is in full defensive/alarm posture. Many cockatoos use this posture to manipulate and control people. One must pay close attention when working with a bird displaying this posture. The important thing to remember is that just as quickly as the posture appears, it can disappear. The individual bird's personality and history need to be considered to determine your response to such displays. *Diane Schmidt*

Pictured here is a Goffin's Cockatoo (*Cacatua goffini*). Its ruffled feathers and partially extended wings indicate its comfort and security knowing its good friend and protector is close by. The Moluccan Cockatoo on the right is exhibiting ruffled plumage and extended wings and crest, as in a semi-alarmed state. The same posture might, however, indicate a desire for your attention, or "Stay away, don't you see how big I am?" Owners must know and observe their birds closely to interpret correctly their parrots' body language. *Thom Qualkinbush*

Focusing

It can be difficult to remain focused on our efforts. When working with a parrot during PRPT, we need to concentrate our thoughts on what we are doing. It is not possible to work with a parrot on biting and hold an unrelated conversation with a friend at the same time. We have to learn not to let our thoughts wander. Not only might it be dangerous, but also it will dilute the effectiveness of our efforts. When our thoughts are not on what we are doing we risk communicating indifference and disrespect to the parrot. The parrot will sense this lack of focus.

Focusing on your efforts will accelerate progress in the relationship. Focusing means to put your heart and soul into the process. All thoughts should be focused on what it is you are trying to accomplish. A good friend taught us this extremely useful relaxation and meditative exercise to use ourselves and with our clients. We recommend practicing it frequently, especially prior to working with your parrot.

1. Sit or lie flat on your back, spine straight.

2. Close your eyes.

3. Breathe in through your nose and out through your mouth.

4. Focus on your breathing.

5. Follow the breath as it enters your body all the way down to the diaphragm and back up through the throat and out of your mouth. Let the breathing become rhythmic.

6. Let thoughts come and go at will. If you get stuck on a thought, go back to concentrating on your breathing.

7. Practice this until you can completely focus on your breathing.

8. Now…in the same way you learned to focus on your breathing, focus on your parrot and what you are specifically trying to accomplish with each encounter.

Whether you practice an exercise like this or not is up to you. The point is not to work with your parrot if you are overly stressed, nervous, upset about something, angry at the parrot or preoccupied with something else. The parrot will sense it and respond accordingly.

Summary

We have presented a great deal of material in this chapter. Use it to tailor an approach that will work for your bird, and create the relationship you both deserve. When all is said and done, the best advice we can give is to observe with all your senses and reach deep into your heart and feel. Be guided not only by your intellect, but also by your heart. But don't forget to practice devoted discipline first, last and always.

Behavioral Case Studies

In this chapter we will present case studies from Parrot Responsive. The reader should understand that outcomes of training are not always what owners expect at the beginning of the process. The owner may come to realize that he cannot release his ideas and prior expectations of the parrot. He may decide that another home may be better or that another type of parrot would have been a better fit for him—or perhaps a dog or cat would be more compatible with his situation and desires. At this point the owner can make a sound decision in this regard, if necessary.

...I only hope you can forgive me...
Diane Schmidt

Given the space limitations of this book and the many reasons underlying parrot behavior problems, there is much valuable case material that was necessarily omitted. We have included cases in which bird and owner "live happily ever after," as well as situations where problems between parrot and owner could not be resolved. We believe these situations may still be considered successful because they resulted in decisions that mutually benefited parrot and owner alike. It is hoped the material in this chapter will clothe the bones of basic information with the flesh of reality, thereby helping the reader gain a better understanding of the reasons for his parrot's behavior and aiding the formulation of useful approaches to his situation.

The studies are told in a narrative style by Thom, who was the person involved with the "hands-on" aspect of these owners and their birds.

Case Study #1:

Slugger, three-year-old male Moluccan Cockatoo (*Cacatua moluccensis*); domestically bred/hand reared. **Presenting problem:** Incessant screaming

Parrot Responsive received several frantic phone calls from Ann and David requesting help for their bird's intractable screaming. In addition, Ann stated that Slugger "terrorized" her. He did this by sitting on the sofa next to her shoulder and staring at her for long periods. He would then make a sudden leap to the floor and commence biting her ankles. Then, as she ran in fear, he herded her into the bedroom. If Ann emerged from the bedroom, the whole performance was repeated by Slugger with great gusto.

Although Ann was upset by Slugger's aggression toward her, both she and David saw the bird's screaming as the primary problem. I counseled them concerning techniques they could use to modify Slugger's unwanted vocalizations. After several weeks Ann and David called once again, reporting that the screaming had continued unabated. They were desperate. In addition to Slugger's screaming and aggression, he had begun to destroy their possessions—furniture, stereo, books, records—nothing was safe. Slugger was admitted to Parrot Responsive's in-house behavioral modification program. When the bird arrived, it became apparent that Ann and David had not exaggerated Slugger's screaming problem. It was continual and extremely loud, and nothing made him stop.

CURRENT SITUATION

Ann and David loved Slugger, in spite of his screaming and the fact that Ann was mortally afraid of the bird. The couple lived in a three-room apartment in a new building with thin walls and were afraid they would either be evicted or forced to get rid of Slugger.

Their lifestyle had been completely destroyed by Slugger's behavior. When the bird was admitted to our program, the couple had resorted to going out to dinner after work, followed by a lengthy stay at the neighborhood bar playing darts. They came home at midnight and tiptoed into the bedroom without turning on any lights, used the bathroom in the dark and went to bed. They lay rigidly still, not even whispering. This was the only way they could prevent the bird's ear-splitting screeches. Ann and David had been literally living in the bedroom for three months, because every time Slugger saw or heard them, he turned their lives into a nightmare.

In addition, Ann, early in her relationship with Slugger, had mistaken his energy, playfulness and nibbling of her fingers for aggression and biting. She became afraid of the parrot, who turned more and more to David for companionship. He eventually became "David's bird." Hence Slugger's determined and highly successful efforts to rid himself of Ann's presence, which he considered to be an intrusion on his relationship with David. Eventually Slugger began to bite both Ann and David, often drawing blood. Having learned that he could intimidate Ann and get away with it, Slugger felt free to exercise his aggression whenever he felt like it, and his behavior became completely uncontrolled.

HISTORY

Slugger's history revealed that he had had a previous owner. This owner had purchased the bird as a hand-fed baby. Making the fatal mistake of giving Slugger unlimited attention with no behavioral guidelines, he created a creature that thought it was the center of the universe. Eventually Slugger began screaming for continuous attention, which the owner could not possibly provide. Ultimately Slugger was sold to a pet store.

When Slugger arrived at the pet store, he refused to have anything to do with other birds. He did not recognize that he was a bird and had never developed flock skills necessary for relating to them. The pet store compounded Slugger's egocentrism by allowing him to sit wherever he chose. In addition, this particular pet store's method of merchandising its domestic birds was to allow them to sit out all day in an open play area in the company of many other birds, at night enclosing the entire area with wire. This in itself can and does create many behavior problems, for what owner can provide this type of living situation for his bird when he buys the bird and takes it home? The bird will suddenly have to adjust to a cage, probably for many hours of the day. Additionally, the bird is no longer continually surrounded by other birds and the attention of many people all day. His day becomes relatively solitary, as his humans are at work or going about their daily activities.

Slugger's experience at the pet store had severely exacerbated his screaming problem. When Ann and David bought him they had no idea of this problem, for he was beautiful and affectionate as only a Moluccan Cockatoo can be. (The personalities of Moluccan Cockatoos are extravagantly affectionate, demanding and intelligent. Because of this and their great beauty, they are eminently "spoilable." Behavior problems arise before the owners even realize what is happening.) Ann and David had no knowledge of the cockatoo personality and could only react with helpless frustration and deep disappointment as their lovely bird's undesirable behavior escalated, creating a truly miserable situation.

ANALYSIS

When Slugger arrived in the program, the two main goals were to stop his continual, inappropriate screaming and to improve his relationship with Ann and David.

Three difficulties had to be surmounted to achieve these goals:

1. Ann and David, as mentioned previously, were unaware of normal parrot behavior. They did not realize that a parrot is not a domestic animal, as is a dog or cat, and that techniques to alter a domestic pet's behavior are ineffective and inappropriate for use with a parrot. The pet store had instructed the couple to use such methods with Slugger. Believing that this advice was "expert," Ann and David unwittingly aggravated and compounded the bird's problems.
2. They equated discipline with punishment.
3. They did not know how to set realistic behavior guidelines and enforce them with Slugger.

BEHAVIORAL MODIFICATION PROTOCOL

Slugger needed to learn the following behaviors to exist happily in his human family:

1. To learn to respond consistently to commands to stop screaming. Ann and David had to learn what constitutes a normal amount of noise from their bird and accept and learn to live with this. (Ordinarily we would not attempt to teach the parrot to respond to a command to stop screaming. In this extreme situation it was a necessity due to the living accommodations.)

2. Ann had to establish a positive attitude toward Slugger, based on her new understanding that nibbling, wing opening and crest raising were not aggression toward her on Slugger's part. (In some birds, this may be aggressive behavior. But in Slugger's case, at least initially, they were simply the behaviors inviting interaction with his humans.)

3. Slugger needed to learn that he was not the center of the universe, and that attempts to gain attention with undesirable behavior would not be rewarded with attention, positive or negative.

IMPLEMENTATION

To achieve these goals, the following steps were taken.

1. Ann and David were requested to visit Slugger once per week to put into practice, with my guidance, the techniques being used with Slugger every day.

2. Slugger was taught to stay on a T-stand until I removed him. This required much persistence and patience, because Slugger climbed down at every opportunity to seek my attention. Every time he did this, he was returned to the stand with the command "Stay" delivered in a firm tone of voice. Once back on the T-stand, Slugger was given no further attention.

3. Initially, every time Slugger screamed, a gentle tap on the beak was delivered to reclaim his attention, accompanied by a loud "No!" Following this, the bird was once again ignored. Eventually just a verbal command sufficed to stop his screaming. Slugger was only given attention when he was quiet. (It is important to understand that this is not a recommended method to be used to correct screaming. The tap on the beak was to regain this particular parrot's attention, because he became completely self-engrossed when screaming. Under normal circumstances, I believe the tap on the beak and the firm "No" would only serve to encourage the screaming.)

4. Slugger was allowed to socialize with my own and other cockatoos here for training on a limited basis. Initially, he refused to have anything to do with the others. After a while, he consented to sit with them in the training area. He then gradually attempted to place himself in a position of dominance in the group, but the other cockatoos refused to allow it. This reinforced what Slugger was slowly but effectively learning—that he would not be allowed to take control of whatever situation he found himself in.

5. Slugger was given no attention by me, Ann, David or other visiting clients for attention-seeking tactics or screaming; however, when he sat quietly and behaved in the presence of other people, he was given praise and affection.

6. Slugger received attention and play activity from me regularly every day for a limited period of time. After playtime, he was placed on his T-stand or cage, and all his attempts to seek attention were ignored.

8. I counseled with Ann and David to make them aware of normal cockatoo behavior and to help them understand that some of this could not be modified, nor would it be desirable or appropriate to do so. I also helped them understand that the techniques I was using with Slugger were not punishment, but discipline and limit setting. Into this category fell such things as refusing him access to the floor of the training area. Ann and David also learned that caging Slugger, in combination with supervised time out of the cage, helped him feel more secure. It also encouraged Slugger to behave while he was out, because he felt less dominant.

9. I helped Ann learn how to hold and cuddle Slugger in a way that allowed her to control the bird's movements. Ann felt more secure with Slugger, and he began to feel relaxed and accepted by her. Slugger was then able to respond to her in a very positive way, seeking her attention and affection and returning them with enthusiasm.

FOLLOW-UP

Once Slugger went home all went reasonably well. Ann and David said the screaming was reduced by at least 200 percent. Occasionally Slugger would test to see if he might get away with some old behaviors, but using the techniques they had learned, Ann and David let him know they were "in charge." Ann and Slugger had a substantially improved relationship. Slugger was able to amuse himself in his cage with toys when necessary, and no longer conducted raiding forays with the intent to destroy everything he could get his beak on.

Ann and David had looked forward to Slugger's return home. They loved him and missed him and wanted to live happily with their parrot. However, several months after Slugger's return, Ann and David realized that a three-room apartment was not a place for even a well-behaved Moluccan Cockatoo. Unable to move, they decided it would be best to find a home for Slugger where he could vocalize in a normal manner. In my opinion, as hard as this decision was for them, they had reached their goal: a level of mutual understanding of and respect for Slugger, and he for them. They made a tough decision in their own and Slugger's best interests. Slugger now lives with a new family that loves him and provides an environment for him that many parrots would envy.

Paco, eleven-year-old male Yellow-Naped Amazon Parrot (*Amazona ochracephala auropalliata*); domestically bred/hand reared. **Presenting problem:** Screaming

Chris and Alex had just about reached the end of their rope with Paco's screaming. This behavior began about two years prior to the first phone call Chris made to Parrot Responsive. The screaming had started as an occasional outburst, but steadily spiraled out of hand.

Chris had an exceptional relationship with Paco. Alex and Paco did not have a relationship, as Paco, unless caged, would lunge to bite when Alex was near. This created a great deal of stress among the three. Chris began to think the best thing to do would be to give Paco up. But after ten years, this alternative was devastating to Chris. Calling me was a last attempt to solve the problem.

HISTORY

Paco was acquired through a local breeder at ten and a half months of age.

CURRENT SITUATION

Paco was fed a varied diet. I was informed that he would absolutely not eat pellets. His cage was in the living room, a room infrequently used by anyone but Chris. Her job required that she do a fair amount of paperwork at home. This is when she would spend most of her time with Paco—with him on her shoulder as she did her work. When Paco wasn't on Chris's shoulder he was on top of his cage. Chris had attached a simple play area to the top of the cage bringing the total height to about seven feet. There were food bowls placed on top of the cage as well. Paco's cage door was left open so he could go in and out at will. The only time Paco was placed in the cage was when the cage tray was being removed for cleaning by Alex. Chris told me that Paco hated being placed on a T-stand. She felt it made him very unhappy.

One major problem Alex had with Paco (in addition to the screaming and biting) was the mess around the cage. The play area allowed Paco's droppings to fall to the floor around the cage, and the food bowls on top of the cage added to the mess.

As much as Chris loved Paco, she realized it was no longer fair for Alex to have to live with the screaming that she herself was getting exasperated with.

ANALYSIS

The primary goal was to relieve the stress Paco's constant screaming had created. A relationship between Alex and Paco was not important to any of them, so eliminating the parrot's screaming became our main focus, to allow Chris to keep her beloved Paco. Two problems were encountered while trying to achieve this goal. First, because of the extremely close relationship between Paco and Chris, it was difficult to educate her. Chris felt there was no need to change how she related to her bird. Second, theirs was a long-term relationship, and only in the past two years had the problems surfaced. Unacceptable behavior was therefore well entrenched and not amenable to overnight change, regardless of the behavior modification techniques implemented.

BEHAVIOR MODIFICATION PROTOCOL

Paco needed to relinquish some control and learn that he was not the dominant one in the flock. Devoted discipline was not something that had been part of Paco's life. Chris needed to learn the importance of the changes necessary in their relationship to achieve some relief from Paco's screaming. For example, she had to acquire the attitude that teaching Paco to sit on a stand instead of his cage was a necessary skill that would help diminish screaming, rather than serve as punishment for Paco.

Alex needed to learn about normal Amazon behavior and decide if it could be tolerated and allowed in their household any longer. If Paco were to remain there, Alex would decide later whether he wanted to pursue his own relationship with the bird.

IMPLEMENTATION

To reduce the screaming, Paco was no longer allowed to come out of his cage on his own and to perch on top all day. He was taught to come out of the cage on Chris's arm and then to sit on a T-stand. This gave Paco a much improved understanding of how much time each day he was routinely going to spend with Chris. In addition, it brought him down to a level that placed him in a less dominant position, thereby removing an important stimulus for screaming.

We reworked the inside of the cage to allow for more exercise inside now that Paco was going to be spending more time in than out. Before rearranging, there were eight toys and four perches in a standard size parrot cage. Uncluttering the cage allowed greater ease in teaching Paco to step up to come out. I recommended that the toys be saved and rotated on a regular basis.

Paco came out for an hour or two each day until he became accustomed to sitting on the stand. No matter how unhappy Chris thought he was about sitting on the stand, he was to be either left there or returned to his cage. She was allowed limited time with him for petting and moral support. This use of time was to help teach Paco to be comfortable on the stand. Once this was comfortably underway, it was recommended that Chris start to bring the stand into other areas of the house where the family interacted. This allowed Paco to feel more a part of the family and lessen his need to scream for Chris's attention. However, I advised that it would not be a good idea to allow Paco to perch on her shoulder while watching TV, reading or working.

Although at first it might appear that Paco's relationship with Chris was being taken away, in fact, it still existed, and he was able to experience more interaction with Chris and Alex because of his improved behavior.

FOLLOW-UP

Upon last contact with Chris the screaming had diminished considerably. I advised that adherence to the program should continue to provide positive results. (A frequent mistake is to slack off and go back to the old comfort zones as soon as things seem to be improving.) She assured me that she would continue to carry out the program, so as to be able to keep Paco. Alex had decided that a closer friendship with Paco was not something he wanted to pursue. Chris was content with that decision as long as she could keep Paco.

Case Study #3:

Africa, nineteen-year-old male African Grey Parrot (*Psittacus erithacus erithacus*); imported/wild caught. **Presenting problem:** Biting

Africa had been biting for the past ten years. Obviously, then, he had not been handled much for the past ten years either. Bill and Cathy were seeking to find a way to reinstate a good relationship with their parrot. Both had been bitten to the point of drawing blood. Africa refused to step up on hand or stick, and allowed only minimal head scratching before he bit. Interestingly, Cathy and Bill felt that Africa was basically a friendly bird that bit people!

HISTORY

Africa was purchased from a pet shop when still young. Bill and Cathy were aware that he was an imported, wild-caught bird. Bill "tamed" Africa over a period of about a year after acquiring him. The parrot remained tame for the first eight or nine years. At his "tamest" he would not step up inside his cage. He would come out on a stick or climb out onto the top of his cage and then step up on Bill's hand. The biting started when Bill became busier with his career, not allowing much time for interaction between himself and Africa.

CURRENT SITUATION

Over the past ten years Africa had been left pretty much alone. He spent time out on top of his cage for a maximum of perhaps five hours a week. If someone accidentally leaned on his cage, Africa sneaked up and bit the person.

Bill occasionally and briefly was able to pet the bird on top of the head, or until the parrot tried to bite. If Bill tried to pet Africa while the bird was in its cage, a confrontation occurred. He was not afraid, but did not like being bitten. Cathy could sometimes pet Africa inside the cage, but was afraid of being bitten and exhibited her fear of the parrot.

Africa's flight feathers had been allowed to grow in fully and he had been fully flighted for eight years. The vocabulary Africa developed over this time was quite remarkable.

ANALYSIS

It seemed clear that Africa's biting was related to the development of independence and dominance resulting from dramatically reduced time spent with Bill. He became dominant in his very small and limited world. (The same set of circumstances with a hand-fed Grey would likely have resulted in feather picking.) Some interaction was present. For example, Bill could pet Africa on the head until he tried to bite. This of course only reinforced the biting/ negative behavior.

The goals were to stop the biting and improve the quality of the relationship among the three of them. Africa's age was a significant factor in the time needed to accomplish these goals, because the negative behavior had been in place for quite a long period. Necessary attitude changes for Bill and Cathy would not be easy either.

BEHAVIOR MODIFICATION PROTOCOL

Africa needed to be eased from his current dominant position and shown once again how to interact with people without biting. Bill and Cathy needed to learn to use devoted discipline consistently, with the result that quality time spent with the parrot would be increased. Cathy had to learn that handling Africa appropriately would reduce both her fear and the risk of being bitten. All of this would require time and patience.

IMPLEMENTATION

My first encounter with Africa was amusing as well as interesting. I approached Africa's box perch slowly and cautiously, calculating every move. Because of this bird's age I wanted to be extra careful not to overstress him. As I nervously approached, Africa nonchalantly stated, "It's okay, just relax." I nearly collapsed! I immediately became aware that my mind-set was not in the right place, and decided to take a break to work on it. I was being overly cautious.

PRPT was not immediately effective. Surprisingly, petting and stepping up from the stand progressed rapidly. Attempts to get Africa to step up inside the box perch usually resulted in the "crouch and growl" position. After about two weeks Africa simply capitulated and stepped up. He was finally willing to relinquish some of that control! Understandably it was not easy for him, but persistence and consistency in technique paid off. (He was given one or two opportunities to step up, and if not, then he was toweled and brought to the stand.)

Cathy and Bill came in once a week and were excited with the progress. I worked closely with Cathy to help her overcome her fear. Bill was busy learning to practice devoted discipline with the parrot, and continued working with Cathy at home to help her build the confidence she needed to work successfully with Africa.

FOLLOW-UP

Relationships were dramatically improved, and Africa is now able to spend valued time with his old buddy Bill. He understands now that he has his time each day to socialize with his family. Cathy is still taking it slow, trying to move beyond her fear and develop a growing relationship with Africa. I imagine Africa is "in heaven," with his restored friendship with Bill, and Cathy making every attempt to become his friend, also.

Case Study #4:

Mike, six-year-old male Blue and Gold Macaw (*Ara ararauna*); imported.
Primary problem: Feather picking/plucking

Mike's owners, Paul and Janice, called regarding Mike's feather picking. On a recent visit to their avian veterinarian they learned that the feathers Mike had removed were not likely to grow back. He had damaged the follicles to the extent that new growth would not be likely. The veterinarian suggested they call Parrot Responsive in the hope of preventing further damage.

Janice wanted to be able to pet Mike, but had never been able to. The most she was able to do was pet him on the beak briefly through the cage bars on a few occasions. Paul had developed a limited relationship with Mike in the four years they had owned him.

Blue-Fronted Amazon (*Amazona aestiva aestiva*) showing typical feather plucking pattern involving breast, abdomen and legs. *Scott McDonald, DVM*

The picking had started six months earlier, when Paul suddenly became much busier with his business. Janice wanted to fulfill the bird's social needs by learning to handle him herself.

Mike had become much noisier, and was starting to bite Paul when he did have time to spend with his macaw.

HISTORY

The parrot had been acquired from a pet shop, where Janice was told that he had recently been imported. She purchased him impulsively for Paul as a Christmas present. Paul liked the idea of a large parrot as a pet and developed a relationship with Mike.

CURRENT SITUATION

Mike's legs, crop area, chest and the undersides of both wings were picked bare when I first saw him. The relationship Paul had developed with his bird was a good, yet limited one. Mike was stick trained, and came off the top of his cage onto Paul's arm occasionally. No one except Paul could handle Mike. He stepped up on the stick for Janice when she needed to put him back in his cage.

Mike was allowed to sit on top of his cage during the day when Janice was alone with him. He wandered down once in a while, and Janice would then put him back on top of the cage. Although she was afraid of Mike, she wanted to be able to relate to him, and substituted food to make up for lack of Paul's attention, giving Mike treats when he got noisy or started picking.

ANALYSIS

Mike definitely perceived the lack of attention from Paul as neglect; he was being deprived both emotionally and socially, since the social stimulation he had become accustomed to had been withdrawn.

Janice was a very fast-moving sort of person who used her hands fluently when talking. When she talked to Mike she moved her hands around him with gestures that looked as if she were going to touch him but never actually did. Mike then lunged at her fingers because he interpreted her actions as teasing.

One goal was to stop the picking. As Paul was truly unable to spend more time with the bird, the second goal was to help Janice and Mike develop a relationship that would fulfill the macaw's need for socialization. The major obstacle was Janice's fear.

BEHAVIOR MODIFICATION PROTOCOL

I spent a great deal of time with Janice, teaching her how to move around Mike without inducing lunging and biting. This allowed her advances to be less threatening to Mike, with the result that he eventually allowed her to handle him. Mike also needed to become less dependent on Paul for attention and learn to relinquish his dominance over Janice. In addition, Mike's diet needed improvement, as it consisted primarily of seed.

IMPLEMENTATION

PRPT was the main factor in Mike's almost immediate cessation of picking and plucking. He thrived on attention and being petted, responding in a very positive way. This fulfilled the need for the social and physical contact he had been lacking.

A stick was utilized for a short time to get him out of his cage and onto a stand. After working with him on petting while on the stand, he soon began stepping up from his stand, and then from inside his cage.

Mike was bathed daily, and his feathers began to grow back in areas that had recently been plucked.

Self-inflicted wing web injury by Amazon parrot. *Scott McDonald, DVM*

Some parrots will not express their pleasure with the bath until they feel the moisture, after it has filtered through the feathers and onto the skin. *Diane Schmidt*

Janice continued to have a very difficult time with her fear. She had this way of moving her hands in a way that really did look as if she were going to touch Mike. He would then lower his head and ruffle up his nape feathers for the expected head scratch, and Janice would quickly pull her hand away. By the time I realized what she had done, she would already be repeating the same action.

It was very frustrating to Mike, and to me, also. I think it was equally frustrating to Janice. She needed to focus her thoughts on Mike's willingness to have contact with her, instead of her fear.

The major problem in trying to help her with her fear was that Janice and Paul only came in twice during the nine weeks Mike was here. They explained that they traveled frequently in connection with Paul's business, and although I explained that it was essential Janice be present to work with Mike, it just never happened. Both times Janice and Paul came in, Janice was able by the end of the session to pet Mike on the top of his head. She left ecstatic on both occasions. Because of this, Janice decided she would like to take Mike home and work with him at her own rate now that she had a better understanding of how to approach him.

FOLLOW-UP

Progress was slow, but Janice did seem to be losing some of her fear. Mike's picking did not resume. During their frequent trips, Mike was boarded with me, but I was out of town lecturing when Janice tried to call to board the bird once again. Unable to reach me, they decided to take Mike to a local pet shop to board. For some reason Paul decided to sell Mike to the pet shop owner for breeding. When I returned, Janice called to tell me what had happened. She said if they were going to give up the bird she would rather have it live here. To my surprise they brought Mike that evening. Mike was in terrible shape. I don't really know what the circumstances were—only that Mike was not the bird I knew a few months before, and the picking and plucking had returned.

I started pumping Mike full of good nutrition, and working with him on a regular basis. He calmed down, but the picking remained a problem. I started him on Annedda (pycnogenol), along with some other natural herbal preparations. He went into a molt, and his remaining feathers began to shine and glow with an iridescence I'd never seen in another Blue and Gold. The picking and plucking stopped, and some of the feathers that were never suppose to grow back did so. As of this writing, Mike has not resumed his picking/plucking.

Case Study # 5:

Lucia, two-year-old female *Eclectus* (*Eclectus roratus vosmaeri*); domestically bred/hand raised; **Presenting problem:** Feather picking/plucking

Lucia was brought to Parrot Responsive for severe feather picking and plucking. She had a few down feathers left on her body, and head feathers out of beak's reach were intact. Otherwise wings, tail and body were bare. Additionally, Lucia was screaming, biting and resisting being handled as she had been in the past. She was most receptive to her owner, Carl, and didn't want much to do with anyone else.

HISTORY

Lucia was purchased from a pet shop, which in turn had purchased her from a breeder. Lucia was approximately one year old when Carl went into the pet shop and discovered this beautiful bird. Lucia was out on a playpen, where she spent about eight hours a day. At night she was returned to a cage. We are uncertain how long Lucia actually lived at the pet shop.

Lucia, a female *Eclectus* Parrot, exhibits physical signs of complex stress with the underlying physical problem, giardiasis. *Diane Schmidt*

Lucia was treated for the physical problem, as well as implementation of behavior modification. *Diane Schmidt*

CURRENT SITUATION

Six months had passed by the time Lucia came to Parrot Responsive, but she had begun picking about one month after Carl had brought her home. When she started picking, Carl called the pet shop. They advised him to leave her out of her cage most of the time and to stop bathing her, because in their opinion this would encourage overzealous preening! The diet consisted primarily of seed.

Carl was a young college professor. He was also a single parent and his schedule was an erratic one. Therefore, it was difficult for him to supervise

219

consistently his children's behavior around Lucia. The joy and relaxation Carl had originally experienced with Lucia was disappearing.

ANALYSIS

Complex stress was the major factor here. Coming from a pet shop that allowed Lucia out of her cage to interact with customers all day, and then going to a home where she was caged for a portion of the day, was a significant change. Lucia appeared to be a victim of the "open air" concept that many pet shops now use. It's good marketing strategy, but what about the parrot when it moves in with a family that can't allow that amount of attention and freedom?

Poor diet was also a factor to be considered. In addition to looking smaller than normal because of the missing feathers, Lucia was considerably underweight.

The unsupervised children were a part of Lucia's complex stress, too. Children can do things to a parrot unintentionally, but which are nevertheless extremely stressful for the bird.

BEHAVIOR MODIFICATION PROTOCOL

We suspected an underlying physiological problem, combined with psychological stresses, so our first goal was to discover the state of Lucia's health.

The second goal was to provide some sort of relief for this obviously miserable little bird. She needed to learn to become comfortable with at least minimal handling again, and she also needed to learn to spend time comfortably in her cage on a routine basis. Her poor diet needed improvement.

IMPLEMENTATION

The veterinary examination revealed that Lucia was indeed harboring the protozoan *Giardia*. We treated her with several different medications to eradicate the parasite. In each instance the symptoms of picking were stopped but resumed shortly after medication was discontinued. She was retested for *Giardia* several times between periods of medication, only to find she was still positive. We experimented with different dosages and lengths of treatment. The longer the course of treatment, the longer before she started picking again after the treatment was stopped. But we could not keep her on medication indefinitely.

I put Lucia on Annendda (pycnogenol). After a week administering it in her distilled drinking water, she began to pick up weight and become more active. She began to play with her toys and become more playfully vocal. She started to seek attention from people when they approached her cage. Feathers began to grow back, and her skin lost its dry, dead look. She became more receptive to petting. After a few months of this natural plant derivative, Lucia had feathers on her wings and legs and a brilliant yellow tail, and was sprouting purple feathers on her chest.

We continued to work with her on adjustment to her cage for part of each day, and acceptance of petting and handling. We also provided her with a well-balanced pelleted diet and fresh foods. We resumed light bathing on a daily basis, as well as providing regular daily rest periods for her.

Carl and other family members were counseled about the goals of behavioral modification for Lucia, and what constitutes normal parrot behavior. Carl religiously visited Lucia and accepted the failures with the successes, and he was genuinely concerned about relieving Lucia's stress and improving her quality of life.

FOLLOW-UP

At the time of this writing, Lucia remains on Annedda (pycnogenol) with no side effects, and has grown many feathers. Although we do not know if she is cured, she is substantially better than she was. She picks on occasion when she is stressed by some extreme change, but this behavior has improved by 60 percent and her emotional state is 95 percent better. Only time will tell how successful we have been in permanently eliminating Lucia's stress and plumage-destructive behavior. But for now she is happy and healthy, and we feel very hopeful that she will remain so.

Case Study #6

Pepper, three-year-old male Blue-Fronted Amazon (*Amazona aestiva*); **Primary problem:** Wild-caught/not tame

Our avian veterinarian referred Pepper and his owner, Melisse. Melisse had received Pepper as a birthday present one and a half years prior to our meeting. Melisse had tamed her Umbrella Cockatoo a few years earlier, but she had not been able to make progress with Pepper. He was extremely hand shy. He rarely tried to bite, but he could not be handled. Melisse said he seemed very stressed all the time. She didn't expect miracles or require that he become a super cuddly pet. She just wanted him to be happier and less stressed.

HISTORY

The pet shop Pepper came from dealt primarily with imported birds. While Pepper lived in the shop he was placed at the mall entrance to the store. He was poked at, bumped into and more than likely tormented all day long. His diet in the store was inadequate and substandard.

CURRENT SITUATION

Melisse was somewhat frustrated and discouraged with attempts at taming Pepper. She was concerned because she didn't want to tamper with his personality. He had developed quite a vocabulary, and she enjoyed watching his clever antics while he played. They had a very pleasant relationship as long as she didn't try to touch. Still, she didn't want him to be well behaved at the expense of his personality, sitting like a "bump on a log," as she put it.

Pepper was in a large cage to which a play perch was attached, and he was allowed to sit on top of it from two to seven hours a day. His diet consisted of a high-quality parrot mix and varied fresh foods. Not a bad diet, but there was room for improvement in terms of balance.

ANALYSIS

Pepper had more than likely been affected by his stay at the pet shop. Melisse had been handling different animals all her life, and her handling of Pepper reflected her love and respect for him, but a year and a half later it was time for Pepper to give up his idea that close relationships with humans were harmful. Pepper was in control. He was using his fear to manipulate and control what he believed to be the safe way to live in this relationship. Parrots are excellent at exercising this sort of control. The only problem with their way is that if they haven't experienced it any other way, they don't know it can be much better when a caring, sensitive, conscientious human is in charge. This was the goal with Pepper: to show him a better way.

Melisse was not afraid of Pepper, which made things easier.

BEHAVIOR MODIFICATION PROTOCOL

The goals for Pepper were to relieve his fear of hands and build trust and confidence in humans. This would add a physical, touching dimension to the trust in Melisse he had tentatively begun to develop.

The goal for Melisse was to teach her how to handle Pepper and to gain control of Pepper's behavior and their relationship. I also needed to reassure Melisse that taming would not "break" Pepper, but would provide him with social skills that would allow his personality to bloom even more.

IMPLEMENTATION

PRPT was implemented as outlined in Chapter 7. Pepper was one of the Amazons that vocalize their displeasure about loss of control with a type of vocalization called machine gunning. It eventually stopped as he became comfortable with his newly adjusted relationships. (We basically ignore machine gunning during PRPT unless signs of overstress are exhibited.)

The outstanding memory I have of working with Pepper is that once we got to the stage of petting while on the arm, I found that he was afraid to be on the arm and facing an open room at the same time. I spent many hours standing with my face about eighteen inches from the corner, Pepper on my arm. Eventually we got to the point where we could do a quarter turn into the room, then a half turn—and finally a full turn.

During the training, Pepper remained rather subdued, and Melisse wondered if the old Pepper she knew would come back. I assured her that the personality she had grown to love would return. He was undergoing many changes. His antics and vocabulary were in waiting—much like a bird that has an excellent vocabulary but refuses to use it until it is comfortable. Melisse said what helped her overcome her concern about the absence of Pepper's "old" personality was the fact that he seemed so much calmer. She could see the fear disappearing.

I recommended that Pepper be furnished with a smaller cage at home, to prevent his refusal to come out on his owner's hand, should he decide to be stubborn. Melisse was not thrilled with this idea at first, but later came to realize that it made sense. I also recommended that he not be allowed to come out on his own and sit on top of his cage now that he knew how to come out on Melisse's hand.

FOLLOW-UP

Clients are supervised while they work with their parrots, forming their relationships. *Thom Qualkinbush*

Melisse now has over fifty breeding birds. Pepper started something big! Melisse says Pepper is the best behaved of all her birds. His personality returned along with his vocabulary, and he is now very calm. It's been about five years, and their relationship continues to grow. She doesn't plan to breed Pepper unless he shows signs of wishing to do so. Melisse is astounded that he has not exhibited signs of the sexual aggression that often manifests at maturity. Pepper's story shows that when parrots are properly socialized as young birds, the chances of sexual aggression appearing are much reduced, often never appearing at all.

Case Study #7

Magoo, two-and-a-half-year-old male Timneh African Grey Parrot (*Psittacus erithacus timneh*); **Primary problem:** Wild-caught/not tame

---

Magoo was wild-caught, and acted it when Cheryl and Kent brought him in. They had been unable to make any progress in the year they'd had him. Cheryl really wanted to be able to handle and enjoy Magoo, which at present she couldn't do. Indeed, on several occasions she had seriously considered selling him. She was afraid of the parrot and was not, under any circumstances, going to attempt handling him. Nevertheless, she had seen an article in a national bird magazine about Parrot Responsive and decided to call and see if there were any chance for her and Magoo.

HISTORY

Magoo was purchased from a pet shop. The shop owner told Kent, when he bought the bird as a birthday gift for Cheryl, that Magoo had been tame at one time.

CURRENT SITUATION

Magoo's diet consisted mainly of parrot mix the pet shop had recommended, and he also ate a few fruits and vegetables, though reluctantly. He occasionally took a seed from Cheryl's hand through the cage bars. Magoo came out of his cage when it was quiet, climbing out of the open door and up to the top of his cage. The door was left open all day.

Cheryl and Kent could not touch Magoo or get him to step on their hands. Cheryl felt that if these things were not possible, it would not be fair to herself or the bird to keep him. She thought that perhaps training might help and stated that she wanted Magoo to be "the perfect bird." Further, it was very important to her that Magoo talk, because of the outstanding reputation African Greys have for their ability in this area.

Kent was not very interested in developing a relationship with Magoo, although he liked Magoo, found him entertaining and felt it would be nice if he could handle him. But he was very supportive of Cheryl and her wish to work at a relationship with the birthday gift.

ANALYSIS

Magoo was not extremely wild. He probably had been handled in the past or had been properly exposed to people. Although Cheryl did not know a great deal about parrots, she was an animal lover and had a strong desire to make this work. It appeared she should easily be able to overcome her fear. Once calmed and comfortable, Magoo would probably even talk—a logical and expected progression in developing parrot/human relationships. The basic goal would be to teach Magoo and Cheryl, together, to relate to each other physically as well as emotionally. This meant that Magoo would be able to stay with Cheryl and Kent.

BEHAVIOR MODIFICATION PROTOCOL

Cheryl needed to learn there was no such thing as "the perfect bird." She also needed to learn to trust Magoo and become confident in handling him.

Magoo needed to develop trust in both his people. As with most situations involving wild parrots and inexperienced handlers, the bird controlled the situation with his natural fear responses, which had to be overcome.

IMPLEMENTATION

As Cheryl visited each week, she gained more and more confidence through PRPT, as did Magoo. We started with getting Magoo used to being lightly petted on the back, followed by scratching on his head and progressed to stepping up. He learned this quickly. In Magoo's case we pretty much followed PRPT by the book. Through consistent handling and persistence, PRPT was effective. It didn't take long for Cheryl to realize there really was no such thing as "a perfect bird"; PRPT and the accompanying discussions usually clarify this sort of misconception. The program is designed to help parrots and their people to notice and appreciate little advances as well as big ones, and to make the most of them.

FOLLOW-UP

The relationship between Cheryl and Magoo continues to grow. Every time we are in contact there is some new development in the relationship. Magoo now talks, and he and Kent have even developed a relationship. However, Cheryl is Magoo's preferred person. Cheryl loves her bird and is happy that she didn't let him go when the going was rough. She also now enjoys feeding Magoo a varied, interesting and well-balanced diet, which he accepts and consumes with gusto.

Case Study #8

Mickey, two-year-old male Yellow-Naped Amazon Parrot (*Amazona ochrocephala auropalliata*); domestically bred/hand raised. **Primary problem:** Physical abuse from previous owner

---

Mickey's story is an especially heartbreaking one. Mickey was a physically abused bird. Whether this occurred because of ignorance on his first owner's part, or because this person deliberately sought to inflict pain, cannot be determined with any certainty. However, Mickey's first owner subsequently purchased a large macaw, which was then resold because it developed problems similar to the ones for which Mickey was brought to Parrot Responsive.

The first contact I had with Mickey's new owners, Ellen and Mike, was a telephone call. Ellen was discouraged, heartbroken and deeply concerned about Mickey. She and her husband lived a ten-hour drive away from Chicago and were experienced pet owners. They shared their lives with dogs, cats and a few other, smaller birds. They had never had such desperate problems with an animal. For Mickey was exhibiting such an overwhelming fear of Mike and Ellen that he had beaten his wings bloody while repeatedly flailing about his cage in desperate attempts to get away from them.

Although Mickey's reaction to Ellen was not so extreme (Ellen could scratch the bird's head through the cage bars), any attempt on her part to enter the cage to clean and feed was met with panic and bleeding. The Yellow-Nape's bleeding problem had been caused initially by breaking blood feathers at the skin line, and Ellen took Mickey to a veterinarian because of this. The veterinarian recommended trimming Mickey's broken feathers but was unskilled, and the resulting inexpert trim exacerbated the bleeding problem. As new feathers emerged, they were broken repeatedly as the parrot desperately tried to escape Mike's presence. When these feathers were removed to stop the bleeding, they regrew and were broken once again. And again, and again, and again. However, it was this same veterinarian who recognized the severity of Mickey's problem and urged Mike and Ellen to seek help.

Ellen and Mike were at a loss to understand why Mickey was so deeply terrified of Mike. Mike had never handled or even verbally reprimanded Mickey. Because of the severity of the parrot's problems, and the potential for life-threatening hemorrhage, it was agreed that Mickey should be brought to Parrot Responsive immediately. It is a tribute to the love and concern of Mickey's people that they were willing, indeed eager, to make the ten-hour trip to bring the bird to Chicago. And that further, every weekend without fail, they visited the bird, staying the weekend so they could both work with Mickey with my guidance. So began Mickey's first visit with me.

At the outset, effecting positive changes with Mickey was hampered by lack of an adequate history of this bird's life before he came to live with Ellen and Mike. When Mickey arrived for his first stay with me, he was a little less than a year and a half old. Ellen only knew that Mickey had had a previous owner who had sold him to the pet store where she first saw him. Mickey was the store mascot. His communication skills endeared him to owner and customers alike. Although he refused to allow men near him, he allowed a few women to scratch him through the bars of his cage. According to the pet shop owner, Mickey had followed his first owner around like a puppy. She told Ellen that this person had stated that Mickey was the most lovable young bird he had ever seen. Although he wasn't for sale, Ellen finally convinced the pet store owner to sell Mickey.

When Ellen and Mike arrived, I was distressed by the bird's obvious terror and the condition of his wings. I also felt great concern and compassion for Ellen and Mike, who I realized had "been through the ringer" with Mickey. Mickey had been through the ringer, too. The only other piece of information that could be elicited about Mickey's history was that he was supposedly a hand-fed baby. Ellen and Mike both doubted this because of Mickey's terror of anyone who approached his cage or tried to handle him. (Mickey did have a closed band, which ordinarily indicates a domestically bred bird. But in the last few years, smugglers have developed a counterfeit closed band that is very difficult to tell from a genuine domestic band. So in certain instances, one might purchase a bird that appears to be domestic but in fact has been smuggled.)

One thing in Mickey's favor was that he had been given, and accepted, an adequate diet. This probably helped him to replace lost blood more quickly and suffer fewer problems because of blood loss than another bird on a poor diet might have experienced.

ANALYSIS/FIRST VISIT

Although I knew that Mickey's present owners had not abused the bird and were caring people who would never harm an animal, I felt strongly that

Mickey had been physically abused, probably by his first owner. There was no information about this, however. Lack of concrete facts that would explain Mickey's behavior made it difficult to devise a specific approach to the bird's problem. There were, nevertheless, two goals that I felt could be realistically achieved for Mickey. First, a complete physical examination and laboratory workup would be undertaken by our avian veterinarian to determine if the bird's behavior had its basis in a physical health problem. The second goal involved teaching Mickey simple skills in a supportive, nonthreatening environment. This was meant to help him lose his terror of people (particularly men) and therefore decrease his panic thrashing and risk of further wing injury.

BEHAVIOR MODIFICATION PROTOCOL

A trip to the avian veterinarian revealed that Mickey's health was good. There was nothing physical that could account for the Yellow-Nape's terror of people.

Mickey's wings were carefully evaluated, but short of helping him to feel comfortable in the presence of people, there was little that could be done to prevent reinjury. I provided thick padding on the floor of the training area, as well as a ready supply of coagulant. Clean towels were kept at hand so Mickey could be quickly restrained if he began to flail and cause his wings to start bleeding.

Working with Mickey was challenging. His extremely slow response coupled with the risk of bleeding required endless care and patience. Simple things, such as cleaning his cage or replenishing food and water, drove the bird to panic and thrash, resulting in reinjury. Often he and I, as well as cage, floor and walls, were splattered with blood. It became necessary to work with Mickey only every three days, allowing him two days between sessions to rest and recover.

The first step was to teach Mickey to stay on a T-stand, away from the security of his cage, and to learn that nothing bad would happen to him in this "exposed" position. Many times Mickey jumped to the floor, and despite the thick padding and low perch, injured his wings. He would then have to be restrained quickly and gently with a towel to stop him from beating his wings to pieces. Once in the towel, the bird would calm immediately, only to begin screaming and thrashing as soon as he was released.

The second step was to teach Mickey to accept petting. Saying "Touch beak, Mickey," I gently touched his beak, progressing to scratching his tummy and finally the bird's head and cheeks. Mickey came to enjoy this and learned that the word "touch" would be followed by a pleasant experience. He would not, however, allow his back to be touched. These first two steps were accomplished in my office. Mickey remained there, keeping me company for long periods, as I completed paperwork and made telephone calls.

Finally, the third step was taken: to teach Mickey to step onto my arm and feel comfortable doing so. As expected, it took a great deal of time for Mickey to learn this and feel secure. But eventually the goal was accomplished.

All through the weeks that I worked with Mickey, Ellen and Mike came every weekend, spending Saturday and Sunday, then making the long, tiring drive home late Sunday afternoon. When Mickey began soliciting Ellen's attention by climbing on her arm and ruffling his neck feathers for a comfortable scratch, she was ecstatic. Mickey also seemed to be developing a great deal of confidence with Mike.

As Mickey progressed, Ellen found that she could do things with the bird that he had never allowed her to do before, and still would not permit from Mike. I advised Ellen to go slowly and refrain from these activities until Mickey would allow Mike to do the same things.

At the end of six weeks, Ellen, Mike and I decided Mickey was ready to go home. He had come a long way from the panic-stricken, bloody bird that had arrived. His wings were healing. Ellen and Mike felt they would be able to continue working with Mickey successfully at home. If questions arose, I was only a phone call away. With a great feeling of accomplishment, I saw Mickey and his family off on their final journey home.

FOLLOW-UP

After Mickey had been home for a week, Ellen called to say that Mickey was doing very well. She and Mike continued to be amazed and gratified by the bird's responsiveness to them. And both were deeply relieved to know that Mickey was no longer the victim of crippling fear.

Two weeks later I called to monitor Mickey's progress, leaving a message on the answering machine. Ellen called back in tears. Mickey had reverted to his old behavior. She and Mike were discouraged, upset and thinking seriously of giving Mickey up. To make matters worse, Mike's father, who had repeatedly expressed a lack of faith in the whole idea of "a shrink for a parrot," was now indulging the "I told you so" syndrome. He told the couple that they should give him the parrot so it could live out its life in solitude in a cage, not having to deal with people. Ellen and Mike did not know what choice to make to provide the best quality of life for Mickey. But they loved him dearly and had seen for themselves what a wonderful bird he could be. They had experienced his genuine enjoyment, if only for a short time, of a good relationship with them.

I strongly encouraged them to bring Mickey back. I asked Ellen to contact the pet store from which she obtained the bird, to find out anything that would help them help Mickey. The young couple agreed to both requests, and so Mickey returned to Parrot Responsive for the second time.

HISTORY/CURRENT SITUATION/SECOND VISIT

When Mickey arrived the second time, his wings were once more bloody. He reacted to Mike and me with screaming panic. Mike, at this point, had stopped all overtures to the parrot because of its obvious terror. Mickey's reactions to Ellen were not so extreme. He tolerated her presence without damaging himself, but only if she did not attempt to enter his cage to clean and feed him. If Ellen attempted these activities, Mickey immediately threw himself into the same panic behavior he exhibited around Mike.

Two things may have been significant in causing the parrot's regression. First, because of Mickey's progress at the time they took him home, Ellen and Mike felt they might have expected too much in terms of his ability to socialize. However, they placed his cage in a bedroom in an attempt to make his reentry into family life less stressful. This led to the second possible cause of Mickey's regression. He left his cage and crawled under the bed. He refused to come out by himself, so Mike and Ellen had to move the bed. This may have confused and frightened Mickey, causing him to react with his old panic behavior. There was also an incident with a friend of the family at a party that Ellen and Mike gave. It was never quite clear to me what exactly happened, but Ellen felt that it resulted in the first indication of regression.

In the meantime, Ellen made every effort to uncover any facts pertaining to Mickey's life with his first owner. The pet store owner, faced with Ellen's concern and persistence, finally "fessed up." Mickey's first owner had, indeed, purchased him as a baby from a breeder in Alabama. Mickey had been brought home, hand fed and weaned.

At about four or five months of age, the bird went through his "teething" stage. All young parrots develop in this manner for two reasons. First, the beak and tongue are used instinctively to explore the environment. The bird makes no distinction between tender flesh and inanimate objects. Second, at this time the bird begins to establish its independence from its parents (either wild or surrogate), using behavior such as lunging and/or nipping. Many people, including Mickey's first owner, interpret such behavior as meanness and do not understand how to handle it. Mickey's first owner reacted by hitting the bird as often as Mickey nipped him. This response occurred many times, several times sending Mickey crashing into the wall. In addition, Mickey's first owner physically resembled me, but had a very loud voice and belligerent manner. No wonder that Mickey was terrified of hands, men's in general, and mine specifically. Mickey had indeed lived through hell. A loving youngster, indulging his wild instincts with an owner who had no understanding, and less tolerance, of such behavior, had become an emotionally crippled and physically abused bird. In the wild a bird can fly from danger. In a home setting he can only react with biting and/or fruitless escape attempts in an effort to protect himself.

PROTOCOL/IMPLEMENTATION/SECOND VISIT

What to do for and with Mickey? Ellen, Mike and I decided that the bird should remain with me for as long as it took him to learn that men, even those resembling his first owner, could be trusted. Mickey was scheduled for a visit to the avian veterinarian for another evaluation of his wings. Following this, it was decided that no further work should be done until his wing feathers had completely regrown, to avoid any possibility of injury. This little parrot would occupy a safe, nonthreatening place at Parrot Responsive while he healed and observed my interactions with the other birds (birds can often learn a great deal about relationships with people from this simple tactic).

A complicating factor in Mickey's situation was that he was now two years old. It is at this age that many hand-fed Amazon parrots begin to experience preadolescent hormonal surges preparatory to sexual maturity. In this group of species, aggression accompanies elevated hormone levels.

In consultation with Mickey's avian veterinarian, the possibility of placing the bird on a short course of steroids to alleviate hormonally mediated aggression was discussed. In this way Mickey would be much more amenable to learning the skills necessary for a good relationship with his family. They, in turn, would have to learn how to deal with the sometimes problematic behavior that accompanies sexual maturity in the Amazon parrot. This is much easier when a firm basis of love, trust and limit setting (devoted discipline) have already been established.

Viewing the steroids as a last resort, I decided to try a different route. Mickey's nerves seemed to be shot. I wondered about possible nerve damage or other conditions that might have resulted from the physical abuse Mickey had received. One thing was clear. Mickey was stressed, day in and day out. He spent most of his days just hanging in the corner of his cage. Bleeding was once again a daily occurrence.

Again in consultation with the avian veterinarian, we decided to give Mickey vitamin B complex injections once a week. If nothing else, it might alleviate some stress. After the first injection there was marked improvement in his stress level. After the first month of injections, when Ellen and Mike came to visit Mickey, they were amazed at the difference in him. Ellen stood with the door of the cage open and her hand inside the cage, which had not been even a remote possibility before this. Over the six months Mickey was on the injections, we saw varying degrees of improvement. There was much less thrashing in the cage at the beginning of each week (after his injection) and noticeable regression toward the end of the week. Mickey began to seek relationships with people even when outside the cage. The vitamin B complex, although not explainable in scientific terms, seemed to enable Mickey to relate to people again and get past some of his fear.

In addition to the vitamin B complex injections, Mickey was worked with on a regular basis. Various phases of PRPT were used, depending on the circumstances of each particular day and Mickey's ability to interact on that day.

FOLLOW-UP

There were many heartbreaking moments with Mickey, many discouragements and many rewards. Now Mickey is living happily with Ellen, Mike and the other birds and animals in the household.

I received a letter from Ellen a few months after Mickey went home the second time. Her words made the work with Mickey well worth the effort.

> Much has happened since Mickey came home. He is my miracle bird. Even though progress has been slow, it has been sure. Mickey has learned to trust again, not just me but others also, including Mike. Mike can now reach around Mickey to get his food dish out of his cage and Mickey doesn't react at all. He can clean his cage and it is no big deal. The fear is all but gone from Mickey's life. He is much more relaxed, talks all the time, has been singing his own songs, is very active and is no longer cage bound. He takes discipline in stride. I never could have disciplined him before as we all know I couldn't even touch him. Now he begs to be touched. As far as personality, he has the best personality of any of my birds. And that is a statement I thought I would never make about Mickey. He makes us laugh all the time. When he eats, he giggles under his breath or expresses his joy. One thing I am very careful about is visitors. Mickey, however, usually makes the first move, begging visitors for attention. Everyone is in love with him: they pet him, he gets on their hands, he charms everyone. Mickey never had joy in his life before. The fear is gone from his eyes. I don't think anyone could imagine unless they have experienced this: the great joy I feel every day in having Mickey be just a normal Amazon.

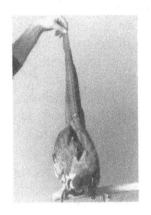

Once the parrot is comfortable with hands, having the trainer moving all around it, and stepping up—we begin working on petting while the parrot is on the arm. This macaw had the reputation of hating to have its tail touched when it first arrived at Parrot Responsive. Now the bird views it as a pleasant chance to display its beautiful tail. *Diane Schmidt*

With patience and persistence the same level of comfort that can be achieved on the T-stand...

...can be accomplished on your arm. This usually becomes a milestone in the relationship. It is hoped you will never forget the process that led up to the moment, or its meaning—the start of a truly mutual relationship where affection can be shared. *Diane Schmidt*

A Plea to All Parrot Owners and Would-Be Parrot Owners

We don't often encounter birds that have been physically abused. Far more troubling are birds that are abused emotionally. This type of abuse we encounter far more often at Parrot Responsive. When we speak of emotional abuse, we refer to the parrot that is overindulged to the point that people don't want it around any more. In other words, it's "spoiled rotten." These are the birds that generally end up going from home to home, sometimes finding haven with a breeder. But in some severe situations the bird is so distraught and confused that breeding isn't even the solution. We are not referring to the owner who unknowingly overindulges his young parrot and then realizes that things are not developing properly and tries to rectify the situation. We are talking about the situation in which the person *wants* the bird to be overly dependent, coddling it to the point that the parrot becomes totally neurotic. The bird may appear fine while in this situation, but inevitably the situation changes, rendering the owner unable to continue with his self-imposed slavery of the bird. I recall a situation when a Sulphur-Crested Cockatoo was brought in to me because the owners could not keep it any longer. This cockatoo literally moaned for weeks. The moan actually sounded like a long, drawn out "Mom." It wouldn't eat. It was neurotic beyond belief. To help a parrot with this kind of grief is not an easy task, and some never get over it.

The point we would like to make is this: Think about your parrot's future as you go about your daily activities. How do you think it would react if you suddenly were not there? What can you do to help prepare it for that possibility? Remember the long life span of your parrot. If you are considering a parrot for a pet, contact a reputable behavior modification specialist and ask him what you can do to avoid overindulging your bird. Start off on the right foot, *for the bird's sake*.

A Miscellany
of Issues

In this chapter the authors will examine various issues that have been raised in previous chapters, as well as considerations not yet addressed. Some pertain directly to the companion bird owner, others more directly affect the parrot breeder. Yet these issues should still be of interest to *any* individual keeping parrots, for the parrot breeders of tomorrow are the companion owners of today. In any case, all owners of psittacids must realize that parrot ownership is not viewed by the conservation, zoological and animal rights communities in quite the same light as domestic animal ownership. There are those in positions of public power and credibility who feel those sharing their lives with these most fascinating of all birds are holding them in public trust. It therefore behooves us to be well acquainted with all facets pertaining to parrots, and to exercise our guardianship of them with the utmost care and responsibility, lest in the future we are denied the honor and privilege of having them in our homes and aviaries.

Additionally, those issues that directly affect parrot breeders eventually impact companion parrot owners. For example, the recently enacted federal legislation that prohibits the import of all parrots for sale as pets has been a matter of grave concern to aviculturists, who worked hard to ensure that some wild-caughts would continue to be imported for breeding programs, thus keeping captive gene pools healthy and viable. Although this consideration was not of concern to most people with one or two pets, the fact that the only birds available will be domestically bred, hand-reared parrots with price tags much larger than those of their wild-caught cousins will be. Further, because

...If we encounter some misunderstandings while determining what our relationship will be—GoTizo, an African Grey Parrot. *Diane Schmidt*

aviculturists will have access to very few imported birds for their breeding programs as a result of the Wild Bird Conservation Act of 1992, problems of inbreeding will inevitably lead to genetic problems that plague purebred dogs and cats, unless captive gene pools of various species are rigorously and responsibly managed. For example, outcrossing, use of species studbooks and participation in cooperative breeding programs are techniques that must be utilized to attain this end. If responsible management of gene pools is not implemented, health problems will then become the concern of the individual who has acquired a parrot so afflicted.

USE OF PSYCHOTROPIC DRUGS FOR TREATMENT OF PSITTACID BEHAVIOR PROBLEMS

General Considerations

We have mentioned elsewhere that mood altering drugs (psychotropics) are sometimes used in the treatment of stereotypic (perseverative or obsessive-compulsive) problems of parrots. In this section, we will explore the reasons for this therapy and some of the medications that are beginning to be used with greater frequency in parrots with feather picking disorders (FPD) and self-mutilation tendencies.

Although these drugs are used commonly for humans having various emotional health problems, their use with psittacids is in its infancy. In human medicine these medications are most usually used in conjunction with appropriate forms of psychiatric or psychological counseling. They should never, except in the most unusual of circumstances, be used alone for treatment of FPD and automutilation. Psychotropics should be used as an adjunct to a good program of behavioral modification. They are not the first choice of treatment for this class of behavior problems, but should be considered only after the modification program has been in place and consistently implemented without noticeable effect. If this is not done, the situation creating the problem is never identified and remedied, and only the symptom (i.e., FPD or automutilation) is treated. No lasting benefit can be expected, for once the drug is discontinued, the "symptom" will usually reappear.

Use of Psychotropics
for Psittacine Aggression

Psychotropics, to our knowledge, are not used for control of aggression in the parrot, nor have we found any evidence in the literature that this has been done. It is the opinion of at least one expert who works with canine and feline aggression problems that the use of psychotropics on dogs and cats for control of aggressive behavior may aggravate it, and that a good behavioral modification program is the best and perhaps only treatment modality with a chance of success (Marder 1991).

When Should the Use
of Psychotropics be Considered?

For those parrots which prove refractory to behavioral modification after a long period with consistent owner compliance, and for whom the avian veterinarian feels psychotropics may be of benefit, the owner's responsibility has not ended. It has begun again on another and extremely important level, for parrots on these medications require constant monitoring to assure that proper response to medication is being obtained, and that side effects are being kept to a tolerable level. These drugs are not without serious side effects, and their use is so new that dosage adjustment is still somewhat an art and may always be. Further, treatment of obsessive-compulsive behavior such as automutilation and FPD with these very potent drugs is subject to species differences in dosage and response. "Species differences most likely play a much greater role in FPD than cultural differences exert in OCD [obsessive-compulsive disorder] of humans" (Ramsay and Grindlinger 1992). This group of veterinary clinicians and researchers goes on to say that many more studies are needed to differentiate among species differences regarding the use of psychotropics in the treatment of FPD and related problems.

Scarlet Macaw (*Ara macao*) with chronic feather plucking disorder. *Scott McDonald, DVM*

Veterinary and Owner Responsibility

Parrots that are candidates for psychotropic drug therapy require prior laboratory evaluation. Because these drugs can cause kidney and liver problems, birds already having undetected diseases of this nature could experience severe difficulties if placed on them. Once on psychotropics, parrots will need periodic laboratory work to determine if the drugs have caused health problems. Owners must be constantly on the alert for any side effect symptoms and report them to the bird's avian veterinarian immediately.

As with any medication that will be given over a period, the owner will need to decide if he is able or willing to provide this care. The decision will be partially based on the method of delivery. If the medication can be given in water or placed in soft food, it is a simple matter to ensure the daily dose has been given. If the parrot must receive the drug by mouth once or twice a day, then it becomes more difficult and time consuming. If this should be the case, then the owner will not be able to leave the bird for extended periods unless there is another competent individual who can administer the medication properly. Obviously, finding such a person can be difficult.

Rationale for Treatment

There are several human mind-altering drugs that have been adapted for use with avian patients. It has been documented clinically and experimentally that constant stress depletes certain chemicals (neurotransmitters) in the brain, specifically the limbic system and the hypothalamus. (These areas are linked to emotions, reproduction, sexual behavior, rage, fear, aggression, defensive reactions, biologic rhythms and various other "automatic" functions.) Deficiencies of involved neurotransmitters result in various kinds of emotional problems. Stereotypic behavior such as FPD and self-mutilation may be two such difficulties. Treatment of these disorders by use of psychotropics is aimed at replenishing normal levels of neurotransmitters so that nerve function can return to normal levels (Johnson 1987).

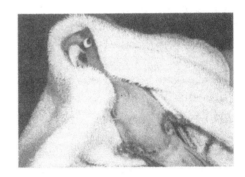

This Peach-Fronted Conure (*Aratinga aurea*) has inflicted serous wounds to its feet. *Scott McDonald, DVM*

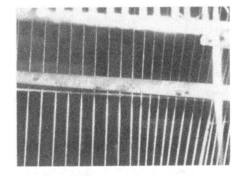

This perch belonging to the same conure (shown in previous photo) is saturated with blood from the parrot's automutilation behavior. *Scott McDonald, DVM*

We suspect that there will be readers (not necessarily aviculturists) who will mentally wring their hands at the thought of using a mood-altering drug as a therapeutic adjunct for what most have customarily thought a consequence of living in the domestic setting. Traditionally, FPD and related problems have been considered a result of chronic stress induced by inadequate environment and management of domestic and companion animals. There is no doubt that these situations do create such problems. However, we speculate that wild parrots may also manifest self-induced feather problems, which are never seen by field workers because these birds would not long survive with extensive plumage damage.

Indeed, even if such a bird were found dead and exhibiting feather damage, it would probably be ascribed to the attentions of a predator, and not the actual cause of the parrot's death. Further, given the almost instant destruction of small carcasses by scavengers, it is highly unlikely that these birds would ever be observed under normal range conditions. We have pointed out elsewhere that the flock situation is not without stress for its members, especially those at the bottom of the social structure, and that various kinds of emotional dysfunction have been noted by field researchers studying wild species.

If these conditions do exist in wild individuals (and this has yet to be documented), then it is not surprising that they would manifest in the domestic setting also. Additionally, breeders may unknowingly contribute to the increase of feather-related problems in domestics by breeding feather pickers. It then follows that supervised and cautious use of psychotropic medication to alleviate behavior painful and distressing to the parrot is not at issue ethically. In human society, we do not deny the benefits of lithium salts to those suffering with manic-depressive disorder, or medication to the person with stress-induced stomach ulcers. We should therefore provide the most effective drug therapy to the parrot (or any other domestic/companion animal) whose emotional status is less than ideal. This is an act of kindness, not of irresponsibility.

Kinds of Psychotropics Currently Used, and Side Effects

There are two types of medication that have been used in the treatment of FPD and related disorders: drugs from mainstream, traditional Western medicine and medications from the holistic, homeopathic approach to disease treatment.

Of those agents from traditional mainstream medicine, the following are most commonly found in use: lithium salts, Valium (diazepam), Sinequan (doxepin), Elavil (amitriptyline HCl), Aventyl (notriptyline HCl), Anafranil (clomipramine HCl) and Haldol (halperidol). As drug research continues, there may be more effective medications for use with FPD parrots. For the present, the agents listed have been used with varying degrees of success with several species of parrot.

Side effects may include (depending on dosage, length of use and species) drowsiness, lethargy, thyroid enlargement, decreased thyroid function, sharply increased water intake and urination, impaired kidney function, increased appetite, tremors, weakness and liver impairment (Gilman and Goodman 1985; Johnson 1987; Leuscher et al. 1991). Symptoms of acute toxicity can include nausea and vomiting (regurgitation in parrots), convulsions and diarrhea.

There is another group of psychotropics called monoamine oxidase inhibitors. At present these drugs are not used in veterinary medicine, but as research continues they will no doubt eventually find their way into the veterinarian's armamentarium. When this group of drugs is used, there are important dietary restrictions that must be observed. Any protein-containing food that has undergone degradation, aging, smoking, pickling or fermenting must not be eaten. Examples include any cheese except cottage and ricotta, brewer's yeast, Italian green beans, liver, sausages, smoked fish, canned or overripe figs, avocados and raisins in large amounts (Johnson 1987).

For obvious reasons, none of these medications should be given to parrots that are breeding or feeding nestlings.

African Grey Parrot (*Psittacus erithacus erithacus*) demonstrating severe feather-picking disorder and automutilation. This parrot has removed feathers, picked at its skin, and seriously scratched the area surrounding its eyes. *Scott McDonald, DVM*

So far, we have discussed medications from traditional Western medicine. There are, however, various nontraditional substances that have been used with some degree of success: homeopathic herbal remedies. In the last few years there has been an upsurge of interest in alternative medicine for people, and this interest has now reached the veterinary community (Griffith 1993; Stephanatos 1992). Various holistic and herbal remedies are now being tried, either alone or in tandem with traditional veterinary therapy for FPD and related problems. They have also been used to stimulate the healing process in various disorders (Harrison 1993; Murphy 1993). Substances such as belladonna, nux vomica, arnica and nat mur are mentioned as having some positive benefit for parrots with feather destruction disorders, and *Echinacea* has some clinical value as an immune system booster. Use of such substances will continue and probably increase as they demonstrate their clinical usefulness. They may offer real help for picking, plucking and self-mutilating parrots as veterinarians gain familiarity with their application in these cases.

The holistic approach to wellness/illness includes the spiritual. Donn W. Griffith, D.V.M., says, "Spiritual considerations include the power of prayer, good thoughts, good intentions, tender loving care by a client and hospital staff, and a belief in powers beyond our ability to measure, that are an integral part of the healing process" (1993).

THE "NEUTERING" OR ALTERING QUESTION

"Can I have my parrot neutered?" is a question sometimes asked by bird owners, especially new ones. Although this seems a perfectly logical question taken in the context of cat and dog ownership, it is not appropriate when speaking of parrots for two major reasons. First, because of the anatomic position of the gonads (which are located in extremely close proximity to the kidneys and adrenal glands), their removal or destruction by conventional, laser or cryosurgery is not possible without killing the bird.

Second, because many parrots are endangered or threatened in their range countries, destruction of the breeding capabilities of those in captivity is irresponsible, even if it were possible to alter them. Those individuals who feel they cannot deal with a parrot during its hormonally charged annual breeding season, and who do not wish to follow a behavioral modification program, should feel honor bound to place such birds in a good breeding program. Preservation of these parrots' genetic material into succeeding generations is critically important and a responsibility to be taken seriously by those who feel, for whatever reason, that their parrots are no longer happy or suitable as companions.

Hysterectomies are performed on breeding hens with a history of chronic and/or life-threatening egg-binding episodes (Doane 1991). This avoids placing a bird at future risk. Ovaries are usually left intact, although once the oviduct has been removed, no further egg laying will occur. (The oviduct in a bird serves the equivalent function of the uterus in humans.) It is marginally possible that because the ovaries remain, hens could possibly still experience breeding behavior. In no case, is hysterectomy a viable alternative for preven- tion of sexual aggression or other behavioral difficulties in the parrot.

PLACEMENT OF PARROTS IN BREEDING PROGRAMS

Reasons for Placement

Regrettably, the human/parrot interface sometimes fragments beyond repair. There will always be some few birds, for whatever reason, that do not respond to behavior modification, although the authors wish to emphasize that this is the exception, not the rule. Owners exist who do not wish to submit to the rigorous responsibility of carrying out a long-term modification program with their birds.

There are also instances in which the human/parrot system intermesh continues to function well and in a mutually satisfactory way, but the owner feels his parrot would be happier with a companion of its own species and opposite sex. Often we hear the comment, "I still get along fine with my bird, but it just doesn't seem as content as it used to be." Still another scenario involves the owner who has kept a rare and endangered species as a companion. Sometimes during the period in which the parrot has lived with its person, its status in the wild has worsened in the long slide to extinction. Owners in these cases often cannot morally justify keeping their birds as singletons and take the responsibility for rectifying the situation.

In addition to these examples, there are situations in which severe allergy or hypersensitivity pneumonitis (which can become life threatening) neces- sitates placement of a companion parrot elsewhere, and sometimes a change in living quarters precludes keeping one's bird. Certainly in these cases, if the parrot is happy being with humans, placement with another individual or family as a companion is acceptable. However, even in these situations, breeding placement is an alternative the owner may wish to consider.

When any of the foregoing exist, it is time to consider placement in a breeding program. It is not surprising that many owners feel reluctant to take this step, no matter how difficult the situation has become. Because our society is rife with reports of puppy mills and some dog and cat breeders who disregard the health and well-being of their breeding animals, many companion bird owners assume this to be the rule for the majority of parrot breeding situations. A further complicating factor is that many owners cannot reconcile the necessity of keeping parrots in breeding flights or cages and equate this with severe curtailment of their "freedom" (even though allowing the bird to occupy their homes with unclipped wings may have led to the breakdown of the relationship in the first place).

The Breeding Situation

It becomes necessary, then, to discuss what a breeding program is, and is not. First, the matter of keeping breeding parrots in flights or cages continuously: Birds that do not live together will not form the necessary bond for breeding. In an aviary full of aggressive breeding birds, an individual with free access to the area is in serious and immediate danger of great injury. Breeding birds are territorial and implacable in protection of cage, mate and nestlings. Second, the assumption that breeding flights, cages and aviaries are sterile environments is faulty. Parrots that are not happy, healthy and secure will not breed. Breeders therefore make every effort to assure that their parrots are in peak physical condition, and that the breeding environment is enriched. Good aviaries have pleasant music, plants, pictures on the wall and sometimes an aquarium or other kinds of visual stimuli. In indoor aviaries natural light is provided, or if this is not possible, full-spectrum lighting is used. Many breeders provide dawn and dusk lights that supplement main lighting. This serves to cushion indoor birds from the shock of being awakened by a "blast" of light. It may also induce the daily hormonal peak of sex hormones birds should experience and that may be necessary to induce normal breeding behavior (Scanes 1986). Often environmental audiotapes are played, sometimes synchronized with daily misting. Breeding flights and cages are usually supplied with a variety of perches, toys and suitable nest boxes. Parrots in aviaries such as this have not only their mates with which to relate and socialize, but also the stimulation of parrots in the surrounding area to watch and with which to interact vocally.

Regarding the matter of mates, many bird owners considering placement of their parrots in a breeding situation would be amazed at the closeness of the bond between pairs of birds. It is touching (and for the inexperienced, eye opening) to see a parrot that has demonstrated its unwillingness or total inability to relate well to people interact with a beloved mate. At the risk of anthropomorphizing, it is quite evident that these birds feel great affection for one another and derive immense pleasure from living with their own kind, breeding and raising young. It is not an exaggeration to state that in such situations the parrot has been given a new lease on life, and that the owner who makes this decision on behalf of his bird's welfare has acted in the kindest and most responsible of ways.

Choices in Breeding Placement: Doing It Yourself

Once the decision has been made to breed a parrot, what choices in placement does the owner have? If the owner and parrot have a long history together, and a relationship that has in the past been happy, the owner may want to consider finding a mate for the bird and breeding the pair himself. Although we would not recommend this to a beginner who has a rare bird, many parrots make suitable choices for breeding by the novice. If the parrot is one of the larger species, it is recommended that the owner find a knowledgeable breeder who will be willing to act as consultant until experience has been gained.

Breeding parrots is not for the fainthearted. It takes an amazing amount of commitment, patience and willingness to persist in the face of frequent failures and sometimes heartbreaking tragedies. Nor is breeding parrots like breeding dogs and cats. As a field of endeavor it is still in its infancy, and what we do not know about the breeding biology of parrots would fill volumes. Additionally, it may take a pair many years to produce young. Very often, the first few clutches are infertile, and many species nest only annually. It also happens with great regularity that for whatever reason (and the reasons are myriad), fertile eggs fail to hatch. Or if they do hatch, the neonates die. Often hens fail to care for their young properly, especially first clutches—parrots learn the art of parenthood by experience, as do humans—and the breeder may have to resort to artificial incubation for pairs that refuse to incubate or care for nestlings properly. This area of breeding is an art, and success only comes with much hands-on experience.

The cost of maintaining breeding parrots can be staggering. Veterinary bills, appropriate food and supplements, the cost of the owner's labor (hard, dirty work), pairs that take years to reproduce, all create a situation in which the owner cannot realistically expect to make expenses, let alone a profit. Nevertheless, for those special people who want their parrots to remain in their lives, and who wish above all else to produce babies, breeding one's own former pet may be the answer.

However, it is not all heartbreak. Words are inadequate to describe the joy of seeing a youngster hatch, and raising babies and seeing them thrive and develop is a privilege few ever experience. There is a feeling of satisfaction in knowing that one is able to give back to parrots a little of all they have given us. There is pride, too, in knowing that one is contributing in some way to the conservation of these birds, either by rearing them for the pet trade, thus removing the incentive for smugglers to bring in illegal parrots; or if one is working with endangered species, knowing that one has contributed to their continued existence on this beleaguered planet.

Breeding parrots opens a whole new horizon of challenge, learning and experience. Serious breeders, because of the nature of what they do, are able to justify keeping species that they would never otherwise be able to observe and learn about. Parrot breeding means taking on new and serious responsibilities for learning for as long as one engages in it. Serious breeders (and there should be no other kind) must subscribe to journals in the field, attend seminars, buy books and join and support avicultural organizations: local bird clubs; regional groups, and national groups, such as the Association of Avian Veterinarians and the Psittacine Research Project at the University of California/Davis. Novice breeders must learn an entirely new concept of parrot health care—that of flock preventive medicine and the closed aviary concept. (The philosophy and practice of aviary health is entirely different from the concept of individual companion bird health with which the breeder is already familiar.) The beginning breeder must learn how to place the weaned youngster suitably when it is ready to leave his care. He must execute this obligation responsibly.

Because of the serious nature of parrot breeding and the need for all breeders to adhere to the highest possible standard of aviculture, we recommend that readers who wish to become breeders investigate the California Model Avicultural Program, and apply for membership. (Model Avicultural Program, P.O. Box 1657, Martinez, CA 94553). This program certifies those breeders and aviaries as meeting necessary standards of peer and veterinary review. This benefits parrots and aviculture in general by indicating to other professions such as conservation and zoological communities that parrot breeders are professional and conduct their affairs in accordance with recognized and approved standards.

Choices In Breeding Placement: Someone Else's Facility

If the parrot owner does not wish to embark on his own breeding program, but wishes to place his bird with another breeder, there are several important considerations of which he must be aware. Finding a suitable program requires care. Also, the terms under which the bird is placed are important and should be *very carefully* indicated and agreed on *in writing* by owner and breeder.

The owner has three choices relative to compensation for his bird. The first is to sell the parrot outright to the breeder. The second is to give the bird to the breeder, with payment in the form of a baby from the parrot and its future mate, or for the price of one of those babies when sold. Sometimes a percentage of the sale price of the entire first clutch can be negotiated. In either of these cases, once the baby or money has been presented by the breeder, the breeder retains sole and unencumbered ownership of the parrot. The third choice is a breeding loan, in which the bird is placed with the breeder, usually for a continuous payback based on the sale price of every baby produced by the pair. With this type of arrangement, the parrot's original owner will be responsible for a specified portion of feed, vet and maintenance costs. This kind of arrangements is basically a partnership.

It is important to realize that with any of these agreements, the owner must accept that the parrot will be placed with a mate with which it will bond for life, usually with deep and lasting attachment. It is therefore morally and ethically reprehensible to demand the return of a bird on breeding loan for any but the most pressing of reasons. Nor will it be possible for the former owner to visit his bird once situated in a breeding setting with its mate. Visits are disruptive to the parrot's adjustment and the breeding activities of other aviary birds. Further, for reasons of security and avoidance of disease spread, breeders do not usually allow visitors to their aviaries for any reason. Another realistic consideration is that as mentioned previously, parrots (even well-bonded pairs) may take years to reproduce, and some pairs never do. Because of this, the former owner must be prepared to wait a long time for a baby from the pair's first clutch, unless he has agreed to take a weanling from another pair of the same or a different species.

Regardless of the agreement decided on by owner and breeder, terms must be specified in a binding contract signed by both parties. This will avoid any misunderstanding. Informal breeding loans and other kinds of transactions in which parrots have been placed in breeding situations often lead to bad feelings, legal disputes and broken friendships. Sometimes friendships disintegrate for other reasons, and the parrot's original owner may demand his bird's return in an act of spite. This is tragic for the birds involved, and only a written, legally binding, signed agreement can prevent such occurrences.

Choosing a suitable breeding program for one's parrot is sober business and should be carefully and thoughtfully accomplished. If the owner does not have friends or acquaintances who breed parrots, the avian veterinarian is a good place to start for recommendations. Membership in a bird club will also provide good information about those who breed, their reputations and track records. We do not recommend placing the parrot with a pet store for sale as a breeding bird. This could result in tragic misplacement of the parrot, with serious consequences to the bird and to the individual or family who purchased it.

Once the owner has recommendations in hand, he may then begin to contact those breeders who might be interested in taking the bird. The owner should do all he can to assure himself of the quality of the program he is considering for his parrot. This can be difficult, for it is rarely possible, for reasons already mentioned, for the owner to see the aviary where the bird will spend its life. However, there are other ways to determine the suitability of a particular facility. It may be possible for the owner to see babies that are being hand reared, and to judge for himself the breeder's credentials in this area. Many breeders are willing for owners to visit their homes, and in this way the owner may judge the degree of cleanliness and care given to companion birds and other pets, and the home itself. The breeder may be willing to give names and numbers of people who have purchased youngsters from him, although, again, many do not wish to have their telephone numbers and names provided without prior permission.

There are also questions the owner can ask the breeder that will give a good indication of commitment and responsibility to his or her program. We caution, however, that the owner should not "grill" the breeder, but try to ascertain the answers in pleasant, general conversation. Most breeders will respect the owner who is caring enough of his bird to have its best interest at heart, unless they are made to feel like suspected criminals by the manner in which questions are asked. Try to find out how birds are housed, and what efforts are made to enrich the breeding environment. Inquire into diet and supplements used, the kind of lighting in place and veterinary care given. Quarantine and isolation procedures in use will give a good indication of the breeder's awareness of the importance of these issues to the health of your bird and those already in his program. In addition, many breeders have special qualifications that enhance their breeding programs: memberships in avicultural organizations, activity in the avicultural legislative arena, authorship, research participation, federal permits to work with endangered species, subscriptions to lay and professional publications in the field—all indicate a more than casual interest in the health and well-being of birds in the breeder's charge.

Choices in Breeding Placement: Where Not to Place

We have already examined the inadvisability of placing parrots in pet stores in the hope they will find their way to a good breeding program. There are also other alternatives sometimes exercised by the owner that are definitely not acceptable, or have only dubious merit. First, never open the window and let the parrot go. It is sad that such a subject even needs discussion. However, there are those well-meaning but misinformed individuals who think that "giving the bird its freedom" is a natural and kind thing to do. Their rationale is that parrots are basically wild and will have the skills to survive in the outdoor environment. *This is not true.* The temperate zone is not the same as the tropics. Food supplies, predators, disease-causing organisms and hazards such as streets, traffic, guns and tall buildings with windows that look like mirrors are things with which parrots have no evolutionary or practical experience. They therefore mean death, sooner or later.

Parrots are not equipped to survive the extreme temperature ranges in this or any other temperate zone climate and will not "adapt," as some people believe. Even in subtropical climates such as the southeastern and southwestern parts of the U.S., hazards of civilization will bring the bird's life to a quick end. Another very important point is that for those parrots that do manage to survive, there is concern, especially in warm climates, that they will preempt the niches of native wildlife. Although this is far from adequately documented, it is just another reason for those with political and quasi-political power to lobby against ownership of any parrot as a companion.

Selling or giving the parrot to another as a companion-quality bird is dishonest and unfair to bird and prospective owner. There are those few individuals who have the capability to take such birds and work with them so that decent quality of life is possible. However, good intentions on the part of the prospective buyer are not enough. Years of experience with problem birds and solid background in the techniques of appropriate behavioral modification are necessary.

Do not contact your local zoo in the hope that personnel will be thrilled to acquire an expensive exotic bird at no cost. Not only do they not have the space to take unwanted parrots (and in many cases the skill required to breed them), but zoo personnel often tend to look with a jaundiced eye indeed on people who have acquired exotic pets and find they cannot deal with them. This is not surprising, because they hear of only the failures, not of the millions of happy, well-adjusted parrots living in harmony with humans. Owners wishing zoos to take their parrots only confirm professionals' attitudes that parrots should not be kept by private individuals for any reason. These same professionals have the ears of legislators, and their opinions are respected as expert, thus they can have great influence on legislation written that may seek to restrict private ownership of exotic birds.

Adoption programs are occasionally found, administered by local bird clubs. Although there are a few that are excellent, the eventual placement of the parrot will be beyond the owner's control in all but a few cases. As with pet stores, the chance that the parrot will be placed unsuitably is high. Very few local animal shelters will accept parrots, either. They do not have the space or expertise to handle them.

Euthanasia is not a choice for parrots who are no longer suitable as companions. The genes they carry are far too valuable to waste in this manner.

A Note on Placement Etiquette

"I just want to find a good home for my bird, but I have to get my money out of it." This is a statement heard countless times by breeders approached by owners wishing to place their birds, and it is not attractive. It indicates that money *is* the primary issue, not the bird's welfare, and casts the owner's motivation into grave doubt. Breeding parrots is time consuming, expensive and hard work. Many parrots offered to breeders will need extensive physical and emotional rehabilitation before they can be given mates, and this involves a great investment of time and money by the breeder. If money is the true issue, owners should be honest about it.

The breeder will either consider buying the bird or not, depending on the price asked and the species involved. (It is sometimes difficult for owners to understand that breeders have varied sources from which to acquire birds for their programs. It is rare for a breeder to pay retail price unless the parrot in question is very hard to obtain and desperately needed.) Breeders will not pay retail price for a less than perfect specimen. Nor do they wish to finance someone else's failure. Breeders recognize that there are good and valid reasons for placing a former companion parrot in their aviaries as a breeding bird, but owners who indicate an overriding determination to receive unreasonable amounts of money will in most cases be turned down flat. Some payment for a parrot is reasonable to expect. It is not sensible to assume that a breeder will pay inflated prices for the privilege of rehabilitating, vetting and caring for one's bird for the rest of its life.

Responsibility of Breeders and Pet Stores When Selling Parrots

The responsibilities of parrot ownership have been covered extensively in this book. They have been emphasized and reemphasized. It is through books such as this, and the efforts of breeders and pet store personnel, that the public will begin to realize that parrots are more than just animated bundles of gorgeous feathers that sometimes talk and *always* squawk. We strongly feel that until those in the position of supplying parrots to the companion animal public take client education seriously, avoidable tragedies will continue to occur. Such misfortunes will always claim the attention of radical animal rights groups, conservation and zoo professionals and legislators. These people rarely, if ever, hear of the successes.

If we do not make every attempt through client education to minimize unfortunate human/parrot relationships, we may find ourselves in the position of no longer being able to keep parrots, either as companions or breeding birds.

The public is quick to seize on that which it is programmed by various sources to perceive as destructive or environmentally immoral (regardless of the true state of affairs, which most will never have a real opportunity to know and understand). This is especially true presently, in a society where, increasingly, the emphasis is on the glib, quick fix, the emotional catch phrase or slogan. Many individuals are too willing to have their thinking done for them by "experts." Many prefer to abdicate responsibility for ascertaining pertinent facts on both sides of a question and to make independent decisions about issues of concern.

For all the above reasons, clients must be discouraged from choosing the wrong parrot. Lifestyle and commitment vary from person to person. It is important to match the parrot and person with regard to personality. Although this may be somewhat difficult, most breeders and pet store personnel spend enough time with their charges to understand when and where appropriate matches can be made. A list of accurate informational reading material should be provided to every new parrot owner. Reasonable health guarantees should be provided, along with a list of *qualified* avian veterinarians from which the client can choose. The seller must make it clear that veterinarians without training in avian medicine are not appropriate for the parrot. Discussion of appropriate diet is most necessary, especially for those who assume that seed is suitable fare for parrots.

It is absolutely essential that new parrot owners be instructed on how to handle their birds when they get home. The do's and don'ts should be clearly explained, with their rationales. The sorts of behavior expected, why they occur and whether or not they are acceptable and appropriate should be reviewed. How new owners should handle common "settling in" behaviors should not be omitted. Sellers must also offer consultation to the new parrot owner on a reasonable basis for the first few weeks of ownership. Guidance and information from an expert during the first crucial weeks when the human/parrot system intermesh is being accomplished will go far to prevent future behavioral problems.

With regard to "advice from an expert," it must be every breeder's goal to become such an expert. Knowledge of psittacine behavior as well as health and illness issues are indispensable. Professional reading, participation in seminars and workshops and membership in avicultural organizations should not be viewed as frills, but as necessary parts of professional responsibility to one's chosen field. Participation in programs such as the California Model Avicultural Program should be the goal of every breeder. Pet store personnel, too, must take responsibility for ongoing education about the birds they sell.

If all this sounds as if cost-effectiveness and profits were at the bottom of the list, it is because, for the short term, they are. By taking a longer but less immediately remunerative view of the future, all who breed, sell and live with birds will ensure that this most delightful of all companion animal relationships will continue unhindered. It will also ensure that the public will continue to want and purchase parrots, thus providing the ongoing economic benefits so necessary to maintain healthy, productive aviaries and businesses.

BREEDING FOR COMPANION PARROTS OR FOR REINTRODUCTION

Captive breeding of parrots, both for companions and for reintroduction to their natural habitat, is assuming great importance, both of which have to do with conservation of this group of birds as a whole. Breeding birds for the pet trade has obvious value, for such birds learn from infancy to trust humans and thus become better companions. Breeding for this purpose also has relevance for conservation, however, which may not be immediately clear to most readers. When domestic parrots are available as companions, it dramatically reduces the market for wild-caught birds. Populations in the wild are then at much less risk of capture for the pet trade, and can remain in natural habitats to reproduce and renew their kind. Accessibility of domestic parrots also reduces incentives for smugglers to ply their illegal trade. The companion bird purchaser also sees no advantage, legally or in terms of pet quality, to buy a smuggled bird. This, too, protects wild parrot populations.

Breeding some species for reintroduction and repopulation of their original habitat has proven its worth. The peregrine falcon program is one program that has been very successful and has received much positive publicity. The California condor program is another that can claim credit for preventing extinction of the species. Captive breeding of parrots for such programs is a valid conservation strategy that is beginning to be implemented for a few species, such as the Thick-Billed Parrot (*Rhynchopsitta pachyrhyncha*), some species of Central American macaws and at least one of the Caribbean Amazon species. Undoubtedly, as knowledge and expertise increase in this relatively new conservation strategy, more such programs will follow.

Reintroduction of parrot species has a threefold benefit. One, the wild populations will have a chance to thrive and increase. Two, the habitat in which these birds exist will gain more value and thus a better chance of protection. Third, parrots have been shown to have value as a draw for ecotourism, again boosting the value of the ecosystems in which they live, and subsequent protection of these areas.

Breeding parrots for the purposes of companions and as reintroduced specimens require vastly different approaches by the breeder, however. Qualities required for suitability as a companion are not those needed for survival capabilities in the wild, and in fact are detrimental to survival. A companion parrot should possess a sweet temperament, and a degree of docility and flexibility that allows it to fit comfortably into the domestic setting is necessary. Such birds should possess a reasonable degree of ability to bond with their humans, as well as a willing dependence on them. In other words, those qualities we prize in our dogs and cats are also prized in the companion parrot. Captive breeding of these birds for the pet trade is still in its infancy, and such traits are far from fixed at this time. However, as time goes on and our ability to breed parrots with consistent success increases, those who breed for the companion bird sector will be better able to select for desirable pet characteristics and inevitably will do so. This has been true in domestic breeding for companion, draft and food animals throughout human history.

At present, companion-quality parrots are produced solely through the early socialization and environmental enrichment provided by breeders during the hand-rearing process. These techniques, coupled with the increasing ability to select for companion animal traits, should produce superlative psittacine pets. However, this is *not* the way to produce parrots for reintroduction programs.

Parrot breeders who wish to participate in this endeavor must realize that there is a huge difference between pet and conservation breeding. Those who take part in conservation breeding must accept this and make the necessary changes in rearing practices of such birds. Breeders who derive their greatest satisfaction from interaction with their unweaned charges would do well to refrain from this very different kind of breeding. The goal here is to produce a parrot that is *not* dependent on humans, which will have the necessary physical development and stamina to forage, breed and survive in the wild. It must learn necessary mating behaviors. The parrot must also learn to want nothing to do with people. Parrots destined for reintroduction programs must be able to recognize natural predators and master evasion techniques.

It is obvious that such parrots are the exact opposite of the ones we enjoy as friends and companions. Toward this end, youngsters destined for reintroduction are reared with as little human contact as possible. It is the usual practice, if at all possible, to leave these babies with their parents to learn the necessary traits of "parrotness." If hand feeding is necessary, no interaction with the surrogate parent is permitted other than the feeding process itself. All newly weaned youngsters are placed within immediate sight and sound of adults of the same species so that they may learn appropriate sexual behavior and will learn to choose mates of their own kind at maturity. Additionally, large flights are required so flying and other kinds of exercise develop stamina and endurance needed for survival, and the foods these parrots will find in their native habitats must be provided lest the bird starve from a failure to recognize what may be eaten once in its original habitat.

This young man is enjoying the friendship of his Timneh African Grey Parrot (*Psittacus erithacus timneh*) and Mealy Amazon (*Amazona farinos farinsa*). He is comfortable with both of them, and they with him and each other. *B.M. Doane*

It is obvious that breeding for these two very different purposes requires very different approaches. We point this out because breeders themselves often do not realize this and may have unrealistic expectations that any domestically bred parrot could easily be the subject of reintroduction. This belief probably comes from a need (however unnecessary) to justify breeding for the companion market at a time when those wishing to appear politically "correct" ignore or denigrate the valid contributions of aviculture to the conservation of all parrot species. Those who breed companion parrots must learn to understand the value of their contributions to conservation. They should take pride in realizing that their responsible efforts have a far-reaching effect on the quality of life of the birds they raise, and the people who are fortunate enough to share their lives with their parrots, their friends.

REFERENCES

Alderton, David. 1991. *The Atlas of Parrots*. Neptune, NJ: T.F.H. Publications.

Bakker, Robert T. 1986. *The Dinosaur Heresies*. New York: William Morrow.

Baver, Fred. 1990. "Eclectus Parrots." *Bird Talk* (October).

Beissinger, Steven R., and Enrique H. Bucher. 1992. "Sustainable Harvesting of Parrots for Conservation." In *New World Parrots in Crisis: Solutions from Conservation Biology*, ed. Steven R. Beissinger and Noel F. R. Snyder. Washington, DC: Smithsonian Institution Press.

Blanchard, Sally. 1991. "The Parrot Learning Process." *Bird Talk* 9:9 (September).

Bradshaw, John. 1988. *The Family*. Deerfield Beach, FL: Health Communications.

Brice, A. T., B. A. Cutler, and J. R. Millam. 1992. *Cockatiel Embryonic Development*. Oakland: University of California Division of Agriculture and Natural Resources.

Brykczynski, Terry. 1985. "Kea, King of the Mountain." *Bird World* (January).

Budiansky, Stephen. 1992. *Covenant of the Wild: Why Animals Chose Domestication*. New York: William Morrow.

Caplan, Frank. 1973. *The First Twelve Months*. New York: Perigee Books.

Caplan, Frank, and Theresa Caplan. 1984. *The Early Childhood Years*. New York: Bantam Books.

Clark, William D. 1991. "Hyacinth Macaws: Nesting in the Wild." *AFA Watchbird* 28:3 (June/July).

"Cockatiel Embryonic Development." 1992. In *Exotic Bird Report* 4. University of California/Davis, Department of Avian Sciences.

References

Coyle, Patrick G., Jr. 1987. *Understanding the Life of Birds*. Lakeside, CA:

Davis, Christine. no date. *Avian Communication*, audiocasette produced by Christine Davis, P.O. Box 816, Westminister, CA 92689 Summit Publications.

Davis, Christine. 1989. "New Techniques in Pet Avian Behavior Modification." In *Annual Conference Proceedings of the Association of Avian Veterinarians*.

Derrickson, Scott R., and Noel F. R. Snyder. 1992. "Potentials and Limits of Captive Breeding in Parrot Conservation." In *New World Parrots in Crisis: Solutions from Conservation Biology*, ed. Steven R. Beissinger and Noel F.R. Snyder. Washington, DC: Smithsonian Institution Press.

Desborough, Laurella. 1991. "Parrots of the South Pacific." *Bird Talk* (May).

Doane, Bonnie Munro. 1991. *The Parrot in Health and Illness*. New York: Howell Book House.

Dreikurs, Rudolf. 1964. *Children: The Challenge*. New York: Hawthorn Books.

Duke of Bedford: 1969. *Parrots and Parrot-Like Birds*. Neptune, NJ: T.F.H. Publications.

Erwin, T. L. 1991. "An Evolutionary Basis for Conservation." *Science* 253:5021 (August 16).

Fink, Millie. 1992. Lecture at Northern Illinois Parrot Society (July).

Fitzgerald, Hiram, Barry M. Lester, and Michael W. Yogman. 1986. *Theory and Research in Behavioral Pediatrics*. New York: Plenum Press.

Forshaw, Joseph M. 1989. *Parrots of the World*. 3d ed. Willoughby, NSW, Australia: Lansdowne Press.

Forsyth, Adrian, 1988. *The Nature of Birds*. Ontario, Canada: Camden House Publishing.

Gilman, Alfred A., Louis S. Goodman, Theodore W. Rall, and Murad Ferid. 1985. *The Pharmacological Basis of Therapeutics*. 7th ed. New York: Macmillan.

Gordon, Thomas. 1989. *Discipline That Works: Promoting Discipline in Children*. New York: Plume.

Gore, Rick. 1993. "Dinosaurs." *National Geographic* (January).

Griffith, Donn. 1993. "Holistic Medicine and the Avian Practitioner." *Journal of The Association of Avian Veterinarians* 6:3.

References

Groves, Philip M., and George V. Rebec. 1988. *Introduction to Biological Psychology*. Dubuque: Wm. C. Brown Publishers.

Harrison, Greg J. 1993. "Herbal Immune Stimulation." *Journal of The Association of Avian Veterinarians* 6:3.

Hohensee, Michael. 1989. *Land of Parrots: Black Cockatoos*. Turramurra, NSW, Australia: Yoho Productions P/L, dist. by Documentaries of Australia. Videotape.

Horner, John R. 1988. *Digging Dinosaurs*. New York: Workman Publishing.

Jacob, S. H. 1992. *Your Baby's Mind*. Holbrook, MA: Bob Adams.

Johnson, Cathy. 1987. "Chronic Feather Picking: A Different Approach to Treatment." *Proceedings of The First International Conference on Zoological and Avian Medicine, Hawaii*.

Johnson-Delaney, Cathy. 1992. "Feather Picking: Diagnosis and Treatment." *Journal of The Association of Avian Veterinarians* 6:2.

Kavanau, J. Lee. 1987. *Lovebirds, Cockatiels, and Budgerigars: Behavior and Evolution*. Los Angeles: Science Software Systems.

Kerr, Michael E., and Murray Bowen. 1988. *Family Evaluation: An Approach Based on Bowen Theory*. New York: W. W. Norton.

Levinton, Jeffrey S. 1992. "The Big Bang of Animal Evolution." *Scientific American* (November).

Low, Rosemary. 1980, *Parrots: Their Care and Breeding*. Poole, Dorset, England: Blandford Press.

Luescher, U. Andrew, Donal B. McKeown, and Jack Halip. 1991. "Stereotypic or Obsessive-Compulsive Disorders in Dogs and Cats." *Veterinary Clinics of North America: Small Animal Practice: Advances in Companion Animal Behavior*. Philadelphia: W. B. Saunders.

Maier, Henry W. 1969. *Three Theories of Child Development*. New York: Harper and Row.

Marder, Ann R. 1991. "Psychotropic Drugs and Behavioral Therapy." *Veterinary Clinics of North America*.

Michel, George F. 1991. "Human Psychology and the Minds of Other Animals." In *Cognitive Ethology*, ed. Carolyn A. Ristau. Hillsdale, NJ: Lawrence Erlbaum Associates.

Munn, Charles A. 1992. "Macaw Biology and Ecotourism, or 'When a Bird in the Bush is Worth Two in the Hand.'" In *New World Parrots in Crisis*.

Murphy, Joel. 1993. "Homeopathic Remedies for Feather Picking." *Journal of The Association of Avian Veterinarians* 6:3.

O'Connor, Raymond J. 1984. *The Growth and Development of Birds*. New York: John Wiley and Sons.

Paul, Gregory S. 1988. *Predatory Dinosaurs of the World*. New York: Crescent Books.

Pepperberg, Irene. 1989. "Training Communicative and Cognitive Abilities in an African Grey Parrot." In *Annual Conference Proceedings of The Association of Avian Veterinarians*.

———. 1991. "A Communicative Approach to Animal Cognition: A Study of Conceptual Abilities of an African Grey Parrot." In *Cognitive Ethology*.

———. 1992. *Communication with Alex*. San Gabriel, CA: CMS. Audiotape.

———. 1993. Personal communication to author.

Peters, Robert. 1991. "Keas: their Aviculture and Breeding." *American Federation of Aviculture Annual Conference Proceedings*.

Ramsay, Edward. 1991. "Self-mutilation Syndrome." *Journal of The Association of Avian Veterinarians* 5:2.

Ramsay, Edward C., and Howard Grindlinger. 1992. "Treatment of Feather Picking with Clomipramine." *Proceedings of The Association of Avian Veterinarians*.

Reisner, Ilana. 1991. "The Pathophysiologic Basis of Behavior Problems." In *Veterinary Clinics of North America*.

Roediger, Henry L., III, J. Philippe Rushton, Elizabeth D. Capaldi, and Scott G. Paris. 1984. *Psychology*. Boston: Little, Brown.

Rosskopf, Walter J., Jr., and Richard Woerpel. 1990. "The Psittacine Mutilation Syndrome: Management, Incidence, Possible Etiology and Therapy." *Proceedings of The Association of Avian Veterinarians*.

Scanes, C. G. 1986. "The Pituitary Gland." In *Avian Physiology*. 4th ed., ed. P. D. Sturkie. New York: Springer-Verlag.

Skinner. B. F. 1974. *About Behaviorism*. New York: Vintage Books.

Slagle, Priscilla. 1992. *The Way Up from Down*. New York: St. Martin's Paperbacks.

References

Soucek, Gayle. Personal Communication, 1993.

Stephanatos, Jeanne. 1992. *Holistic Pet Care*. Las Vegas: Agape Video Systems. Videotape.

Stettner, Laurence Jay, and Kenneth A. Matyniak. 1968. "The Brain of Birds." In *Scientific American: Birds*. San Francisco: W. H. Freeman.

Toman, Walter. 1976. *Family Constellation: Its Effects on Personality and Social Behavior*. New York: Springer-Verlag.

U.S. Fish and Wildlife Service. 1987. *Appendices I, II, and III to the Convention on International Trade in Endangered Species of Wild Fauna and Flora* (February 20).

————. 1989. *Endangered and Threatened Wildlife and Plants* (January 1).

Welty, Joel Carl, and Baptista, Luis. 1988. *The Life of Birds*. 4th ed. New York: Saunders College Publishing.

Wheler, Colette. 1993. "Avian Anesthetics, Analgesics, and Tranquillizers." In *Avian And Exotic Pet Medicine* 2:1, ed. Alan M. Fudge. Philadelphia: W. B. Saunders.

Wiley, James W., Noel F. R. Snyder, and Rosemarie S. Gnam. 1992. "Reintroduction As a Conservation Strategy for Parrots." In *New World Parrots in Crisis*.

Wilson, E. O. 1975. *Sociobiology*. Cambridge: Belknap Press of Harvard University Press.

Wright, John C. 1991. "Canine Aggression Toward People: Bite Scenarios and Prevention." In *Veterinary Clinics of North America*.

Yoerg, Sonja I., and Alan C. Kamil. 1991. "Integrating Cognitive Ethology with Cognitive Psychology." In *Cognitive Ethology*.

Index

Index

Printed in the USA
CPSIA information can be obtained
at www.ICGtesting.com
JSHW012022140824
68134JS00033B/2824

9 781684 421848